# SERVICE BANKING

# Service Banking

A Commentary on Bank Services
in the United Kingdom
by

D. G. HANSON, LLM, FIB
of Lincoln's Inn, Barrister

With a Foreword by
The Lord Seebohm

The Institute of Bankers
10 Lombard Street
London EC3V 9AS

First published in 1979 by
THE INSTITUTE OF BANKERS
10 Lombard Street, London EC3



ISBN: 0 85297 048 X (Hardback)
ISBN: 0 85297 0498 (Paperback)



Prepared by Hobsons Press (Cambridge) Limited
Bateman Street, Cambridge
Made and printed by The Garden City Press Limited
Letchworth, Hertfordshire SG6 1JS

*For my banking friends and colleagues*

# Foreword by The Lord Seebohm

This book by Derrick Hanson is, I believe, the first to be devoted to 'Service Banking' in contrast to the vast number of excellent and learned publications on all aspects of bank lending and money transmission. It must, therefore, be a very welcome addition to banking literature for all those who are studying or working in the business of banking. So much has happened or been developed in this field during the last decade or so that this book will fill a significant gap in the material available for all those who are interested either professionally or academically in the various services that banks now offer to their customers. The author gives a very complete coverage of the subject and describes in some detail no less than eighteen different major services, some of which are very recent developments.

I can, however, recommend this book to a much larger readership than just those who are studying banking or working in banks. It is skilfully and at times entertainingly written and the fact that the author has had long and deep experience of managing many of these services comes through in every chapter.

Many of us who have spent our lives in banking and more particularly those of us who, like myself, can look back over many years, wonder whether the wide diversity of services which this book reveals is altogether wise. Can branch managers give the time to sell so many different products? Are there not specialist institutions who will usually be better equipped to deal with such matters? Are we sure that the overall profitability of the bank will be improved by such activities? Mr Hanson, quite rightly, does not see it as his business to answer all these questions, but what he has done is to give us a much fuller understanding of 'Service Banking' which will help the rest of us to draw our own conclusions. Thank you, Mr Hanson.

*Frederic Seebohm*

# A Personal Note

There can be few major business activities which have changed so much in the space of a decade as British banking. It so happened that I spent a large part of my banking career in the so-called service departments and I was privileged not only to observe at first hand many of the developments described in these pages, but also to be involved in a modest way in the changing scene. Like many others, I believed that banks should move into the field of total financial management and this very largely is what has now happened. Some problems remain and some questions remain unanswered, but the remarkable thing is that so much has been achieved by the banks in such a short time. The banker of today has to have a working acquaintance with a range of financial services far beyond anything which would have been expected of him years ago. Both as a student and in his bank duties, he will have to learn of banking activities which would have been quite unfamiliar to a former age. This book can only scratch the surface of what in some cases are very wide subjects. It is not strictly a textbook as such and it does not set out to teach the experts anything about their own subjects. It is an attempt to describe to the layman (and in this sense we are all laymen) something of what goes on in the specialist fields of present-day banking. I count it a privilege to have this book published by The Institute of Bankers, but the opinions expressed are, of course, my own and do not necessarily reflect the views of the Institute or the banks. If the book serves as an introduction to some of the less traditional and perhaps less familiar aspects of banking business, it will have fulfilled a useful purpose.

*D. G. Hanson*

February 1979

# Acknowledgements

I am immensely grateful to all those who have helped in so many ways towards the publication of this book. In particular, I am indebted to Lord Seebohm for so kindly agreeing to contribute the Foreword; to Mr Philip Wilkinson, General Manager (Related Bank Services), National Westminster Bank, formerly Chief Executive of Lombard North Central, who helped me in so many ways with introductions and information; to Mr David Barber, a General Manager of Midland Bank, formerly a Director of Samuel Montagu & Company; to Mr Charles Bissell, former General Manager of Midland Bank Trust Company, Mr R. A. M. Coker, Former Head of Trustee and Income Tax Services, National Westminster Bank, and my good friend and former colleague, Mr Oliver Atkins, a Director of Barclays Bank Trust Company, for statistics and other help relating to the trustee, tax and investment services of the banks; to Mr M. A. W. Vale, Chairman of the Association of Corporate Trustees for making available to me the evidence submitted by the Association to the Royal Commission on Legal Services; to my former colleague, Mr K. W. Storry, Director and General Manager of Barclays Unicorn Group, for so kindly reading and commenting on the chapter on unit trusts; to Mr W. J. Burnett, Secretary of the Unit Trust Association, for the statistics he so readily supplied; to my friend, Mr Geoffrey Heywood, former President of the Institute of Actuaries, for so kindly reading and commenting on the chapter on life assurance and pensions services; to Mr B. C. Crittenden, Managing Director of National Westminster Insurance Services, for his help in reading and commenting on the chapter on insurance broking; and to Mr Harry Head, Executive Director, Barclays Insurance Services Company, for the helpful information he gave me; to former colleague, Mr Trevor Hart, Chief Accountant, Barclays Bank Trust Company, for the help he gave me in connection with pensions services; to my old friend and colleague, Mr C. A. Brockbank, Assistant General Manager (Corporate Services), Barclays

Bank and formerly Executive Director of Barclays Mercantile Industrial Finance, for his help in connection with leasing and factoring; to Mr George Gilhespy, Director and Chief Executive of Access, Mr W. B. Hair, Chief Manager, Access, at Midland Bank, Mr Frank Snushall, Divisional General Manager, Barclaycard, Mr M. G. Pinks, Assistant Divisional General Manager, Barclaycard, Mr T. R. Froggatt of Barclaycard, and their colleagues for considerable help and information in connection with credit cards; to my friend, Mr Paul Robinson Jr. of Chicago, who assisted with information on the world credit card industry; to Mr John Padovan, Chief Executive of County Bank, for time given to the discussion of merchant banking; to Mr R. J. Barnes, Chief Executive of Lombard North Central and Chairman of the Finance Houses Association, and his colleagues, Mr R. J. Philo, Mr R. J. Young and Mr R. W. Cottle, for their very considerable help on the subject of hire purchase; to Mr Howard Scholefield, Executive Director of Barclaytrust International, and Mr W. Penman Brown, Director and General Manager of Manufacturers Hanover Bank (Guernsey), for the information they put at my disposal on off-shore services; to Mr Andrew Russell, Treasurer and General Manager of the Bank of Scotland, and his colleagues, Mr R. Scott, Mr J. T. More, Mr J. R. D. Moore, Mr J. Wighton and Mr J. R. Browning, for giving me their time to discuss bank services in Scotland; to Mr R. Illingworth, Chief Registrar, Lloyds Bank, Mr L. C. Hockey, Assistant Chief Registrar, Lloyds Bank, and Mr R. F. Taylor, formerly Deputy Manager, Barclays Bank (London and International), Knutsford, and their colleagues for information on registrar services; to Mr B. Hosh and Mr F. Salinger, Directors of Griffin Factors, and their colleagues for all the help they gave me with the subject of factoring.

I am especially grateful to my old friend and former colleague, Mr Peter Jones, for so kindly undertaking the tiresome chore of reading the manuscript and preparing the index, to Mrs Jennifer Ray for so kindly typing it, often at great inconvenience to herself, and to David H. V. Beckwith, formerly of Midland Bank, who did so much to assist the Institute in bringing this book to a point of publication in their busy Centenary Year.

Finally may I, on behalf of the publishers and myself, express our thanks to Mr D. E. Wilde, for reading the entire text and making most helpful comments, and to the many anonymous readers in the clearing banks who commented on individual chapters: the helpful and constructive comments of all concerned have, almost without exception, been incorporated in the text.

Much of the credit for this modest work must go to these good friends and others whom I have failed to mention. The mistakes, for some there must surely be, are entirely mine.

D.G.H.

# Contents

*'Banking is a trade.'*

CHAPTER 1

# Service Banking

'Like many other beings', said Lord Denning, Master of the Rolls in United Dominions Trust Limited v Kirkwood, 'a banker is easier to recognise than to define'.[1] In that celebrated case his Lordship and his colleagues enunciated a number of essential requirements if one was to enjoy the title of banker, but drew back from offering any precise definition. Indeed the statutory definitions are those which describe 'banker' as 'any person or corporation carrying on the business of bankers'.[2]

One might also reflect on whether the 'business' of banking is a trade, a profession or an industry. (This last appellation almost certainly has its origin in the Ministry of Labour jargon of the 1940s.) Certainly the former Lord Chief Justice, Lord Goddard, considered that 'ordinarily speaking, banking is a trade' and that 'a banker in the proper way refers to his *customer* because he is carrying on the *trade* of a banker – old bankers never refer to their clients – that was left to hairdressers and dressmakers.[3] Be that as it may, we can assume for all practical purposes that the traditional business of banking is that of taking deposits, lending money and providing a money transmission service.

This book is concerned with some other aspects of the business of banking. It is not a textbook on banking as such, a subject which is admirably covered in other works. Equally it is not a compendium of modern bank services. It is an attempt to describe, for the first time within one cover, those services which are in themselves a departure from the traditional banking function. Accordingly, 'personal loans', first introduced in 1958, are excluded because they are no more than a variation in the manner of lending – similarly with budget accounts, standing orders, bankers' opinions, travellers' cheques and documentary credits – and a host of other conventional services – because they belong naturally and tidily to banking in its traditional form. On the other hand, it seems right to include hire purchase, leasing and factoring – all services closely related to the banking function, but different in the nature of the new relationships created.

It was customary at one time to refer to these non-banking activities as 'ancillary services', but this is no longer acceptable, for *ancillary* means 'subservient or subordinate' and this would never do.

A collective term used by the National Westminster Bank for some years is 'related banking services' and this is usefully explicit although probably inaccurate because presumably what it means is 'services related to banking'. At least one senior banker[4] has used the description 'service banking', and this is a useful title although subject to the criticism that all banking is a service.

Not all these related services are new. The executor and trustee services of the banks have been operating for nearly seventy years or so. The Midland Bank Executor and Trustee Company Limited (now Midland Bank Trust Company Limited) was established in 1909 and on the occasion of its Jubilee was referred to with some affection by the then Chairman of the Midland Bank, Viscount Monckton, as 'our earliest subsidiary'. Indeed, it must be one of the oldest subsidiary companies of any British banking group.

For the most part, however, it has been in the last decade that the British clearing banks have come out in a rash of new services. There are now approximately 300 separately identifiable services available over the counters of the United Kingdom banks. It has been a truly remarkable phenomenon and one without any precise counterpart elsewhere in the world.

A former Governor of the Bank of England remarked that 'the supremacy of London as an international banking centre is founded on a freedom from banking legislation equalled in few countries in the world', and on the same occasion referred to 'the arrival of the all-purpose bank in the United Kingdom'.[5] Certainly the freedom of the British banks to engage in almost any business activity of their choosing made it possible for them to embark on the proliferation of their services.

Those given to long-term strategy would no doubt like to think that all this happened like the unfolding of some master plan. It is true that today corporate planning forms an essential part of the decision-making process in the British clearing banks, but it was comparatively unknown a decade ago. The banks tended to pursue an empirical, even pragmatic approach to the development of their business. More particularly, banks were not great originators. They did not necessarily have any occasion to diversify into other activities, nor did they see any particular reason for departing from traditional concepts. That was equally true across the Atlantic. Professor Paul Nadler wrote in recent times of American banks that 'banking's motto has long been "Never do something the first time" '.[6]

One may speculate on the reasons for the gradual and in some cases reluctant diversification into financial services which began in the late 1960s. Some may regard it as no more than a normal organic or evolutionary process, a kind of blossoming to crown the years of sturdy but unexciting growth. Such an idealistic, even poetic, view is probably far from the truth. Until the middle 1960s few, if any, saw banks in the role of financial supermarkets. Not a word in the banking publications of thirty years ago contemplated, even in part, the crop of services which eventually emerged. Banks were banks and that was an end to the matter. Less than twenty years ago, a commentator was able to write: 'Unlike manufacturers, banks are not continually developing new products or improvements upon existing products which can be made the subject of an advertisement or a series of advertisements.'[7] In certain respects, the American banks were ahead of their British counterparts, despite their legal limitations on diversification, but some of their innovations were thought not to be appropriate to the traditional view of banking in Britain.

For the first sign of change we need look no further than the monetary climate of the 1960s. The three basic ingredients which we have already mentioned, viz deposit taking, lending and money transmission, all seemed to be severely threatened albeit for different reasons. With regard to deposits it is now well known that the clearing banks' share of new personal savings has diminished very significantly over the post-war years. This was well recognised in the 1950s and 1960s but the trend has continued. For example, in 1972 the increase in banking deposits from the personal sector amounted to £1·7 billion against a figure of £5 billion for growth in savings through building societies, life assurance and pension funds. By 1976, the increase in personal bank deposits was down to a level of £1·3 billion compared with over £9 billion placed with building societies, life companies and pension funds.[8] More graphically, the evidence of the clearing banks to the Wilson Committee[9] showed that among the deposit-taking institutions in the United Kingdom, the clearing banks' share of deposits fell from 48·8 per cent in 1962 to 35·4 per cent in 1976. Over the same period, the building societies' share of deposits increased from 21·2 per cent to 37·7 per cent and the share of all other banks in the United Kingdom, including overseas banks operating in the UK, rose from 3·8 per cent to 12·5 per cent. In their evidence, the banks also comment on the fact that in the twenty or so years since the Radcliffe Committee reported in 1957, the total number of commercial banks, both domestic and foreign, operating in the United Kingdom had expanded from under 125 to over 300. In the same period, as a result of the mergers of the late 1960s, the number of clearing banks had been reduced from eleven to six. As the following table shows, by the end of 1977 building society savings in the UK accounted for 47·3 per cent of the liquid assets of the personal sector, whereas bank deposits (including all banks) had fallen to 31·7 per cent.

**Liquid assets of the personal sector, December 1977**

| **Category** | **£m** | **% of Total** |
|---|---|---|
| Trustee Savings Bank | 3,912 | 5·9 |
| National savings | 9,837 | 14·7 |
| Local authority short term securities | 203 | ·3 |
| Building society shares and deposits | 31,757 | 47·3 |
| Bank deposits | 21,266 | 31.7 |
| Deposits with other financial institutions | 64 | ·1 |
| **Total** | 67,039 | 100·0 |

[Source: *Financial Statistics*, December 1978]

As regards the flow of money into pension funds and insurance companies, it must be acknowledged that these constitute a large part of the long-term savings market whereas the banks traditionally are in the market for short-term savings. Such a generalisation may, however, be partly fallacious, because a large proportion of bank deposits tend to be long term. In any case, there is only so much disposable income at any one time and that part which goes into long-term savings is obviously not lying in personal banking accounts.

Over the years, the volume of money in private hands has increased enormously, but as we have seen the banks' share of this has diminished. For many years the attitude of the banks was comparatively passive. They showed little aggression in the competition for private savings and the word 'marketing' was not heard in the corridors of British banks until the mid-1960s. Nowadays, the competition is intense and the banks naturally feel aggrieved at the taxation advantages and the comparative freedom from regulation enjoyed by some of their competitors. They were to say with some force in their evidence to the Wilson Committee:

'At present, the national savings movement, the building societies and the life assurance companies in particular can attract deposits and savings on the basis of fiscal and regulatory advantages not available to other types of institution. Such differentiation may have made sense when the roles of the various institutions were more clear-cut than they are today. But now that institutions are increasingly competing with one another in the same market places, the differentiation has become discriminatory and undoubtedly lessens the efficiency of the financial system as a whole.'

Whilst the deposit-taking business was losing ground to competition, the banks' role as lenders was more overtly threatened. For most of the post-war years and certainly from 1951, credit squeezes were successive features of monetary policy. For most of that time, bank lending was subject to qualitative constraints and from 1957 onwards there were quantitative controls. Only for a comparatively brief period, from 1958 to 1960, were restrictions on bank credit removed – long enough for a great upsurge in lending, the advent of personal loans, the new concept (for banks) of fixed-term loans for consumer durables and with that the gradual turning of the banks towards involvement in hire purchase finance. With the return of lending 'ceilings' in 1960, it seemed to many that lending constraints must forever be a feature of the mixed economy.

The third area of traditional banking, the transmission of money, was not and probably could never be a profitable activity in itself, but it is of course an essential aspect of current account management – and even that area was coming under threat from the National Giro.

The threats to traditional banking were very real and bank profits seemed to be a hostage to bank rate. In some banks it was calculated that a return to a period of 'cheap money' would prevent the continuance of profitable trading. Not unnaturally, all the banks, no doubt with varying degrees of conviction, turned their minds to the more profitable use of resources. In the mid-1960s there were approximately 12,500 banking branches throughout the United Kingdom and the staffs of the clearing banks totalled something over 150,000. If conventional banking activities were to be circumscribed, it was essential to use some of those resources in new, profitable channels. It was also thought at the time that automation would release staff to deal with higher grade duties, although it is doubtful whether in the event this happened. In any case, costs were increasing rapidly and it was only a few years later in 1971 that Sir John Thomson in his address to Barclays Bank shareholders said, 'We must continue to supplement our retail service by developing less labour intensive activities, which will gather some of their business from the network of 5,000 branches in the Group'.

Thus the banks began to look in a number of directions at once, but they showed neither unanimity nor uniformity. In November 1954, the Commercial Bank of Scotland had acquired the share capital of Scottish Midland Guarantee Trust and Second Scottish Midland Guarantee Trust, but it was not until 1958 that the English clearing banks took any major investment in hire purchase houses. In July of that year, Barclays Bank and British Linen Bank acquired 25 per cent of the share capital of United Dominions Trust, described by the then Barclays Bank Chairman as arising from 'an unexpected opportunity'.[10] A month later, in August 1958, Westminster

Bank and Martins Bank announced the acquisition of 20 per cent each in the equity of Mercantile Credit Limited; National Provincial Bank acquired the whole of the capital of North Central Wagon and Finance; Midland Bank acquired the whole of Forward Trust; Royal Bank of Scotland acquired 40 per cent of British Wagon Company; Lloyds Bank acquired 25 per cent of Bowmaker and 30 per cent of Olds Discount; District Bank acquired 33⅓ per cent of Astley Industrial Trust; and Bank of Scotland acquired the whole of North West Securities. It was a busy month! The *Bankers' Magazine* was prompted to declare:

'The celerity with which the schemes have appeared certainly suggests that in modern times an association of banking with hire purchase finance is regarded as a natural and desirable development.'

The total investment by the clearing banks in hire purchase companies at that time came to approximately £23 million.

Among the services which had their inspiration outside the United Kingdom – in this case the United States – was the credit card. Here again, however, the banks chose to go in quite diverse ways. Early in 1965 Westminster Bank announced the purchase of 40 per cent (later 48·7 per cent) of The Diner's Club with its international credit card business. In October that year, the first cheque card was introduced by National Provincial Bank, guaranteeing payment of cheques up to £30. Before the year was out, Barclays Bank had developed 'Barclaycard', a true credit card on the American pattern, regarded by Barclays Bank in their announcement 'as a natural extension of ordinary banking facilities'. In March 1966, Midland Bank introduced their cheque card and the following month Lloyds Bank and Martins Bank, together with nine other English and Irish banks, announced the introduction of the 'Bankers' Card'.

There was a similar confluence of activity in the matter of unit trusts. Almost simultaneously with an internal decision in Martins Bank that they would not then go into the management of unit trusts, Lloyds Bank announced its decision to do so. The first issue of Lloyds Bank units was made in October 1966. The following July, Westminster Bank moved into unit trust management jointly with Hambros Bank and within a few months Martins Bank announced the aquisition of 75 per cent of Unicorn Securities. With commendable single-mindedness Midland Bank chose not to enter the field of unit trust management, but to concentrate on the role of trustee. Possibly Midland Bank thought there was the risk of conflict in being managers of their own unit trusts whilst being trustee of others, although other banks seemed to resolve this problem. However, in due time through the acquisition of Montagu Trust and the Drayton Group, Midland Bank found themselves in the business of unit trust management and so they remain.

There we have but a few examples. As we shall see, the banks turned their thoughts in a short space of years to insurance broking, life assurance, advisory services, merchant banking, leasing, factoring and almost every other legitimate financial activity. Sometimes the banks went by different routes to the same terminus. An outside observer may be forgiven for thinking that there were times when the banks did not know their own mind. They moved in no time at all from talk of 'sticking to their lasts' to such terminology as 'one stop banking' and 'banking supermarkets'. Perhaps we may liken each bank to a giant omnibus pausing, however briefly, to take each new service on board, but gathering increasing momentum as it moves towards the goal of total financial management. It must have seemed to many bank managers that service was piled on service and they must have longed to cry halt. On an old sign on the M6 motorway approaching Carlisle, the plea of many a bank manager was graphically summed up – 'no more services'. Indeed, a recent survey among bank managers (see p. 189) elicited at least two graphic comments: 'banks shouldn't sell specialist services' and 'ancillary services are a pain in the neck'!

Let no one think that the services described here will ever dominate the banking scene. Although in their evidence to the Wilson Committee the clearing banks refer to the 'diversification into a wide range of financial activities not previously associated with clearing banking', they go on to say:

'The clearing banks have developed along lines much closer to those of the continental "universal" banks than before, aiming to provide a comprehensive range of domestic and international financial services within a single group of companies. But the blurring of traditional demarcation lines between the clearing banks and other institutions does not mean that they

*'Banking Supermarkets.'*

either seek or expect to dominate all the diverse financial markets, old and new, in which they now operate. Deposit banking remains the staple of their existence and conditions all other banking activities. In particular, it means that by far the largest part of their banking business must be conducted with due regard to the essentially short-term nature of their deposit base.'

And again:

'It is their (the clearing banks) intention to continue to adapt to changing circumstances and needs and to compete robustly with one another and with other institutions. But in so doing they cannot afford to neglect the basic clearing banking services which remain the foundation of their business.'

For the student of banking the following pages are designed to serve as a guide to the non-traditional banking activities of the clearing banks in the United Kingdom. An attempt is made to describe each service in substance; to discuss in each case the market for the service and the environment in which it is offered; to consider the attendant problems and pose some questions for the future; and to look at the structure or framework within which each service operates.

For the practising banker here is something in the nature of a refresher course. In his everyday business the bank official has the seemingly impossible task of assimilating the details of a great number of diverse financial services, seeing each one in its place in the total spectrum of banking activities and calling up the relevant information from the recesses of his memory depending on the needs and circumstances of the customer. Furthermore, for a long time to come, bank officials will be required to attend courses and other meetings to discuss the range of products offered by their group and to consider the marketing and profitability of this or that service.

Finally, this commentary may also be of interest to the external observer of British banking. If it helps the enquirer to understand, in the comfort of his armchair, something of the role of the United Kingdom banks in the field of 'service banking' and if in turn that stimulates imitation, imagination or even inspiration, it will have been a useful exercise.

## References

1 United Dominions Trust Ltd v Kirkwood (1966) 1 All. E.R., at page 979.
2 Bankers' Books Evidence Act 1879 *and* Companies Act 1948, s. 432.
3 Regina v Industrial Disputes Tribunal *ex parte* East Anglian Trustee Savings Bank (1954) 1 W.L.R. 1093.
4 L. C. Mather: *Commercial Banks: Evolution of Services*. International Banking Summer School, Oxford, July 1970. The Institute of Bankers, 1970.
5 Lord (then Sir Leslie) O'Brien speaking to The Institute of Bankers in Scotland, January 1973.
6 P. S. Nadler: *Banking*. Girard Bank, February 1972.
7 G. Riley: 'Banks and Advertising'. *Journal of The Institute of Bankers*, August 1959.
8 Central Statistical Office: *Economic Trends*. January 1978.
9 Committee of London Clearing Bankers: *The London Clearing Banks – Evidence to the (Wilson) Committee to Review the Functioning of Financial Institutions*. Longman, 1978.
10 A. W. Tuke: Address to the Stockholders of Barclays Bank Limited, 12 January 1959.

CHAPTER 2

# The Administration of Estates

The all-purpose bank is often thought of as providing a cradle-to-the-grave service, and in that context it must seem inappropriate to begin with the subject of death. Nevertheless, as we have said, the trustee services of the banks are the oldest of the extra-banking activities and for that reason, at least, they are a good place to start. Trustee services are not of course all concerned with the dead. For both technical and marketing reasons, trust services fall into the broad categories of (a) private and (b) corporate. For this purpose, private customers can be divided yet again between the living and the dead and so let us begin, as it were, at the end.

The oldest of non-banking functions, that of executor and trustee, is perhaps the most anomalous. It was no doubt thought appropriate that banks who look after the affairs of the living should also look after the affairs of the dead; that the friendly bank manager should become the friendly executor; that those big solid institutions that had seen many a customer through many a storm in life should be the repository for his problems on death. In fact, the leap into trustee work was much greater than with some of the services of recent years and the affinity between banking and the administration of estates is not at all an obvious one. In simple terms, the banker looks after his customer's money but an executor takes over the management of the entire estate; the banker acts as agent for his customer and of course as debtor or creditor, but the executor necessarily acts as a principal; and banks in this country seldom if ever accept the responsibility for dealing with a customer's entire affairs during his or her life, but as executors have shown a willingness to jump in at the deep end on death. Furthermore, the traditional skills and training of bankers as such are not specially related to those of the trust man. One cannot resist the thought that the banks' decision to go into trust business might have been different if they had been confronted with the choice in more recent years.

This is not the place to dwell in detail on the history of corporate trustees in the United Kingdom and in any case, the story has been excellently told by D. R. Marsh in a book,[1] now sadly out of print. It was in 1845 that the South Sea Company sought to change the company into a 'Public Trust Company' and to undertake the administration of private trusts on a commission basis. It prompted one commentator to remark that 'instead of its former vocation of fishing in the South Seas, it wished to transfer its operations to fishery of suits in Chancery'.[2] The Charter was granted but apparently owing to some misunderstanding never sealed. In any event, this was the first of a number of Bills laid before Parliament over a period of approximately sixty years, all of which sought to establish companies for the purpose of engaging in trust business and all of which failed. The main reason generally advanced in support of the 'trading' trustee was the alleged unwillingness of private people to undertake the burdens of trusteeship. This was attributed to the decline of the landed aristocracy and the growth of the industrial and commercial classes. The various Bills were opposed not surprisingly by solicitors who saw their business disappearing to banks and insurance companies, but also, more philosophically, by those who could not reconcile limited liability with the concept of a trustee's personal responsibility.

It is a well-known rule of Equity that a trustee may not profit from his trust and only by special agreement or special powers may a trustee benefit, however indirectly, from his trusteeship. Each of the Bills laid before Parliament in the latter half of the nineteenth century on the subject of corporate trustees provided for the payment of remuneration to trust corporations (subject to appropriate safeguards), but Parliament would not have it. This was the more remarkable because in Australia, South Africa, New Zealand and America trustees had the right to charge reasonable remuneration either by statute or the common law. How the trust corporations of today would welcome a Bill similar to Lord Hobhouse's in 1889 when he sought powers for trust companies to administer estates and take on existing trusts even though there was no enabling power in the trust instruments, and to have the right to charge remuneration in those cases on a scale approved by the Board of Trade!

The sense of outrage at the idea of trusteeships becoming a paid business was dramatically summed up by Lord St Leonards in 1858: 'that a trustee should be paid for his services is altogether repugnant to our habits and feelings. The office is to be filled by a friend with whom we can communicate freely and confidentially. A paid trustee would stand in a different character. Undoubtedly some would make a trade of the office and endeavour to attract custom to their own mill . . . the trade of a trustee! The business of an executor! Fancy it written over a shop door!'[3]

By the turn of the century only one Act, the Judicial Trustees Act of 1896, had given any sort of recognition to corporate trustees as such, and yet by this time no less than 290 trust companies were in operation in the United States. Here we might reflect on the quite different experience of the United States in the development of trust business. Although it was not until 1853 that the first American company, the United States Trust Company, was formed for the express purpose of administering estates and trusts, there was already by that time a large volume of trust activity in corporate hands in America. The Massachussetts Hospital Insurance Company of Boston had obtained legislative power to administer trusts as early as 1818 and in the following years a number of other insurance and annuity companies obtained similar powers, including in 1836 the Girard Life Insurance, Annuity and Trust Company, now Girard Bank. The later experience was the reverse of that in the United Kingdom in that many of the American banks had their origin in trust company operations – perhaps a more rational development than we saw in this country.

It is strange that England, where the legal concept of the 'trust' had its origin, should have been the last – after the United States and the 'old' Dominions – to give legislative recognition to the management of trusts as a business. Such recognition did not come until the passing of the Public Trustee Act in 1906. It was the culmination of twenty years of tireless campaigning and sponsorship of various Bills by Sir Howard Vincent, MP. The Act created the office of the Public Trustee with power to charge for his services and also empowered banks and insurance companies and the like to act as Custodian Trustees (with power to charge) where the active management remained with private individuals. This latter provision was of limited use as events turned out, but the dam was breached and the concept of the trading trustee was recognised.

It seems there was something of a reaction in official circles and some fear that the Public Trustee might become a monopoly, with the banking balances of thousands of private trusts being swept into the Bank of England. In 1904 the Union of London & Smiths Bank had amended its objects clause to permit 'the undertaking and executing of any trusts', and one by one, before and after the passing of the Public Trustee Act, the other banks followed suit. In the years from 1908 to 1912 the banks and insurance companies set up their trustee departments and arranged for the training of their staff to undertake this new 'non-banking' operation.

Today the trust companies and departments of the six clearing banks have on their books over 100,000 cases of all kinds with a total approximate value of nearly £10 billion. In the course of a recent twelve months' period they accepted the administration of over 9,000 new estates with an average value of £26,000 and over 1,000 other trusts. At the present time the total number of will appointments, i.e. for living customers, on the books of the English clearing banks exceeds 800,000. The growth of business over seventy years or so has been impressive, but only modest in relation to the development of trust business in the United States.

Trust companies and departments are in the business of asset management. In the course of their activities, they are called upon to deal with almost every kind of asset susceptible to private ownership. Broadly speaking, the business consists of deceased estates, private trusts set up by will or *inter vivos* settlements, trusteeships for pension funds and charities, debenture trusts, unit trust trusteeships and the management of investment portfolios whether for private clients or institutions. The mainstream of that business is the administration of estates.

We need not deal here with the technicalities of estates and trusts for trust administrators. The subject has been dealt with very competently in a number of textbooks over the years, one of the most recent being the excellent book by Mr Sladen.[4] For ease, therefore, we will use the word executor to embrace also the role of the administrator. An executor is the person who administers a deceased's estate, having been named as the executor in the will. An administrator on the other hand is appointed by the Court in those cases where (i) there is no will; or (ii) the will does not name an executor; or (iii) the executor has died before the testator, or does not wish to act. For most practical purposes, the role is the same. A similar function undertaken at times by corporate trustees is that of 'agent' for executors. In such cases, the grant of representation is applied for by the executor or other appropriate person and the bank or insurance company assists with the correspondence and book-keeping, and indeed virtually does all the work for the named executor or administrator. This procedure was occasionally adopted even in the early days of trustee departments in this country and has since been experimented with from time to time, but there are legal and practical difficulties. The service is a little more widespread in the United States.

The work of an executor may be summarised as (i) seeing that the funeral arrangements are dealt with; (ii) collecting the assets; (iii) paying the debts and expenses; (iv) arranging for the assets to be valued so far as may be necessary either for taxation or distribution purposes; (v) discharging any duties and taxes payable on the death; and (vi) accounting for the estate to the beneficiaries entitled.

Where banks are named as executors, they will usually peruse the draft will prior to its execution and offer their assistance, where this is welcomed, to the testator and his solicitor. Quite often, the very considerable experience of trust officials can be useful at this early stage in order to avoid difficulties later on.

Anyone of full age and sound mind can be an executor or administrator and the task is often undertaken by ordinary people with no special financial or legal knowledge. On the first occasion, however, few people know where to start and are utterly dependent on obtaining the right advice and help. To step into the shoes of a deceased person, whether family or friend, is a great responsibility. Few people succeed in managing their own financial affairs adequately and are ill-equipped to take on the affairs of others. In these days of increasing complexity in personal financial matters, executorship is no longer a matter for the amateur, if indeed it ever was. An eminent jurist has described the ideal executor and trustee in the following terms:

'The Trustee of my property, my Executor, must be always well and at home; he must never run away and never steal; must have life everlasting; must be rich and stay rich with all his property pledged to the proper performance of his trust; must have no partialities; must be subject to no political or personal influences; must make no mistakes; must never forget; must do what he is told to do, first, last and all the time; must keep a complete record of what he does; must make only reasonable charges, and must have the learning, the experience, the discretion, not only of one man, but of a number of the most successful businessmen of the community.'[5]

Thus the choice of an executor is not easy. It lies among (i) a relative or friend; (ii) a professional man; (iii) the Public Trustee; or (iv) a corporate trustee such as a bank or insurance company. The banks have always claimed to offer special advantages, notably the continuity of their business, the security which a large bank exemplifies in the conduct of its customers' affairs and the cumulative experience of a highly trained staff, many of whom have spent all or most of their career in trust work.

Why then do all the world not appoint banks as their executors? In the first place, there are of course 25 million or so adults in this country who do not have accounts with a clearing bank and a few million others who, whilst conducting accounts with their banks, do not come into such a meaningful relationship that they would contemplate the appointment of their bank as executor. Leaving such cases aside on the assumption, for the moment, that they are outside the banks' 'market' for trustee work, we enounter two main reasons why the banks have not swept the board.

The first is the often expressed view that banks are impersonal. Taken as a general proposition, this does not stand up. Banks, like other institutions, can only operate through the human beings they employ. They can be as kind and understanding as the man next door; they can be as unimaginative and as obdurate. A bank's trust department is only as good as the people in it. Over the years one has seen cases administered with a robot-like lack of understanding of the human problems involved and a determination to 'go by the book'. But such cases are not typical: there are many beneficiaries of family trusts who have had cause to appreciate and commend the dedicated attention given to their affairs by trustee department staff. They have gone about their work with sympathy and quiet efficiency and many have become 'friends of the family' in a way which used to be reserved for the clergyman, doctor or solicitor.

For the trustee staff themselves, the work provides one of the most satisfying careers that an institution can offer. To adopt the slogan of a well-known newspaper, 'all human life is there'. Trustee work is a happy combination of professional expertise and a socially desirable objective – never more so than in the administration of an estate on death. It is a task which must be done by someone, usually at a time of family distress and anxiety. It is a task which brings satisfaction not only in its own usefulness, but in the sheer variety of the work. The trust administrator may have to deal in his time with almost every conceivable type of asset – from the post office account to the investment in North Sea oil; from tumbledown cottages to elegant office blocks; from flocks of sheep to fleets of tugs; from the well-worn wedding ring to the glistening tiara.

That is a digression. Let us agree that it is very personal work.

The facts remain, however, that at the time a will is made the bank trustee must seem remote and impersonal. It is very seldom that a customer meets the trust official who is going to administer his estate. Some people clearly do not mind. They are comforted by the objectivity and impartiality of the institution which will take over. On the whole, however, most people who give thought to these matters at the time of making a will would prefer to think that family and fortune are in the care of someone they have known in this life. One possible answer lies in the choice of a private executor from among friends or family to act jointly with a corporate trustee, but in practice this can be a cumbersome arrangement. In any case,

*'From flocks of sheep to fleets of tugs.'*

the corporate trusteee should make it his concern to work closely and sympathetically with the family.

It is perhaps a matter for contemplation that banking in the High Street has to a degree become less personal over the years. Computers have contributed to the situation, at least in the minds of the public. Other factors have been the pressures on managers which make it increasingly difficult for them to meet more than a proportion of their customers: population movements and the uniformity, indeed anonymity, of suburban life, and at times the rapid movement of bank managers themselves. It has become increasingly difficult in modern times for banker and customer to build up a friendly, continuing relationship over a period of years. Whatever the reasons, many customers never meet their bank manager, even less look upon him as a personal friend, and so do not naturally turn to the banks to administer their affairs on death. In sharp contrast, the entry of the banks into trustee work had its origin, at least in part, in the close personal relationship of banker and customer, particularly among the private bankers. We are told that on the death years ago of a partner in Hoare & Co., the well-known private bankers, he was trustee of over 200 trusts, and that the practice of the partners acting as trustee had continued over the 275 years of the firm's existence. The banking relationship was a personal thing started in life and continued after death. Today things are different.

The other deterrent to the appointment of a clearing bank as executor is the comparatively high cost of doing so. The privilege of a bank executorship is not for the poor man. This is a pity because there are many people of modest means who do not have a natural executor to turn to. By the nature of things, the less the wordly goods, the less sophisticated the family when it comes to dealing with financial matters. Furthermore, the great mass of people in this country do not have a family solicitor as such, nor any regular contact with a member of the legal profession. In earlier times, the cost of appointing a bank as executor was comparatively small and many people of modest means chose banks as their executors. Not many years ago, nearly 70 per cent of all the estates and trusts in one bank were under £10,000 in value. In recent times, however, banks by force of circumstance have had to price themselves out of the executorship business for Mr Everyman. Strange to say, something of this situation was foreseen in the opposition to the creation of corporate trustees in the long debate towards the end of the nineteenth century, the objecting petitioners pointing out that the charges for maintaining a 'joint stock establishment' would render the administration of an estate as costly as administering it in the Court of Chancery.

To some extent that prophecy has come true. A reasonably well informed clerk can administer an average estate with care and efficiency and everyone will be satisfied. It can be done at a fee which will leave something over as a fair margin of profit. If, however, that clerk has to be trained to a standard where he can deal with a large variety of estates, if for the good name of the organisation his work has to be checked by a senior officer, if a legal department has to be set up as a long-stop, if an inspection team has to be created to keep everyone on the right lines, if a local branch is set up for the convenience of the market, if a manager is appointed to oversee the local business and given the benefit of a car, if all are paid at the present level of bank salaries and adequate transfers made to the pension fund, the cost becomes enormous. The banks have done much to counteract the trend. They have moved cases to low-cost areas and have reduced the number of branches wherever possible. It is significant that the Public Trustee only ever had one country office, at Manchester, and that was closed for reasons of economy many years ago.

Similarly, the banks have done much to rationalise their organisation and methods, but that in itself was an expensive exercise, particularly where the introduction of computers was involved. On the other hand, computers now enable a vast volume of trust work to be done speedily and with economies of scale.

There are many matters in connection with the administration of an estate which are of a legal nature and which are properly the concern of a solicitor. There are two areas, however, where duties are reserved for the legal profession which the banks and other corporate executors could well deal with themselves. In the first place, under the rules of the Supreme Court,[6] it is not possible for a corporate body to make a 'personal' application for a Grant of Probate. A private executor can do so, but a corporation must make application through a solicitor. This is an anachronistic rule because today there are hundreds of trained staff in the banks who can prepare the details for a probate application quite as well as those employed in solicitors' offices. The other rule, perhaps of greater validity, is that no one but a legally qualified person may prepare legal documents – other than a will or other testamentary document – 'in expectation of any fee, gain or reward'.[7] It is doubtful whether the Inland Revenue affidavit sworn for Capital Transfer Tax purposes is a legal document within the meaning of the Act because it is a government form, but the executor's oath more probably is within the scope of the Act. Even in this case, however, the actual wording of the document is normally supplied by the trust corporation to the solicitor for engrossment. The effect of these two rules is that in every case where a corporate body is appointed as executor, it is necessary for a solicitor to be appointed with a consequent increase in costs. It is doubtful whether these rules can be justified any longer on the grounds of public policy, but this is no doubt a matter to which the Royal Commission on Legal Services will turn its attention in due time. It seems reasonable to suggest that organisations engaged in a particular line of business should be free to prepare those documents which relate to its business activity, notwithstanding that an ultimate benefit accrues to the business.

To return, however, to the banks' own costs, it seems unrealistic to suppose that they will ever fall significantly below their present level, particularly if inflation continues. In 1974 some figures produced for the Price Commission in support of a proposed increase in fees showed that the administration of an average estate, involving no particular complexities, cost a bank considerably in excess of the fees then chargeable.

Even on the basis of the fee scales now in force, the administration of a comparatively small estate of, say, £10,000 would still produce little or no profit for the corporate executor. This is to some extent the story of trust business in the banks over the years, although it has been brought into sharp relief by the inflation of recent years.

At one time, the trust activities of the clearing banks were subsidised to the extent that they were not charged specifically with some overhead charges, such as rent and pensions. Taking all costs into account and taking one year with another, trust business in the United Kingdom has so far not been a very profitable exercise. Naturally, one asks why. The most probable explanation is that the public of this country are not accustomed to the idea of paying for their estates to be wound up. It is accepted that a solicitor is entitled to a certain level of charges for preparing a property conveyance, that an estate agent receives a standard commission for selling a house and that the undertaker be paid at the appropriate level of fees for burying the dead. Indeed very many life policies were taken out with the industrial life companies for the very purpose of ensuring that money was there for the funeral, but traditionally the executor who stepped into the shoes of the deceased was either expected to do it as a labour of love or given a small legacy for his trouble. Certainly, people with assets on paper to a value of, say, £20,000 are unaccustomed in their lifetime to paying a £1,000 fee to anyone for anything and therefore do not take kindly to the thought that their executor should receive such a fee, particularly as it would be in addition to legal charges. On the other hand, the view is sometimes advanced that the testator is not unduly concerned about the burden of costs which falls on his beneficiaries provided he is not asked to pay anything in his life time.

The unprofitability of the business is not peculiar to the United Kingdom. Out of the 14,000 or so banks in the United States, large numbers do not undertake trust business because they regard it as unprofitable and, of those who do engage in trust work, only a handful admit to making profits on trust activities as such.

The observer will wonder why the banks continue in this line of business if it be unprofitable. The answer lies partly in the difficulty of extricating themselves from a situation where such vast numbers of living customers have already appointed the bank as executor. To withdraw from this situation would be a mammoth operation, but more particularly would be regarded by many as a breach of faith. The other reason is that executorship services are seen quite properly as part of the concept of total financial management. This is no doubt the better view and it may well be that as the public come to accept more and more the role of the all-purpose bank, they will be readier to pay the costs of winding up their estates.

In any case, trustee work is not without its related benefits – the 'spin-off' to other services. The most important and most quoted benefit is the level of banking balances generated by trust work. The sad thing is that even allowing for the benefit of executorship balances, the service has not always been profitable; and one must remember that if banks did not undertake the administration of estates, many of those balances would remain with the banks as bankers. Then again, the work provides opportunities for the cross-selling of bank services and many an executorship has led to an investment management portfolio or income tax work or perhaps insurance business. Of less tangible benefit but of equal importance is the goodwill created among beneficiaries and others, and the additional points of contact developed between bank and customers or potential customers. These things are difficult to evaluate, but much money can be lost in the name of 'goodwill' or 'service'. True costs should be balanced against true benefits.

A particular feature of trust companies throughout the world is the *ad valorem* system of charging. It is usual to quote a percentage fee graduated according to the size of the estate. This has always been so and probably will remain so. The responsibility for administering an estate is measurable primarily by reference to the size of the assets: thus the *ad valorem* fee reflects the responsibility involved. The weakness of the system is that it does not reflect the varying degrees of difficulty among different estates. Thus, a large estate can sometimes be quite simple and the fee looks disproportionate, whereas some small estates can be difficult and time-consuming and the fee can never recompense for the work involved. The student of these matters might care to consider possible alternative systems. One obvious possibility is to charge on a 'time' basis. This is a professional service and it would be quite in keeping with professional practice in this country to charge on a time-involved basis, allowing a margin for profit. This has the disadvantage of uncertainty and some might argue that the estate would be at the mercy of the executor bank. At least the present system has the advantage of simplicity and certainty.

It is unfortunate that inflation has taken bank executorship services further away from the ordinary man. The market is large and the banks' share of that market after seventy years' experience is not great. At first sight, the total market for executorship business is made up of the adult population of Great Britain. This is of the order of 40 million people. For all practical purposes, however, we can limit the number to those 15 million or so who have accounts with the clearing banks. As we have said, trustee services developed from the banker–customer relationship and the banks in general do not expend their marketing efforts for these services on the unbanked population. There are of course exceptions but they are rare enough to be ignored. The market is further restricted, and very considerably so, by the subtraction of those citizens who have little or no assets to dispose of on death. Out of the 600,000 or so people who die in England and Wales each year, approximately one-half leave 'estates' so small and so simple that no application is necessary for a Grant of Probate or Grant of Letters of Administration.

So much for the market. Let us turn now to the methods by which that market is attacked. It has been said that bank trustee departments are associated with 'graves and worms and epitaphs'. Certainly the image of death has clouded – or should we say shrouded? – the marketing of these services. In the Bankers Almanack of 1907 the announcement by one bank of its executor and trustee services was in the smallest print and most tentative wording compared with the bold type and forthright announcement of the similar services offered by the Northern Trust Company in Chicago. For decades, the banks contented themselves with the cautious announcement that they would 'undertake' executor and trustee business. Even the word 'undertake' did not help and in one bank in the early days a blackedged counter announcement with the word 'undertake' prominent had to be withdrawn hastily. The general approach to the marketing of trust services was just about as low key as one would expect from 'undertakers'. Most banks were satisfied with an announcement on their counters or bank windows and left the rest to the local manager. In later years, the Midland Bank produced an excellent film entitled 'Why not Uncle Willie?' and some of the banks introduced slightly more graphic advertising, but it was all part of the back-up to the local manager's own efforts. Few if any bank people expected to sell executorship business by advertisements. What then of the bank manager? There is of course no prototype for the 12,500 bank managers in the country. Some found it easy and natural to offer executorship services to their customers and thus built up a useful volume of business. Others did not wish to risk offence by talking of such delicate matters and potential business went by default. Success tended to be measured by numbers alone, with the result that large numbers of cases of small value were taken on to the banks' books and, with inflation, it became increasingly difficult to administer these without loss. Also, the higher level of fees bore heavily on small estates and thus it became the practice on the part of the banks to offer to renounce, wherever the estate was small. Definitions of 'small' varied from time to time and from bank to bank, but at the present time bank managers are seldom encouraged by their trust departments to go in pursuit of business worth less than £10,000, and on death the banks will normally offer to renounce their appointment if the estate turns out to be less than that sum.

The banks use different methods to encourage their managers to obtain trust business, but over the years the most usual method has been to pay an introductory commission to the branch concerned. There is some variation of practice among the banks, but the aim has always been to give branch managers some extra inducement to introduce business to the trust department.

Nowadays, few managers find it difficult to raise with their customers the delicate subject of executorship, but it would appear that they do encounter a certain resistance to modern fee levels. Part of the difficulty is that the bank managers themselves find it difficult to accept the need for the current level of charges. Nevertheless, the business still flows in as evidenced by the total number of estates taken on to the banks' books, as quoted on page 16.

Over the years, solicitors in general have been antagonistic to the appointment of banks as executors. As we have seen, they resisted the entry of the corporate trustee into what they regarded as their own field and that attitude has continued, at least in some parts of the country, down to the present time. On the whole, particularly in the south of England, trust companies and solicitors work together in a friendly, co-operative way. The Trustee Departments' Committee of the Committee of London Clearing Bankers have established a regular liaison at senior level with the Law Society and this has been very helpful in resolving particular problems. The fact remains, however, that many solicitors find it difficult to recommend their clients to appoint banks as trustee at the present level of remuneration, which as we have said is in addition to the legal charges. Generally, the duties will be carried out more cheaply and equally satisfactorily if a member of the family is appointed executor, perhaps under the guidance of the solicitor. However, there are many cases where a testator does not wish a member of the family to act and where he is attracted by the professionalism and independence of the corporate trustee.

In one related area there is a market for bank services which is perhaps not fully explored. A large number of people in this country die without having made a will. Their families quite often do not know which way to turn and the bank manager (who is usually one of the first to hear of the death) can be of help in offering the services of the bank's trust department. The banks take on many such cases in the course of the year and can be of very real help to customers at what is usually a very difficult time.

In conclusion, we may say this of the administration of estates:

**1.** It is a service which is here to stay because of the banks' very considerable commitment to hundreds of thousands of customers under existing wills and also because of the substantial deployment of resources on this work, principally in terms of highly qualified staff – resources which could not easily be redeployed, certainly in present conditions, elsewhere in the banks.

**2.** It is a service which the market regards as expensive, almost elitist, notwithstanding that current fee scales are very much in line with those charges which are permitted by law in other parts of the world.

**3.** Profits will be hard earned: it is a sophisticated and personal service requiring high-grade staff and, because of the small routine content of the work, there is but limited opportunity for improving productivity.

**4.** It is valuable as a means of consolidating and developing existing banker/customer relationships and opens up the market for other services.

**5.** It is very much in keeping with the modern theme of comprehensive financial management – it would be inconsistent for the banks to proffer the solution to virtually every personal financial problem in the customer's lifetime and then quietly withdraw at the graveside.

**6.** It is a service which meets a very real market need.

## References and notes

1 D. R. Marsh: *Corporate Trustees*. Europa, 1952.
2 *Legal Observer*. Volume XLVI, p. 300.
3 *Handy Book on Property Law*. 1858.
4 M. Sladen: *Practical Trust Administration*. Europa, 1977.
5 I am indebted to Mr R. A. M. Coker, of the National Westminster Bank, for this quotation.
6 *Non-Contentious Probate Rules 1954*. S.I. 1954, No. 796 R2(2).
7 Solicitors' Act 1957, s. 22(2).

CHAPTER 3

# Private Trusts

Departing from the 'business of an executor' we come, in the words of Lord St Leonard's alliterative strictures, to the 'trade of a trustee'. Although the distinctions between the two functions have become blurred in the public mind, they have their origins in entirely different corners of the law, the one in the law of succession and the other in our singular and fascinating law of trusts. An executor is not *per se* a trustee, but may become one. For practical purposes and with deliberate oversimplification, we may say that an executor or administrator becomes a trustee at that moment when he holds the estate or any part of it on behalf of the beneficiaries. He does not necessarily hold the capital at their disposal: the funds may be 'settled' for a further specified period and such settled trusts are, as we shall see, the hard core of the trustee business of the clearing banks at the present day.

Every student of law knows that the trust is a special creation of the Anglo-Saxon legal system, although not without its points of similarity with the *Fideicommissum* of Roman law which had developed in the last Republic and was given recognition under the Emperor Augustus.[1] The trust had its origin in the thirteenth-century practice of making conveyances ('feoffments') to 'uses'. The word 'use' had its derivation in the latin 'opus', gradually corrupted to 'oes' and 'ues' and ultimately 'use'. Even before the Domesday Book it was not uncommon for a man to make a transfer of property *ad opus* another, but it was not until the year 1230 that we see the first instance of a man holding land permanently to the use of another. With this simple device of holding property for the benefit of another person, it became possible (i) to avoid the cumbersome methods of land transfer; (ii) to devise land by will – not otherwise possible in feudal England; (iii) to avoid feudal dues; (iv) to create future interests in land; (v) to avoid forfeiture for felony; (vi) to get round the Mortmain Statutes which forbade the holding of land by corporations, e.g. monasteries; and (vii) in the case of the clergy, to circumvent the vows of poverty because a Papal Bull of 1279 ordained that a 'use' was not 'property'. It was not altogether surprising therefore that King Henry VIII, like many a modern Chancellor of the Exchequer, sought the 'extinguishment of all such subtle practised feoffments' in order to stave off regal poverty and, after a stormy passage, the Statute of Uses was passed in 1535. The purpose of the Statute was to prevent conveyances to uses. The effect of the Statute was that the transfer of property to A for the use of or in trust for B would give B the entire legal ownership, which of course was not the intention of the transferor. If the matter had ended there we would presumably not have had the development of trust law as we know it today in this country. This is not the place to spell out the subsequent developments, all of which have been written of many times. Suffice to say that with characteristic resilience the English lawyers found a simple and ingenious device for circumventing the Statute and the use or trust was here to stay.

This slight historical excursion serves to illustrate that from the earliest days there was a 'commercial' aspect of uses or trusts to the extent that they were used to mitigate taxes and conserve capital. The whole concept is based on confidence or trust in the wider sense of the word and it has been developed over the years with a flexibility and adaptability which has given the system much of its strength. Today we have a canon of trust law which is the envy of our continental friends.

There is no very satisfactory definition of the trust. One which is often quoted is that of Professor Keeton, viz. 'a trust is the relationship which arises wherever a person called the trustee is compelled in equity to hold property, whether real or personal, and whether by legal or equitable title, for the benefit of some persons (of whom he may be one and who are termed *cestuis que trust*) or for some object permitted by law, in such a way that the real benefit of the property accrues, not to the trustee, but to the beneficiaries or other objects of the trust'.[2]

Within such a definition there is an almost infinite variety of trusts in operation in this country today. For our present purpose, we shall categorise them into (1) private trusts and (2) corporate trusts. The distinction is not clear cut: for example some trusts such as charitable trusts are hybrid in the sense that they fall into either category. In this section we are concerned with trusts set up by private individuals.

Where funds have been 'settled' for someone's benefit, the trust is generally known as a 'settlement' and the person creating the trust is the 'settlor'. Such terminology would be wrong, however, in relation to certain non-private trusts such as pension funds.

Private trusts fall into two broad categories – those which arise under a will or on intestacy and those which are made *inter vivos*.

Turning first to will trusts – let us call them 'settled estates' – we encounter the largest category both in numbers and value of trust business in the United Kingdom banks. The great majority of trusts under administration in the banks today are settled estates arising under the wills of testators who died over the last sixty years or so. They are thought to number in total approximately 50,000 cases. In former years, it was more common than it is today to settle all or part of one's estate for the benefit of successive generations in so far as this was permissible within the perpetuity laws. There were a number of reasons for this. First, there was the testator's concern to protect beneficiaries, particularly female beneficiaries, from either themselves or the exploitation of others. Thus, the daughters would be lucky if they received more than a life interest in their part of the estate whereas the sons would take their shares absolutely. With the 'liberation' of women and greater enlightenment all round, this practice has largely disappeared. Secondly, a widow (and sometimes a widower) would be given a life interest in an estate partly for reasons of protection already mentioned, but more particularly because of the relief which this gave from Estate Duty. With the introduction of Capital Transfer Tax,[3] all transfers between husband and wife are free of tax and thus the old exemption is no longer relevant. Thirdly, it was often the wish of the testators to tie up their fortune in trust for as long as possible in order to give the next generation but one, including those still unborn, a share of the cake. Perhaps this was personal vanity, perhaps a genuine desire to provide for future generations. In any case, swingeing death duties made it increasingly difficult to leave large sums in trust, but more particularly there has been a noticeable change in social attitudes. Testators show diminishing concern about locking up funds for even the next generation, although most parents would rather see their worldly wealth go to their children than evaporate in taxes. The change in attitude over the years probably owes less to egalitarianism than to inflation: people of all financial levels find it difficult enough to maintain standards in this life without worrying too much about future generations.

Are we to conclude therefore that the days of the settled estate are numbered? Certainly it is unlikely that we shall ever again see substantial fortunes locked up for successive generations, but cases will still remain where estates are not immediately distributable on death. One of the largest banks estimate that one in seven of new estates result in a settled trust when the executorship is completed.

*Inter vivos* settlements are those made by deed in the settlor's lifetime. Traditionally they were made for a variety of reasons. Perhaps the most typical was the marriage settlement, usually following a set pattern and embracing the property brought in by the husband and wife into the 'husband's fund' and 'wife's fund' respectively. New settlements in this form are seldom seen, largely because of the fiscal and social changes to which we have referred. Other trusts would be set up for unmarried daughters or for handicapped children and the so-called protective trusts would be created to guard against the possibility of the beneficiaries' bankruptcy. This could be done by the express terms of the trust or by adopting the statutory terms set out in Section 33 of the Trustee Act 1925. The general desire of a settlor, however, would be to set aside funds for the future benefit of the family and to do it, if possible, in a way which would minimise the impact of taxation and the old Estate Duty. The most convenient and deservedly popular vehicle for this came to be the discretionary trust.

All trusts may be swept into one of two broad categories, viz. 'ministerial' (to use an old word) or 'discretionary'. The former requires no more than the exercise of normal prudence and business judgment in carrying out the express terms of the trust; the latter, as the name implies, requiring the exercise of a discretion by the trustee – sometimes in the choice of beneficiaries, sometimes as to the quantum of the benefit and sometimes as to its timing. In their earlier forms, discretionary trusts were usually to protect beneficiaries from themselves or from a trustee in bankruptcy, and in fact the statutory protective trusts provide for the trustees to exercise discretionary powers in certain circumstances. In more recent years, however, the discretionary trust became almost the standard form of family trust.

A discretionary trust combines those two essential features of English trust law to which we have already made reference – confidence and adaptability. The settlor must have confidence in his trustee as a person or institution of integrity and good sense. The trustee must be prepared to adapt to changing circumstances and exercise his discretion with wisdom and understanding. A discretionary trust has three distinct advantages. First of all, it makes for maximum flexibility because the trustee's discretion will be exercised according to changing circumstances over the years. Even in the best regulated families it is impossible to foresee future hazards whether of a financial or matrimonial nature or worse. Secondly, a discretionary trust allows the settlor to have at least a moral say in the management of the trust. He has surrendered his legal right to control the destination of the funds, but the trustee is entitled to have regard to the settlor's wishes and will normally do so not only during the settlor's life, but as far as practicable after his death, always bearing in mind that he, the trustee, must act in the best interests not of the settlor but of the beneficiaries. Thirdly, the discretionary trust may still be an effective vehicle for reducing taxation notwithstanding the efforts of successive Chancellors to close the gap. It is rather sad that successive fiscal legislation has imposed an undue burden of taxation on this most valuable, perfectly legitimate and indeed historic aspect of the English trust.

During the last seventy years the banks have built up an enormous fund of expertise in the management of settled trusts. They have managed the affairs, sometimes for three generations, of some of the most influential families in the land. They have managed over 100,000 settled trusts in a sensitive and professional way and the proportion of error or oversight has been minute. In at least one bank, the settled estates have been referred to over the years as 'automatics'. It arose no doubt from the need to set up arrangements for the automatic collection and distribution of income, but beyond that such cases are far from automatic. The burden of a trusteeship, whether discretionary or not, is considerable and lies heavily on the shoulders of the trustee. He must exercise a wise judgment in such matters as: (i) the advancement of funds to beneficiaries; (ii) the maintenance and education of infant beneficiaries; (iii) the preservation of the trust property; (iv) requests for the partitioning of the trust; (v) applications by the beneficiaries to the Court for varying the terms of a trust under the Variation of Trusts Act 1958. During the life of a trust beneficiaries will die, others will come of age and some new ones will be born. It can be more than a lifetime's task and the continuity of the trusteeship is important.

The most important aspect of a trustee's role is his stewardship of the trust property, whether it be investments, land, houses or chattels. The beneficiaries may forgive him for a technical or mathematical error in some apportionment of income or application of a legal rule, but he will not be excused for negligent management of the assets. Very few people today have the knowledge and the technical back-up to manage trust funds over a long period of years. It is a job for corporate trustees, particularly the banks with their concentration of economic and financial knowledge and familiarity with the principal markets throughout the world. Even so, corporate trustees do not always get it right. Perhaps at times they have seen their task as a legal or technical one, or possibly as an accounting process, rather than the stewardship of investments. It would be unfair to criticise some of the investment decisions made years ago because they should be judged against the climate of the times. Even so, many thousands of family trusts have been diminished in value by an undue allegiance to gilt-edged stocks twenty-five years ago. This applied whether the trustees were private or corporate but, with the passing of the Trustee Investments Act 1961 which gave trustees wider investment powers, the trustee departments of the banks had the resources to move quickly to take advantage of the new legislation. The important point, however, is that nowadays banks hold themselves out as investment experts, for example in the management of pension funds and private portfolios, and thus their management of trusts will be judged increasingly by their performance in the investment field.

Improved investment performance will lead in many cases to higher fees and this will be a useful contribution to the problem of profitability. Many of the settled trusts administered today by the clearing banks were accepted years ago on the basis of fee scales which are no longer relevant. In one bank, out of approximately 20,000 settled trusts no less than 12,000 are on out-of-date fee scales. As we have said, this country is one of the few which do not have a statutory or common law power to charge fees and thus, in all cases the pattern of remuneration is governed by the terms of the trust instrument. All the banks have made approaches to their beneficiaries from time to time to secure an improvement in fees and these approaches have met with varying success. It is a problem which is fraught with difficulties and for the most part the banks are having to live with an uneconomic commitment into which they entered years ago. To add to the problem, the introduction of Value Added Tax in the 1972 Finance Act required payment by the banks of VAT on the fees in these old cases without any corresponding statutory power to charge the tax to the trust. This was almost certainly an oversight in the drafting of the Bill and representations were made to the Treasury, but no one in government circles felt inclined to amend the Act.

There is a touch of irony in the fact that the banks carry this great incubus of old cases on inadequate fees at a time when the market for new private trusts has declined. If all the old cases were on modern fee scales the profitability of trust business would look very different. In fact, the English banks act in approximately 80,000 settled trusts with a capital value of nearly £4 billion, but a very large proportion of these are on old and uneconomic fee scales.

If the flow of private trust business has diminished, the philanthropic instincts of the English settlor still remain and find expression in trusts of a charitable nature. We mention them here because they are private in origin if set up by an individual, but in law they are public trusts enforceable not by the beneficiaries as such but by the Attorney-General. A charitable trust enjoys the advantages of freedom from

*'. . . a touch of immortality.'*

taxation, freedom from the perpetuity rules (and thus may continue for an indefinite period) and freedom from the normal trust rules regarding the ascertainment of the beneficiaries – as the lawyers would say, a charitable trust will not fail for uncertainty. Even in these stringent times, people are prepared to set aside part of their personal fortunes for the public good and who shall deny them a touch of immortality for doing so.

There is one aspect of private trust business which has grown widely in the United States, but has little or no counterpart in this country. It is the so-called living trust. In America there are advantages in settling one's assets on named beneficiaries in either revocable or irrevocable form whilst still retaining the use and benefit of the trust fund at the discretion of the trustees. There is no fiscal advantage, any more than there would be in this country, in a revocable trust and Gift Tax is payable if the trust is irrevocable. Citizens in their declining years find it helpful, however, to pass the management of their affairs in this way to a trust company and on death the procedures are simplified and costs saved because title has already passed to the trust company. A living trust offers flexibility because it may be varied according to family circumstances and yet also certainty, in that the settlor can see the deed operating in his lifetime and thus avoid the problems of interpretation and even of legal contest which may arise where property passes under a will. There is also a greater degree of privacy. There may well be a model here for the English market to adopt, particularly now that there are no death duties payable on the passing of property between husband and wife. Is it too fanciful to suggest that if A settles all his assets on himself in a revocable trust with remainder to his wife on his death, there will be nothing for an executor to do because the assets will already be held for the wife's benefit in the trustee's name?

Another area of trust business, although of comparatively minor importance, is the trusteeship for a life policy. The proposer or 'life assured' under a life policy may settle the proceeds by a simple form of trust in favour of his wife or children or other beneficiaries and thereby avoid aggregation of the policy monies on death with the rest of his estate. Such a policy in favour of a wife was normally expressed to be taken out under the Married Women's Property Act 1882 – an Act which removed the disability of married women to dispose of their property by will – but this is not necessary: any disposition of the policy monies by way of a trust deed will be enforceable. The appointment of a corporate trustee for such a policy is not normally favoured as it would incur extra costs, and thus this is not a significant part of the banks' market. However, of more importance and a creature of our times is the off-shore trust. This is essentially the settling of funds in one of the tax havens of the world, usually under one of the schemes approved by Tax Counsel, in order to put one's fortune beyond the reach of the United Kingdom Treasury. We will come to these matters in Chapter 18 on 'Offshore Services'. They are of interest primarily to persons of substantial means and normally the bank trust departments and trust companies can be of assistance through their subsidiary companies off-shore.

Such is the private trustee business of the clearing banks. It is substantial for historical reasons, it is of diminishing importance, it is unprofitable overall, but there is still a future for the discretionary type of trust with its built-in flexibility to allow for changing circumstances.

## References

1 Justinian ii.23.1.
2 G. W. Keeton and L. A. Sheridan: *The Law of Trusts*, 10th ed. Professional Books, 1974.
3 Finance Act 1975, Part III.

CHAPTER 4

# Corporate Trusteeships

Let us turn, with a little more enthusiasm, to corporate trusteeships. The expression 'corporate trusts' is not in this country a very precise term. We use it here to differentiate between private trusts set up by an individual, as already discussed, and trusts set up by corporate bodies for the purpose of their own business. In the United States the title has a more precise meaning to which we will refer later.

Trusts for corporate bodies may be classified under five particular headings, although the list is not exclusive. They are:

1 pension fund trusteeships,
2 custodian trusteeships,
3 debenture trusteeships,
4 consortium trusteeships, and
5 trusteeships for unit trusts.

The pensions services of the clearing banks will be considered in Chapter 9 and here we are concerned only with the trustee aspect. Occupational pension schemes fall into two categories, i.e. those which are self-administered invested funds and those which are underwritten or managed by a life assurance office. In the former category, it is necessary for a trustee to be appointed to hold the assets of the pension fund. In the case of an insured scheme the trustee will be responsible for the due administration of the scheme and the purchase of the pensions in due course, but will not hold the funds as such, these being part of the life fund of the insurance company. We are concerned here primarily with the self-administered fund. Pensions business is big business. The flow of new money into the pension funds of this country is enormous (see Chapter 9). The scope for trust business is also very considerable.

With the passing of the Social Security Pensions Act 1975 (effective from April 1978) every employed person, subject to minor exceptions, became automatically covered by the new State Scheme unless he or she had been contracted out of the State Scheme to the permitted extent and was covered by a private scheme approved by the Occupational Pensions Board. Thus, the pensions scene, which had been confused for some years, became much clearer. Some schemes continue as before, some have been improved to satisfy the regulations and in all other cases employees are automatically covered by the State Scheme.

Every private pension scheme requires a trustee and the appointment of a corporate trustee is appropriate because of the advantages of continuity. In some companies the pension fund trustees are private individuals, perhaps directors of the company, but this is not an ideal situation. Indeed, many employees would probably prefer the fortunes of the pension fund to be handled outside the company.

The role of the pension fund trustee is to receive the contributions, whether from employer alone or from employer and employee, and to invest these in the pension fund according to the terms of the deed. In due time, the trustee is responsible for the payment of pensions to retired employees. To an extent the work is largely administrative. A 'full' trustee of a pension fund will also be responsible, however, for investment policy. There are usually very wide investment powers and thus the trustees have the very real responsibility of investing the trust fund, with virtually unlimited powers, in an attempt to combat inflation and keep the pension fund solvent.

In other cases the trustees will act on the advice of an investment committee or investment managers appointed by the company, but usually depending on the wording of the deed, the ultimate responsibility will still rest with the trustee. We shall discuss these investment matters at a later point.

The second area of corporate trusteeship is that of custodian trustee. In fact, this role is not limited to corporate situations, and in practice custodian trusteeships tend to be on behalf of companies and other corporations and unincorporated groups of people such as clubs and local societies. The office of custodian trustee is a statutory creation of the Public Trustee Act 1906 and, as we have seen, is the only instance where a corporate trustee has a statutory authority to charge fees. In practice, the statutory provisions are burdensome and it is normal for custodian trustees to be appointed under express powers in the trust deed. It is a useful arrangement where the organisation concerned wishes to retain the managing function whilst having the benefit of a bank or other corporate body holding the trust assets. The custodian trustee retains custody of the trust property and documents, leaving the managing trustees to deal with the day-to-day administration of the trust.

The third main area of corporate trust work is that of debenture trusteeships. When a company seeks to issue debentures or debenture stock, or even unsecured loan stock, it is customary to appoint a trustee to protect the interests of the debenture-holders or stockholders. The issue is normally constituted under a trust deed entered into between the company and the trustee. The powers and duties of the trustee will be set out in the deed. In general, it is the concern of the trustee to see that the obligations of the company are duly performed. The debentures or stock may carry a fixed charge over certain fixed assets, or a floating charge over the undertaking generally, or both. The trustee would normally hold the documents of title to any specifically charged assets and in some cases may be required to ensure that the floating assets of the undertaking are maintained at a stipulated level. If there is a sinking fund for the redemption of the debentures or stock, the trustee will be responsible for seeing that the fund is operated in accordance with the deed. The trustee may have a particularly active role where there are a number of dealings in the charged assets by way of sales, purchases, leases, etc. The security property can be released only with the consent of the trustee and such consent would also be necessary where, for any reason, it is proposed to reduce the value of the security property by the withdrawal of assets from behind the debentures or stock without replacement. The trustee will also be responsible for seeing that freehold and leasehold properties are properly insured and that all outgoings are duly met.

The trustee's role will be comparatively passive unless and until the security becomes enforceable, when some action will be necessary by the trustee, usually the appointment of a

*'... to protect the security property.'*

Receiver, to protect the security property for the benefit of the debenture-holders or stockholders. The trust deed will specify the circumstances in which the security shall become enforceable and these will normally include default in payment of principal or interest on the debentures or stock, the winding-up of the company, the cessation of business or breaches of covenant by the company. It is fortunately rare that a trustee has occasion to appoint a Receiver, but it does of course happen from time to time and the responsibility of the trustee can then become an onerous one. The author had the unusual experience of appointing a Receiver for a well-known undertaking in Israel where the debentures were held worldwide – an interesting experience but not generally to be recommended.

Debenture trusts are usually of long duration and call for trustees of standing and business experience. The banks and insurance companies are therefore well equipped for the task and, in the ordinary way, the business is remunerative.

Whilst the duties are normally of an undemanding nature, they cease to be so if the security becomes enforceable and it is usual to provide that in such circumstances the level of remuneration shall be doubled, or even trebled.

As far as the banks are concerned, the business of debenture trusteeships has had a chequered career. It was not uncommon for a bank to accept debenture trusts in the pre-war and immediate post-war years, but it became a matter for comment in the Report of the Cohen Committee on Company Law Amendment in 1945, which suggested that a conflict of interest might arise in cases where a bank was both the creditor of a company and trustee for the debenture-holders. Following the Report, the Rules of the Stock Exchange were amended to provide that the trustee for the debenture-holders of a listed company must not have an interest in relation to the company which might conflict with the trustee's role as such.

Whilst recognising that a conflict of interest can arise where a banker is in the dual role of lender to a company and trustee for the debenture-holders, it should be noted that banks are not unaccustomed to apparent conflicts of interest between their rôle as banker and as trustee. In practice such issues are resolved with commendable independence by both sides and nothing is likely to deter the bank as trustee from acting in the best interests of its beneficiaries or, in this instance, debenture-holders.

After the Stock Exchange ruling it was therefore left to the banks to take in each other's washing, but in practice this did not happen. Some banks were reluctant to become trustee for debenture-holders in a large public company if it might inhibit the possibility of their becoming bankers to the company at some future date. Others felt that the conflict was more apparent than real and continued to take debenture trusteeships. In more recent times the Stock Exchange rule has been relaxed and the problem no longer remains, but in the years of uncertainty a considerable amount of debenture trusteeship business was lost to insurance companies.

Perhaps a more esoteric aspect of company trusteeship is the development in recent years of consortium trusts. They usually arise where a major development or exploration is financed internationally by a consortium of leading names. Provided the consortium are prepared to adopt the Anglo-Saxon concept of a trust, the appointment of a London clearing bank or trust company as trustee can solve a lot of problems. The day-to-day financial administration of the project becomes the responsibility of the trustee who will deal with stage payments under the contract, insurance, performance bonds, bank guarantees, currency conversion, investment of surplus funds and generally act as stakeholder for the parties. In such cases, the trust becomes the focal point for the legal, accountancy and administrative aspects of the project and a vehicle by which enforcement is ensured of the diverse legal rights of the contracting parties.

This is perhaps a good place to mention the development of corporate trusteeships in the United States. One important role there is the trusteeship of local authority bonds. This is similar to a trusteeship for debenture-holders in the United Kingdom, but there is no counterpart in this country in relation to local authorities. The local authorities in America enjoy a considerable degree of independence and autonomy and are responsible for their own local commitments such as schools, hospitals, roads and bridges. For these purposes money is raised in the market and there are over 80,000 municipalities issuing bonds in the United States. Corporate trustees are required to act in connection with such issues and this work falls to the banks and trust companies. They have an obligation to ensure that an issue is sound, but there is no legal liability on the trustee in the event of a failure of a local authority.

We come then to the last major area of corporate trusts – the trusteeship of unit trusts. It is surprising that even at this stage in the development of unit trusts a large number of people, some of them in the business world, do not know what they are. In fact, market surveys show that the man in the street is remarkably ignorant on the subject despite having been bombarded by newspaper advertisements for a good many years. Perhaps many people would say 'I know what it is, but I can't describe it'. That is understandable because a definition is not easy and unit trusts are almost *sui generis* in that they do not fall naturally within the scope of company law or the vast body of trust law in this country. And while it is true that unit trusts have their origin in the basic trust concept – particularly in the use made of trusts to hold property for unincorporated associations – unit trusts on the whole owe little to the general body of trust law. Considering the growth of unit trust business, there is remarkably little statutory or case law on the subject. This is no doubt attributable both to the good sense of those engaged in the business, whether as managers or trustees, and to the very shrewd control exercised by the Department of Trade.

We will deal more particularly with the nature and development of unit trusts in a later chapter, but perhaps a brief historical note would be appropriate here. Dr Pennington, of Birmingham University, in his admirable book, *The Investor and the Law,*[1] refers to the trust funds set up in Victorian England for the purpose of spreading investors' risks, the equalisation of income, the gradual re-investment of capital and ultimate disbursement of capital profit. These foundered on the company law rule that associations 'formed for the purpose of carrying on a business that has as its object the acquisition of gain' may not have a membership exceeding twenty.[2] Although the decision was overruled in the later case of Smith v Anderson[3] and the way cleared for the development of investment trust funds, it was the investment company rather than the trust concept which was to be developed in England during the 1930s.

The subsequent development owes something to the

experience of investment trusts in America, a large number of which were created in the 1920s, not all with satisfactory results. Some of them were very hazardous and became worthless when Wall Street collapsed in 1929. These early trusts (which were in fact companies) were 'fixed', in that the subscriptions from investors were committed to a stated portfolio which remained fixed throughout the life of the trust. When all the units of a trust had been issued, a second trust would be set up on identical terms with an identical portfolio, and so on with successive trusts. There was some confusion of terminology when these trusts were introduced into the United Kingdom because over here each separate trust was called a unit and the 'shares' held by the public were known as sub-units. The first British trust of this type was launched in 1931 by Muncipal & General Securities Company Limited (now the M. & G. Group) under the name of First British Fixed Trust. In the ensuing years a number of other similar trusts were launched, but it soon became apparent that fixed trusts were too inflexible and that the managers could not vary the investments. Thus, the flexible unit trust was introduced and the first of these was The Foreign Government Bond Trust, which was launched in 1934. By the beginning of 1938, seventy-three unit trusts were in existence in this country with a total market value of approximately £80 million.[4] All existing fixed trusts were either converted to flexible trusts or wound up, and all the newly-formed trusts were 'open-ended' in that the number of units in issue could vary according to the level of purchases and sales. The term 'sub-unit' was dropped in this country and the individual shareholdings became known as units or shares.

The principal difference between the British and the American pattern of development lay in the fact that, under company law in this country, it was not and still is not possible for a company to buy its own shares.[5] This limitation did not apply in the United States with the result that their mutual funds, as they are known today, grew out of the concept of the investment company.

In December 1935, the London Stock Exchange published a report on 'Fixed Trusts' and recommended that legislation be introduced for the protection of the investing public.[6]. This was followed in August 1936 by a Board of Trade report which in turn recommended that there should be legislation on the subject of fixed trusts.[7] There was no statutory regulation of unit trusts however until some clauses were inserted at the Committee stage in the Prevention of Fraud (Investments) Bill 1939, which became law on 8 August 1944. Those provisions were updated and re-enacted fourteen years later in the Prevention of Fraud (Investments) Act 1958. Under the Act, the regulation of the unit trusts movement was brought under the then Board of Trade and is now the responsibility of the Department of Trade. Among other matters, the Act serves to emphasise the importance of the role of the trustee and it is that aspect with which we are principally concerned in this section.

Although the powers and duties of a unit trust trustee will be laid down in each case in the unit trust deed, the trust will not be 'authorised' (see Chapter 6, p. 76) by the Department of Trade unless the deed complies with the requirements of the first Schedule to the Act.[8] Certain duties of a routine or procedural nature are also imposed on trustees by the Unit Trust Records Regulations.[9]

In general terms, we may summarise the functions of the unit trust trustee as follows.

1. To secure the vesting in the trustee or his nominee of the trust property prior to the issue of units.[10]

2. To be given reasonable time to consider or propose advertisements and related documents and to prohibit their issue if he, the trustee, disapproves.[11]

3. To require the managers to retire from the trust if he, the trustee, is satisfied that it is in the interests of the unitholders that they should do so.[12]

4. To hold the investments of the trust and any cash deposited by the managers, to collect and distribute the income from the trust assets, to sign and issue certificates to unitholders and to supervise the maintenance of the Register of Unitholders.[13]

5. To ensure general compliance with the terms of the trust deed.

The trustee of a unit trust does not have any specific responsibility for the content or performance of the portfolio, but if, for example, an investment were purchased outside the investment powers of the trust, it would be proper for the trustee to draw attention to the matter and require its rectification.

A trust deed will normally absolve the trustee from liability in respect of breaches of trust and he will not normally be liable for loss or damage to the trust property unless he has acted fraudulently or negligently. Nevertheless, the burden is an onerous one. The trustee must carry out his duties in a diligent and prudent fashion. It is not a passive role, it is not a perfunctory patrolling of a quiet street, it is not a mere custodianship. It is an active, day-to-day supervision of the manager's role to ensure that the terms of the trust deed and the Department of Trade regulations are observed, and that the interests of the unitholders are protected.

The statutory requirements and the nature of the duties effectively limit the choice of unit trust trustees to the clearing banks, merchant banks and insurance companies. It is a role which has fallen naturally to the clearing banks because of their trustee experience over the years and at the present time, out of 393 unit trusts in this country, some 361 have English and Scottish clearing banks as trustees. The Midland Bank Trust Company has actively sought unit trust trusteeships over the years and for a long time stood aside from active participation in the management of unit trusts. Perhaps for that reason the Midland Bank Trust Company has a larger number of unit trust trusteeships than its competitors.

Those banks which moved into the management of unit trusts in the early days did not however, necessarily, suffer in the development of their trusteeship business. For instance, Barclays Bank, although managers of the Unicorn Group of trusts, one of the largest in the country, was also for many years the trustee of the giant Save & Prosper Group. The two roles were exercised in separate pockets of the organisation and there was no apparent conflict and certainly no breach of confidence.

It is a statutory requirement that the effective control of the management company is 'exercised' independently of the corporation acting as trustee.[14] Thus a bank or other corporate body may not be trustee of a unit trust of which it is manager, even though the functions may be exercised separately in the same group. There are cases where the two roles are exercised side by side – indeed in some instances there are 'managing trustees' – but such trusts cannot be 'authorised', a subject which is dealt with in Chapter 6.

The business of unit trust trusteeships can be profitable if conducted on a reasonably large scale with streamlined methods of administration. The fees are a matter for negotiation between managers and trustees and are usually expressed as a percentage of the value of the funds under management. As this is in itself the subject of Department of Trade control, the scope for improving the trustee's remuneration is very limited. Where the trustee is a bank, the uninvested cash balances can be an added source of remuneration to the banking group, provision having been made for this in the trust deed, and such balances used to be very substantial although probably less so in recent years.

If there be any special problems of unit trust trusteeship, they almost certainly lie in the area of supervision and control. Troubles can soon arise if the management company does not have an adequate administrative system. There may also be problems over the monitoring of advertisements, but nowadays the Unit Trust Association (see p. 85) exercises a very firm influence on its members in such matters. Fortunately, it seems to have been exceedingly rare that a trustee has had to intervene to the point of requiring the manager to resign. (The author was closely involved in such an incident years ago, but knows of no other case.)

It has been said that unitholders are given less control in the management of their medium of investment than the shareholders of an investment trust company.[12] One might go further and say that unitholders have less 'say' in the affairs of their trust than a shareholder in any company. It is usual for the deeds of authorised trusts to provide that holders of, say, one-tenth in value of the units in issue may convene a meeting of unitholders. Such a meeting cannot, however, vary the terms of the trust without the approval of the managers, the trustees and the Department of Trade. The unitholders cannot remove either manager or trustee and they have no say in investment policy or any other matters concerning the day-to-day running of the trust. The unitholder has the right to request the Department of Trade to appoint inspectors to investigate a unit trust,[16] but the

Department may do this only where it is satisfied that it is in the interests of unitholders and the matter is one of public concern. The remedies of two million or so unitholders in this country are minimal: thus the role of the trustee is an important one.

**Other corporate trusteeships**

The concept of the trust is one of the most versatile in English law and thus, in a changing environment, new forms of trust arise depending sometimes on fashion or ingenuity, but occasionally from statutory requirements. Two such examples are:

(a) trusteeships for insurance companies. Under a comparatively recent statutory provision,[17] the Department of Trade (or more correctly the Secretary of State) may require insurance companies to set aside in the United Kingdom a fund equal to the whole, or some specified proportion, of their domestic liabilities and may require the whole or part of the assets set aside to be held by a person, approved by the Secretary of State, to act as trustee for the company.

This enactment has led to a substantial flow of business to the banks who are, of course, natural custodians for this purpose.

(b) trusteeship of profit-sharing schemes. Although there is nothing new in the concept of profit-sharing schemes for employees, they have not been widespread in the United Kingdom, partly because of taxation considerations. Under the 1978 Finance Act, however, provision was made for a degree of tax relief for profit-sharing schemes with effect from April 1979. Under the Act, an employer may make up to £500 per employee available in shares, free of tax, provided a special trust has been set up for the profit-sharing scheme. The shares must remain with the trustee for the minimum period of five years. Thereafter, if the shares are sold, income tax will be payable on a reducing scale to a point where no tax will be payable after a fifteen-year period. It remains to be seen whether such schemes are introduced on a wide scale, but if so there may well be scope for useful business for the banks.

All in all, the banks have few major competitors in the field of corporate trusteeships. It is a role they fill with great experience and efficiency and one which they will no doubt continue to carry out profitably, whether in relation to the particular areas described in this chapter or for some future categories of trusteeship as yet not contemplated.

## References


1 R. R. Pennington: *The Investor and the Law*. MacGibbon and Kee, 1968.
2 Sykes v Beadon (1879) 11 Ch.D.170.
3 Smith v Anderson (1880) 15 Ch.D.247.
4 M. J. Day and P. I. Harris: 'Unit Trusts'. *Oyez*, 1974.
5 Companies Act 1948, s. 54.
6 Report of The Stock Exchange Sub-Committee on Fixed Trusts, 1935.
7 Board of Trade: 'Fixed Trusts' – Report of a Departmental Committee, Cmd 5259. HMSO, 1936.
8 Prevention of Fraud (Investments) Act 1958.
9 Statutory Rules and Orders 1946. No. 1586.
10 Prevention of Fraud (Investments) Act 1958, Schedule 1, para. 2.
11 Ibid, para. 4.
12 Ibid, para. 7.
13 Unit Trust Records Regulations 1946, para. 5.
14 Prevention of Fraud (Investments) Act 1958, s. 17(d).
15 M. J. Day and P. I. Harris: op. cit., p. 174.
16 Prevention of Fraud (Investments) Act 1958, s. 12(1).
17 Insurance Companies Act 1974, s. 32.

CHAPTER 5

# Investment Services

The clearing banks in Britain have always been rather shy of any activities bearing the name 'investment'. Until comparatively recent years, the banks did not regard themselves as being in the investment business other than for the purpose of managing their own gilt-edged portfolios and their own pension funds. Today the banks are four-square in the investment business and under that heading have probably built up the most comprehensive package of investment services to be found anywhere in the world.

A straight catalogue of these services is as boring as a laundry list, but perhaps in this instance it will help if we consider in sequence all that the banks offer their customers under this heading. The word 'investment' requires some explanation or definition, particularly as it is often linked almost synonymously with 'savings'. The act of saving is an accumulation of a capital sum: investment, at least for our purpose here, is the putting of that capital sum to work.

We need not take much space over those investment services which are of an administrative or procedural nature. They are:

(a) **custody of bearer securities and collection of income** Many bank clerks will have spent time in the strongroom cutting coupons from bearer bonds and sending them for payment. This task of collecting the customer's income goes back well into the last century and is referred to by Bagehot in his book *Lombard Street*, in 1873. Nowadays, to the extent that these bonds are foreign securities, they will normally need to be held by the banks as 'authorised depositories' and the collection of coupons is a natural corollary of this. It is of advantage to the customer, who does not need to keep a look-out for dividend announcements and other company notices.

(b) **nomineeships for shareholders**
All the banks operate nominee companies for the convenience of their customers, as do other financial institutions. It has been estimated that over 25 per cent (by value) of ordinary shares in the leading UK companies are held in nominee names.[2] The banks offer this service as a convenience to stockbrokers, charities and other associations, and to customers living abroad. It is a convenience to customers in that it saves a lot of work and other administrative chores. The banks will not knowingly allow nominee services to be used for tax avoidance or other abuse of our fiscal legislation.

(c) **valuation services**
Most of the banks, as an extension of their computer services, will provide customers with valuations of quoted securities for a modest charge.

The next category of investment services is really no more than an extension of the banking function in that it covers alternative avenues for placing liquid funds within the banking group itself, which therefore appear in the bank's balance sheet. They include:

(d) **negotiable certificates of deposit**
The principal United Kingdom banks, whether through their merchant banks or other subsidiaries, issue negotiable certificates of deposit denominated in sterling and usually offering a higher rate of interest than that available on normal deposit accounts. The minimum amount accepted in this way is usually £50,000. These are bearer certificates and are negotiable. Dollar certificates of deposit are also available to non-residents or UK residents with exchange control permission, and are issued by the international subsidiaries of the London banks. Foreign currency deposits will also be accepted from customers who are resident abroad or UK residents who have Bank of England permission. All these services offer great flexibility, coupled usually with a rate of interest higher than that available on domestic deposits.

(e) **market rate deposits**
The London banks will offer market rates for substantial funds, the usual minimum being £50,000, placed direct with their Treasurer's Department. Here again, the arrangements are flexible and the rate of interest higher than the normal seven-day bankers' deposit rate.

(f) **deposit receipts**
Most of the London banks will issue a deposit receipt for a fixed sum on the basis that interest, which will be at current rates, will not be paid until the date agreed with the customer. The scheme is useful for tax planning and income equalisation purposes.

In all the foregoing cases, the banks are acting in their primary role as bankers and to that extent the services listed are strictly outside the scope of this book. They have been included in order to present a full picture of investment services. In other instances the banks act as intermediaries for their customers and these services include:

(g) **purchase of stock exchange securities**
A survey conducted in 1966[2] showed that 53 per cent of all owners of stocks and shares made their purchases and sales through their banks. This has been borne out by subsequent surveys and there is no doubt that the clearing banks play a major role in stock market investment on behalf of their customers. The procedures adopted by the banks vary, but the result is the same – the banks buy and sell investments for their customers through stockbrokers, usually of the banks' choice. Traditionally this service has been provided free by the banks for their customers, the banks receiving a share of the stockbrokers' commissions. It is a great advantage to the private customer to be relieved of the paperwork in such cases and to have the transaction settled by the bank on his behalf. The service extends to all ordinary stocks and shares, and gilt-edged stocks and bonds, quoted on the principal stock exchanges in this country or abroad.

(h) **local authority investments**
All the banks will place funds with local authorities on behalf of their customers, whether by way of mortgages or bonds, usually for periods of one year upwards.

(i) **Treasury bills**
The banks will purchase Treasury bills on behalf of their customers – these are bearer instruments issued by the Bank of England for ninety-one days – and usually take a small commission for their trouble. The minimum amount is £5,000 and the bills may be discounted with the Bank of England or negotiated in the market.

(j) **insurance contracts**
The banks also act as intermediaries in placing investment funds in various forms of insurance contract. These include annuities, single premium policies, income bonds and pension plans. These are discussed in Chapter 8.

There remain two very considerable areas where the banks demonstrate an investment capability. These are investment advice and investment management.

(k) **advice on investments**
Various surveys have shown, not surprisingly, that most people regard their bank managers as financial advisors and indeed it is customary for letters of allotment and other documents to contain the suggestion that the investor in need of advice should consult, among others, his bank manager. Paradoxically it has been a standing instruction in the English banks down the years that their managers must *not* advise on investments. The banks' reluctance to be seen in this role is understandable. It would be unthinkable that 12,000 or so bank managers should hold themselves out as being sufficiently expert in the art of investment to advise their investing customers. We are not a litigious nation, but such a pose by the banks would inevitably lead to a spate of claims for negligence on the part of disappointed customers. Such a claim did in fact reach the Court in the rare and unfortunate case of Woods v Martins Bank (see p. 147).

The Woods case provided a platform on which to rehearse the law on the subject, but it was not a typical case and the decision turned very much on the rather singular facts in question. However, it is reasonably clear that if banks allowed their managers to advise on investments, they would have to do so with that standard of care expected of a clearing bank, which would be a very high standard indeed. It would almost certainly be that same standard of care as the bank exercises in the management of its own investments. In other words, the advice would have to be backed by those processes of research and analysis which are conducted in great depth by the banks, but the results of which are not available, nor would it be feasible to make them available, to the managers in the front line. For that reason and others which we shall discuss, it would be wrong to expect the bank manager in the High Street to be an investment advisor. The present system is that the manager is a channel for investment advice and information between stockbroker and customer. The manager who is asked for his 'advice' on the investment of a sum of money or on whether or not a particular 'rights' issue should be taken up or whether indeed certain investments should be bought or sold, will obtain the comments of one of the stockbrokers allocated to the branch and pass these on without embellishment to the customer. The system works well enough and keeps everybody happy.

There are occasions however when customers seek not the second-hand advice of a stockbroker, but the opinion of the bank itself. In such cases, the information or advice must come from the centre where in all the banks a degree of investment expertise is concentrated. In fact, there is no formal enquiry service of this kind, partly because the demand is not apparent and partly because the cost of providing such a service would be more than the market would bear. Perhaps the nearest thing of its kind was the Investment Report service introduced by Barclays a few years ago. This provided the customer with a detailed report on, and valuation of, a customer's portfolio at intervals selected by the customer, together with up-to-date comment on the stock market and the economic climate. The management of the investments remained with the customer and there was no continuing services between reports. A fee was charged according to the number of holdings in the portfolio. This was perhaps the nearest approach to an advisory service as such, but it had limited appeal and has now been discontinued. Most owners of stocks and shares prefer to have the comments of a stockbroker, passed on to them by the local branch manager, no doubt believing that they are receiving some kind of combined opinion which of course is far from the case. Let us conclude by saying that the High Street banks are not prima facie in the investment advice business.

(l) **management of investments**

We have already remarked on the reluctance of banks in this country to manage the affairs of their living customers, although willing enough to do so on death. Perhaps the dead are more reasonable to deal with. Certainly, years ago it would have been unthinkable that the banks would undertake the management of customers' investments, but out of the business of administering estates and trusts has grown a very considerable investment management capability.

In discussing private trusts, we have stressed the importance of the investment role but, as we have said, the active management of the trust investments was seldom seen as a matter of primary responsibility. None of the trustee departments conducted any basic investment research but were satisfied with a distillation of stockbrokers' circulars. Each trust had a stockbroker advisor and an investment review would be conducted with the stockbroker at least once a year. The system was not without merit – it was perhaps unimaginative but it worked, although the banks did not regard themselves as investment experts and were slow to take the initiative in investment decisions.

On the winding-up of an estate or trust it would quite often happen that the investments passed into the absolute ownership of a beneficiary, perhaps a widow or daughter, who did not feel able to take on the responsibility of management. In other cases, parents would not wish their children, albeit of full age, to have the control of their inheritance. In these and similar cases, the bank would agree to continue to hold the investments and execute a 'declaration of trust' to the effect that they were held absolutely for the beneficiary who could call for the transfer of the investments at any time. Thus, the banks moved with apparent ease into the business of managing the assets of the living. With very few exceptions the assets of a declaration of trust were always quoted securities, and investment decisions would not normally be taken without the approval of the beneficiary and then only on the recommendation of the stockbroker. It was the beginning of investment management and it was only a matter of time before 'declarations of trust' were entered into for bank customers at large, regardless of any trustee connection already existing.

There were visionaries in all the banks who saw a great

future for investment management business, but it was Lloyds Bank from among the English clearing banks who first moved overtly into the investment management business and changed the name of 'declaration of trust' to 'investment management account'. The Scottish banks too, perhaps a little less affected by the constraints of the English 'trust', saw the opportunities for investment management work, and in time all the banks followed suit. Today the investment management business of the English and Scottish banks is enormous. They manage, on the basis of recent figures, approximately 35,000 portfolios for private clients and the total value is of the order of £1,500 million.

To some extent the banks had been hidebound by their own traditional attitudes. On the one hand they could not hold themselves out as investment experts without training or recruiting a team of people for the work, but on the other hand the time-honoured method of managing trust investments did not seem to call for, nor justify in terms of cost, the employment of analysts, accountants and economists. When, in 1964, Martins Bank (perhaps a little unexpectedly for a provincial bank) set up a small investment research unit, it claimed to be the first of the clearing banks to do so, although there were no doubt varying degrees of research activity in most of the banks by that time. Three years later, Martins Bank Trust Company, the first of the new style trust operations, was devised as an investment-orientated operation. It claimed to be in the business of asset management, for the living and for the dead, for private people and for institutions. On its takeover by Barclays Bank, the combined operation became one of the largest investment houses in Europe.

Even when the banks broke away from their traditional thinking and developed investment management business, they did not readily accept the full responsibility for investment decisions. In most cases, an investment transaction would be put through merely with the approval of the owner. Some customers did not want this. They preferred the bank or trust company to take whatever action they thought necessary and report afterwards. Thus, the discretionary account developed and today one-half or more of new investment accounts undertaken by the banks are of a discretionary nature, i.e. the bank takes a decision and tells the customer afterwards. Indeed the investment specialists prefer it this way.

The decision-making processes in the field of investment management vary in detail, but follow substantially the same pattern. The amount of time and money spent on research differs from bank to bank and generally reflects the degree of importance attached to investment research. The individual analysts will normally follow the fortunes of particular sectors of the market and as many as possible of the companies in those sectors. This is achieved by day-to-day contact with the market, detailed study of the financial press, distillation of stockbrokers' reports, visits to companies and a continuing awareness of the political and economic climate in which the companies are operating. Depending on how it is used, investment research can be an expensive luxury or the very stuff of which investment decisions are made.

Whatever the quality of research, and whether it be from internal or external sources, it must be fed into the policy-making machine. Investment policy operates functionally at three distinct levels: (a) the degree of liquidity which is considered to be desirable across the board in all the portfolios under management; (b) the balance of the portfolio among the various market sectors, e.g. gilt-edged, equities (UK and overseas) and property; and (c) the designation of individual investments for purchase or sale.

There is little doubt that the first is the most important. Some would say that the only decisions that really matter in portfolio management are those that call for liquidity at the top of the market and full investment at the bottom. Certainly the more graphic performance is achieved by overall timing rather than switching activities within the portfolio, however desirable this may be at times. Judicious switching can of course improve the performance of the portfolio. It can be a mistake to chase the winners in a market where there are only losers. In the tragic 'bear' market of 1972–74 the honours went to those investment managers who took their clients out of the market in good time instead of worrying about which shares would perform best. However, as we know, it is not all that easy. A large bank managing scores of thousands of portfolios cannot readily take such across-the-board decisions. There are always a great many subjective considerations which have to be interpreted at local level, and it is not always possible to do for one what is done for another.

In the choice of shares for purchase or sale it is the common practice among banks to have a 'shopping list' circulated to their local offices. The list and the grading within the list are usually arrived at by informed debate in the investment department. Such lists are usually intended to be a general guide and are not always expected to be followed slavishly. Nevertheless, a branch office which persisted in buying a stock marked in the list as a 'sale' would do so at its peril.

Ideally, in the interests of scientific management, all the portfolios which a bank has under management should be centred in one place, preferably in one room, where investment decisions may be translated quickly into action and where there would be a uniformity of treatment. This is the normal practice among merchant banks and other investment houses who do not operate through a branch network. On the other hand, the management of private portfolios is a very subjective business and many customers attach great value to the facility for discussion at local level. Mr Hoyt Ammidon, former Chairman of the United States Trust Company, is credited with saying that investment management is 10 per cent know-how and 90 per cent public relations – a conscious hyperbole which nevertheless serves to emphasise the personal aspect of the investment business.

Thus far we have looked only at the management of personal portfolios, but the banks are equally in the market for institutional business – the management of portfolios for corporations, pension funds, charities and other institutional investors. Such business is much sought after because the portfolios are usually substantial, the investment guidelines are generally clear cut and devoid of subjective considerations and the work can be centralised in the investment department. Traditionally, much of this work has gone to the merchant banks, largely because of the low profile maintained by the clearing banks in investment matters until recent years. We will look more specifically at pension fund business in Chapter 9, but it is noteworthy that institutional business of all kinds, administered by the clearing banks and their subsidiaries, whether as trustee or investment manager, amounts to over £4,000 million spread throughout nearly 500 portfolios. This is in

*'90 per cent public relations.'*

addition to the very considerable funds managed by the banks in their own pension funds.

Not surprisingly, investment management on such a scale has its problems. One of these is the difficulty of dealing with the smaller portfolios. To maintain a sophisticated investment department is an expensive business and it becomes disproportionately expensive when portfolio managers have to be employed to deal with large numbers of small cases. Historically the banks have had more than their share of smaller portfolios. This stemmed from the practice of taking on very small declarations of trust which, as we have seen, were the origin of the present-day investment business. There is also the very real point that the bank in the High Street seeks to provide a service for all-comers – to be all things to all men.

There are two aspects of this problem. The first is the very real difficulty of managing a small portfolio in an economical way. Only a few stocks can be purchased so that the portfolio is not truly representative: just one 'mistake' can be unduly expensive and costs are disproportionately high. If there were no satisfactory alternative one might make a case for portfolio management of amounts of, say, £20,000 and above. In practice, however, there is in this country the very real alternative of unit trust investment which generally is a far better medium for sums up to, say, £50,000 or indeed well above that. This is something we shall consider separately in Chapter 6. There will, however, always be those investors who wish to have their own separately managed portfolio, however small the value.

The second problem is one of costs. The American trust departments will not normally accept the management of portfolios of less than $250,000 and sometimes the minimum size is very much larger. In this country few merchant banks undertake the management of portfolios of less than £100,000. Over 90 per cent of the portfolios administered by the clearing banks today are less than that figure. The banks will have differing views as to the break-even point in terms of portfolio size, but it is improbable that individual portfolios of less than £100,000 can be managed profitably at current fee levels when one takes into account present-day salaries and pension provisions, the cost of a branch network, proper allocation of overheads and some contribution for marketing costs. On a sample costing in one bank, it was found that with comparatively small cases, of which there were a large number, the cost of setting up the records and doing the preparatory work for a new investment management account exceeded the amount of the first year's fee. Taking a typical fee of 60p per £100 on a portfolio of, say, £50,000, the client will be paying £300 per annum for the service. Whilst this is modest for the responsibility of managing a fund of that size, it is large in relation to the net return which the investor will have annually after tax. Unfortunately in this country such charges for the management of assets are not allowable for taxation purposes as they are in other countries, notably the United States. Despite the increase in fees in recent years, however, the banks' charges are still competitive and they have succeeded in increasing their share of the market very substantially.

Another problem area is the multiplicity of holdings. Although we are considering at this point the investment management service for private and institutional customers, the banks have a vast investment business in connection with their estates and trusts. In general these require the same degree of investment management as the investment management accounts. The result is that the total number of portfolios under management might be as many as, say, 30,000 and many of the individual investments in these portfolios would not have been chosen from a select list but 'inherited' from deceaseds' estates and retained for various good reasons. In one bank, on a simultaneous scrutiny of the portfolios, it was found that no fewer than 2,600 separate equity stocks were held, i.e. in separate companies, in addition to large numbers of fixed interest stocks and bonds. It is quite impossible, of course, to monitor adequately such a wide range of holdings. It is doubtful whether a well staffed investment department can follow more than, say, 250 stocks in a meaningful day-to-day fashion and it may well be that the banks will have to limit their investments under management to a more modest number.

If the multiplicity of individual stocks is a problem, so too is the number of portfolios. It is the norm in this country for each estate, each trust, each investment management account and each fund of any kind to have its own separate portfolio which may have a selection of ordinary stocks and a proportion of fixed interest investments. Apart from the investment aspects, this calls for a very considerable administrative operation. If, for example, a bank or trust company administers 30,000 portfolios with an average of only ten investments in each, there are 300,000 separate investments to be recorded and designated, and if on each investment there are two dividend or interest payments per annum, there will be 600,000 separate items of income to be collected and distributed. In some banks, the problem is alleviated by the practice of mandating interest and dividend payments direct to the banking accounts of the beneficiaries. Whatever system is used, the basic pattern of trust business in the United Kingdom remains the same – that each case of whatever size has its own individual portfolio. In recent years, this has been alleviated to some extent by the use of unit trusts, but for legal reasons it is not possible to merge portfolios into common funds as is done in the United States. The objections are (a) that as the law stands at present, a common fund or unit trust for fixed interest stocks would be at a disadvantage for taxation purposes and (b) that a common fund of equities would have to be constituted as an 'authorised' unit trust if it were to qualify as a wider range investment under the Trustee Investments Act 1961. Quite often the authorised unit trusts within each banking group can be used for such purposes, but (i) this is possible only where the trust instrument permits it (otherwise the trustee would be benefiting from his trust to the extent that fees were charged in the unit trust), and (ii) in many cases there would still be a residue of fixed interest investments so that there would be almost as many separate portfolios as before.

Whatever the administrative problems there is also an investment problem, although perhaps of an administrative nature. It is not uncommon for a popular stock to appear across a wide range of portfolios under the management of the same business house. Some years ago, on a sample check in one bank, it was found that a certain leading company was represented in no fewer than 20,000 portfolios under the bank's management. Those portfolios were administered in thirty or so separate offices round the country and the total investment was in excess of £20 million. A decision on investment grounds to sell the shares in that company or even to reduce the holdings substantially on a proportionate basis in all cases, would have been quite impossible to execute except over an unacceptable period of time. If the banks are to continue to act for an ever-growing number of investment clients, they would be well advised to seek a change in the law to permit much wider use of in-house common funds.

The Bank of Scotland have taken a step towards solving the problem not only of smaller portfolios, but of the multiplicity of holdings. They offer their customers what is known as a Managed Portfolio Service, which is in fact a participation in one of two master portfolios, one offering high income, the other offering capital growth with some income. The scheme has some of the merits of a unit trust in that the investor achieves a wide spread of holdings, whilst being relieved of all administrative problems of managing his own investments. From the bank's point of view, there is also the advantage that two major portfolios take the place of a variety of smaller ones. It is not, however, a unit trust as such. Each individual investor owns a cross-section of the master portfolio and, to that extent, has his own list of investments on which he receives regular detailed reports.

The last area of special difficulty is one which is not always recognised or acknowledged. It goes without saying that a bank is prima facie in the business of banking and this involves the bank in a very considerable awareness of the financial and economic climate, as well as in a detailed acquaintance with a large number of quoted companies. If then, as has happened, a bank turns its hand to the management of stock exchange investments, to what extent (a) ought it to use or (b) ensure that it does not use, its knowledge as a banker in exercising its role as investment manager. (The author, as a junior bank official, was aware on one occasion of a highly valuable international contract won by a leading company and saw the same day an instruction emanating from the investment department to reduce the shareholdings in that company because of its poor investment prospects: he maintained a proper silence.) The general view in this country is that the two functions must be divorced and if the investment side is a separate entity within the group, so much the better. This may, however, be too facile a view and it may be that a Court would take the view that if a bank cares to divide its functions and its knowledge, that is a matter for the bank itself, but that so far as an investment client is concerned, he expects in the management of his portfolio that the bank will use all the resources at its disposal, although presumably excluding the use of insider knowledge as such. What, for example, would be the view where a bank as investment manager last month bought for its client shares in a company and where this month the bank in its role as banker has appointed a Receiver? Is it so improbable? To add to the problem, the research analyst from the investment department might have visited the company and come to the view that it was a good recovery stock! Such conflicts are not necessarily so specific. It may be that a bank in its role as banker may have come to a very firm view on the state of the economy, industrial confidence and investment intentions, whilst the investment subsidiary could well have come to a contrary view and fashioned its investment policy accordingly. Perhaps these problems are more apparent than real. They have never been tested in the Courts and the first occasion would be a very interesting one. In the United States it is a very live subject, but there the climate points increasingly to a clear demarcation between the role of banker and that of investment manager or trustee.

As we have said, banks are not alone in the business of investment management. Their principal competitors are stockbrokers, merchant banks and a number of investment counselling firms of varying size. For the most part it may be wrong to regard stockbrokers as competitors. Not all stockbroking firms operate an investment management business for private clients on a continuing day-to-day basis. In contrast, some stockbrokers are more than happy to work with a bank as investment manager. The retail outlets of the clearing banks in this as in other matters help to ensure a continuing flow of new business. More and more people with an investment management problem tend to think in the first instance of the High Street bank.

Nevertheless, the market is not considerable. Although there are believed to be over 2 million private shareholders in companies quoted on the London Stock Exchange, many of these shareholdings are quite small and others are in the hands of executors or trustees who cannot readily delegate their responsibility to an investment manager. It is difficult to arrive at accurate statistics for the distribution of personal wealth, but on one estimate there are only 320,000 people in Great Britain with net personal resources in excess of £50,000, inclusive of all assets and not merely Stock Exchange investments.[3] Furthermore, among those private individuals who have been traditional investors in Stock Exchange companies, there has been considerable dis-investment in recent years. In 1977, net sales amounted to £1,850 million, the highest dis-investment by private shareholders in company securities for four years.

If the scope for the management of private portfolios is limited (although there is still a worthwhile market to tap), there are two areas where the potential is very considerable. The first is that of pension funds, which we shall look at in Chapter 9, and the second is unit trust investment. The view has been expressed here that for all but the larger investors – probably those with portfolios approaching six figures – unit trust investment is the right answer. That is not to say that unit trusts are appropriate for everyone. The first question which every investor must answer is 'is investment in the stock market right for me?' It certainly is not right for persons of modest means to put the whole of their savings into ordinary stocks and shares whether via unit trusts or not; and it is certainly not right for any investor whose resources or temperament are unsuited to the vagaries of the stock market. By the end of 1974 many investors had seen their nest eggs reduced to approximately one-third of their value only eighteen months earlier.

On the other hand, we believe that in our type of mixed economy long-term growth can come only from successful enterprise in industry and commerce. In the long term one expects to see the success of the enterprise reflected in the level of stock market prices, but there are many ups and downs on the way.

We have looked briefly at the history of unit trusts in this country and considered the role of the trustee. We turn now to the part played by the banks in unit trust management.

## References

1 Royal Commission on the Distribution of Income and Wealth: Report No. 2, Cmnd 6172. HMSO, 1975.
2 'How does Britain save?' – a survey for the London Stock Exchange by the British Market Research Bureau.
3 Royal Commission on the Distribution of Income and Wealth: Report No. 1, Cmnd 6171, HMSO, 1975.

CHAPTER 6

# Unit Trusts

We have considered in Chapter 4 the role played by the banks over many years as trustees of unit trusts and we referred to the distinction between trusteeship and the management of unit trusts. We also noted, in the introductory chapter, the movement of the banks, begun by Lloyds Bank in 1966, into the business of unit trust management. In some ways it was a surprising development. As we have seen, the banks were somewhat demure in matters of investment advice and investment management – and it must be admitted that in the minds of the public, banks did not readily come to mind as investment experts.

Furthermore, the fact that the banks were engaged in the trusteeship of unit trusts would be seen by many as a deterrent to their entering the management side of the business. Perhaps for that reason some of the banks set up their unit trust management activities under separate control from that of their trustee departments. In matters of investment policy this could hardly be justified – the same overall view of the market must apply in managing unit trusts as it does in the management of private investment portfolios.

The banks entered the unit trust movement by widely differing routes and this is understandable. In new business ventures it is often a matter for deliberation whether to evolve from within or purchase an existing organisation, and whether to 'go it alone' or jointly with another business house. Some developments, as we have already said, are a matter of conscious decision and others arise without being consciously sought. So it was that Lloyds Bank chose to set up their unit trust organisation from their existing resources and this met with immediate success. The first offer of units in Lloyds First Unit Trust in October 1966 produced £2·3 million – the first time that an English bank had sold its own units over its own counters. Two years later when the Second Unit Trust was launched, the initial offer brought in just under £10 million, an all-time record for the initial launch of any unit trust.

Westminster Bank chose the 'joint' road with Hambros Bank and they too were pleased with the immediate response. The first trust was launched in July 1967 and six months later the Westminster Bank Chairman, Mr D. A. Stirling, was able to report that the value of the units in issue had grown to over £10 million.

That same year Martins Bank chose the direct acquisition method by its purchase of Unicorn Securities, which gave the bank control of over £40 million worth of unit funds and gave Martins Bank the lead, in terms of size, which it and subsequently Barclays Bank have since maintained over their competitor banks.

To enter the unit trust business was not by any means a natural step for the banks to take, particularly for those banks heavily committed to the trusteeship of unit trusts. Barclays Bank, on the acquisition of Martins Bank, looked hard and long at the lively unit trust baby which had been acquired with its parent. It was some months before Barclays Bank came to terms with what it had bought because it had hitherto taken the view that it wished to be a trustee of unit trusts rather than their manager. If the Barclays approach was a little cautious at first, it was to develop in a short time to almost an excess of enthusiasm as unit trust sales flowed through the branches of the Bank and Unicorn's share of new investment in the industry rose as high at one point as 70 per cent. This was not without its consequences, which we shall look at a little later.

It was in fact the Unicorn Group which, under the Rt. Hon. Edward du Cann and Mr Bill Fowler, had led the way in 1957 in the post-war development of unit trusts. The general forms and procedures adopted in the next few years were to become the pattern for unit trust management and have remained so to this day. The following table gives some indication of the growth in the unit trust movement in the last twenty years.

| Year | Value of funds (at year end) £m | Sales £m | Re-purchases £m | Net investment £m | Holdings (millions) |
|---|---|---|---|---|---|
| 1959 | 200·0 | n.a. | n.a. | n.a. | 0·52 |
| 1960 | 201.·4 | 26·88 | 13·37 | 13·51 | 0·66 |
| 1961 | 236·6 | 21·57 | 14·21 | 7·36 | 0.67 |
| 1962 | 272·5 | 45·01 | 11·07 | 33·94 | 0·82 |
| 1963 | 371·2 | 77·46 | 17·78 | 59·68 | 1·05 |
| 1964 | 428·9 | 99·64 | 22·60 | 77·04 | 1·31 |
| 1965 | 521·9 | 80·80 | 21·78 | 59·02 | 1·42 |
| 1966 | 581·8 | 129·69 | 24·26 | 105·43 | 1·64 |
| 1967 | 853·6 | 126·56 | 42·64 | 83·91 | 1·71 |
| 1968 | 1,482·4 | 328·93 | 70·45 | 258·48 | 2·15 |
| 1969 | 1,411·9 | 262·70 | 76·53 | 186·17 | 2·39 |
| 1970 | 1,397·7 | 171·15 | 73·35 | 97·80 | 2·40 |
| 1971 | 1,991·2 | 204·10 | 127·45 | 76·65 | 2·32 |
| 1972 | 2,647·5 | 436·86 | 195·59 | 241·27 | 2·29 |
| 1973 | 2,060·4 | 357·90 | 171·75 | 186·15 | 2·24 |
| 1974 | 1,310·8 | 194·87 | 110·17 | 84·70 | 2·20 |
| 1975 | 2,512·4 | 321·21 | 130·90 | 191·31 | 2·20 |
| 1976 | 2,543·0 | 333·40 | 165·88 | 167·52 | 2·12 |
| 1977 | 3,461·3 | 372·32 | 257·90 | 114·42 | 1·99 |

[Source: Unit Trusts Association]

The 393 unit trusts in existence at the end of 1977 were managed by a total of ninety-three groups. Of the total unit trust business, 8·65 per cent (thirty-four trusts) by number and approximately 15·5 per cent by value are controlled by the English clearing banks and the Scottish banks. Thus the involvement of the banks is very considerable and the other unit trust groups look enviously on the branch network available to the banks for the sale of units.

In considering the basic procedures in the management of unit trusts, it has to be noted that unit trusts are, unfortunately, not easy to define. There are a number of descriptions used for the benefit of the general public which are adequate for that purpose, but are not always technically accurate. It is sometimes said that a unit trust is a joint investment venture. In common parlance it is, but it is not so in any legal sense. Sometimes the expression 'association' of investors is used, but this again would be legally unacceptable. The essential point is that a unit trust is a trust. It is established by a trust deed, the parties to which are the 'managers' who are the promoters of the trust and undertake certain obligations in the trust deed, and the 'trustees' who, as we have seen, are responsible for holding the trust assets which are divided into units for the benefit of the 'beneficiaries' or 'unitholders'. Under the trust deed the managers may offer units in the trust fund to potential investors who thereby become unitholders, and the managers are obliged under the trust deed to buy back such units from any unitholders who wish to sell them. Thus we may say that a unit trust is a form of trust where the trust fund is divided into units and held for the benefit of the unitholders, who become unitholders by the purchase of units from the managers of the trust and who at any time may re-sell their units to the managers of the trust, at a price determined in each instance in accordance with the terms of the trust deed. The basic value of a unit is always the value of the trust fund divided by the number of units in issue. Thus, if the trust fund has a current value of £1 million and there are a million units in issue, each unit will be worth £1. The price of a unit for the purpose of purchase or sale will, however, take into account the dealing expenses. A purchaser of units will pay a price calculated according to the underlying value of the units plus dealing costs, on the basis that his investment increases the value of the trust fund and additional securities will therefore be purchased. The seller of units will receive a price based on the underlying value of the units less dealing costs, on the basis that his sale of units results in a reduction of the trust fund and the corresponding sale of securities. Thus there is a margin between the 'offer' and 'bid' prices.

In calculating the offer and bid prices the rules laid down by the Department of Trade must be strictly followed. Under these rules, the maximum price at which units may be offered to the public must be calculated by reference to (a) the lowest price at which the underlying securities may be purchased on the Stock Exchange at that time – *plus* (b) stock exchange commissions, (c) stamp duties – 2 per cent on purchases and ¼ per cent instrument stamp duty, (d) the managers' initial charge of, say, 5 per cent, (e) accrued income in the fund and (f) a 'rounding' adjustment in the final figure in order to avoid fractions (this must be limited to 1 per cent or 1.25p whichever is the lesser amount). Thus the maximum purchase price is arrived at.

On the sale of units by a unitholder to the managers, the minimum price which must be paid by the managers under the Department of Trade rules is calculated by reference to (a) the highest price obtainable at that time on the Stock Exchange for the underlying securities *plus* (b) the accrued income in the fund *less* (c) stock exchange commissions and (d) the permitted 'rounding' figure.

The margin between the maximum purchase price and minimum sale price permitted by the Department of Trade rules will normally be of the order of 13 per cent and such a margin would quite rightly be unacceptable to the investing public. In practice, the managers of unit trusts operate on a dealing margin of 6–7½ per cent, subject to certain exceptions. This is primarily because at any one time the manager will be buying or selling existing units so that some of the costs of creating, or as the case may be liquidating, units can be avoided.

When a trust is expanding, i.e. when the managers are selling more units than they are re-purchasing, the offer price will be pitched as high as the Department of Trade regulations permit because that reflects the price which would have to be paid for new securities on the market. When a trust is contracting, i.e. because more units are being sold back by unitholders than new units are being bought, the bid price, i.e. the price which managers will pay for units, will be as low as the Department of Trade regulations permit reflecting the fact that securities will have to be sold on the market. One should visualise, therefore, the managers' buying and selling margin of, say, 7 per cent moving up or down the much wider scale of, say, 13 per cent permitted by the regulations. When a trust is expanding, the price will be nudging the top of the scale, usually referred to as being on the offer basis: when a trust is contracting, the price will move to the lower level, i.e. the bid basis. It is thus an advantage to existing unitholders that their trust should be on the offer basis so that if they sell their units (at the bid price of course), the price will be nearer the top of the Department of Trade scale. For the purchaser of units, it would be an advantage to buy when the price is on the 'bid basis' because the price he pays (the offer price) is that much lower.

A large part of the profits of unit trust groups comes from

dealing in existing units. Equally it can be a source of losses. It is part of the managers' skill to fix the unit prices at the right level within the permitted range. If, for example, investors are selling back more units than they purchase, a manager who kept the trust on the offer basis, i.e. at the top of the range, would make a loss because he would be paying unitholders at the higher price and having to liquidate units in the market at the ruling bid prices.

For a unit trust to be 'authorised' by the Department of Trade, it must be invested in 'securities' as defined in the Prevention of Fraud (Investments) Act 1958 (s. 26(1)). The term, for all practical purposes means stocks or shares or government securities. It is impossible therefore for an authorised unit trust to be invested in freehold or leasehold property. Property bonds and similar investments which we shall consider at a later stage are not authorised unit trusts.

Within the definition of 'securities' it is permissible and quite usual to launch unit trusts with a special investment emphasis. Most of the early unit trusts were 'middle of the road' trusts. They sought the kind of performance which would give a mixture of capital growth and a medium level of income. They were designed for the every-day investor. It was the pattern to follow up with a 'growth' trust designed to seek capital gain – if necessary at the expense of income – and an 'income' trust to suit those investors who were looking for as much income as possible from their equity investment. In practice over the years many of the income trusts have had good capital performance and some of the growth trusts have been disappointing. There then followed over the years a variety of 'specialist' trusts with investment policies geared to individual sectors such as financial institutions, small companies, commodities, gold shares, energy shares, recovery shares and so on. The management of unit trusts is very much a marketing operation and many groups launched new funds with popular labels attached to them, but which over the years bore little relation to their investment merit. In more recent years, as anxieties increased over the UK economy, a large number of 'international' funds have been launched designed for overseas investment.

To obtain Department of Trade authorisation, it is necessary for the trust deed to contain a provision that no investment shall exceed 5 per cent of the total value of the fund with the proviso that this may be increased to 7½ per cent in respect of not more than six separate holdings, provided that the number of separate holdings shall not be less than twenty and the aggregate value of the trust's holdings of investments in any ten separate holdings shall not exceed 55 per cent of the total value.

The normal rule is that investments shall be made only in securities quoted on recognised stock exchanges. Some of the older trust deeds do contain power to invest in unquoted securities, but under the modern deeds a total of no more than 5 per cent of the fund may be invested in this way.

In the unit trust industry there is a great variety of schemes, usually referred to as 'plans', designed to encourage savings and investment in unit trusts. Most of these are available in one form or another among the clearing banks' trusts. They include the following.

**Savings plans**

We have seen the importance of maintaining a unit trust on an expanding basis and we should also add that the system of charging is such that unit trusts generally depend for their profitability on their ability to sell new units. Thus, from an early stage, most groups recognised the importance of regular savings schemes. The only contractual form of saving permissible in equity shares in the United Kingdom is the life assurance policy. We shall look at life assurance in the next chapter and, in particular, deal with the practice of linking life assurance contracts to unit trusts. It should be noted, however, that this practice has become so important in the unit trust industry in this country that approximately one-quarter of all unit trust sales are now effected through a life assurance link. Approximately 750,000 investors have chosen to buy their units in this way. From the management point of view, it is extremely valuable to have a regular and ascertainable flow of new money each month regardless of the state of the stock market at the time.

The ordinary savings account is also very valuable. This enables the investor to contribute so much a month for investment in the unit trust of his choice. No legal obligation rests on the saver and he is free to vary his monthly investment, or cancel or defer it, entirely at will. The great advantage of any regular saving in this way is that it helps to even out any fluctuations in the stock market. There is also the purely arithmetical advantage of 'pound cost averaging': when prices are low the fixed regular investment buys more units – when prices are high fewer units are purchased. The effect is that the average purchase cost of units is less than the average price of the units over the period of regular investment.

Regular savings plans can be used to re-invest unit trust income as well as, if desired, any additional monthly sums. For the re-investment of income, however, it is more economic to use one of the accumulation trusts designed for the purpose. This is because in an accumulation trust the value of the units is increased by the accumulated income and there is no manager's initial charge on the accumulations as there would be if they were treated as new investments.

There is no doubt that for most investors the regular savings plans are attractive in that they reduce the importance of timing and take a lot of anxiety out of stock market fluctuations.

**Withdrawal plans**

In the ordinary way the income of a unit trust is the amount of interest and dividends on the underlying investments less a deduction for fees and expenses. All the income has to be distributed to the unitholders or re-invested in the ways we have discussed. If the dividend performance of the underlying investments is good, the income distribution to the unitholders is that much greater: if it is poor, the distribution is reduced. To the extent that companies increase their dividends from improved profits over the years, unitholders can see substantial increases in their unit trust distributions. For example, an investor in the Unicorn Capital Trust at its launch in 1957 would have received initially a yield of 4·84 per cent so that for £1,000 invested, the annual distribution would have been £48.40. That same investor during 1977 would have received an annual distribution of £183.27 representing a yield of 18·33 per cent on his original investment. In times of inflation the prospect of seeing an increase in one's income is important and is one of the particular attractions of equity investment.

In some cases, however, investors wish to have a higher 'income' from their unit trust investment than the amount of the annual distribution, and some investors prefer to see that annual distribution expressed as a fixed percentage of their investment. The withdrawal plan (or selective income plan) was devised for that purpose. The investor in a withdrawal scheme can choose, within certain limits, the annual payment he wishes to have, e.g. 8 per cent on the sum invested, and if the annual distribution is less than that, the managers will sell units to make the payment up to the required level. In other words, the investor is receiving a regular annual return made up partly of income from the underlying investments and partly from the sale of capital. This is very satisfactory on a rising market because the investor is merely receiving a part of the capital profits. The danger is that on a falling market the initial investment is already diminishing in value and that process is accelerated by sales of units to make up the annual distributions. Such erosion of capital will usually result in a fall in the annual dividend distributions so that even further sales of units are necessary to make up the required annual payments.

The response to withdrawal plan advertising was considerable. In one group alone, the withdrawal plan sales in two years amounted to approximately £100 million. The dangers we have described were very evident in the 'bear' market of 1973 and the Department of Trade became very concerned on behalf of investors. Unitholders were invited by the management groups to suspend their withdrawals of capital until the market recovered and many investors did this.

Another disadvantage of the withdrawal plan is that many investors, no matter how precisely the advertisements and leaflets are worded, believe they are entering into an investment where they receive a fixed percentage for life. They come to regard it rather as an annuity and are greatly concerned when the true effect of a withdrawal plan in a falling market is made clear to them. Nevertheless, there is a place for withdrawal schemes for investors who understand them and who wish to have a regular source of 'income', partly out of dividends and partly out of capital.

## Share exchange schemes

A number of investors with private portfolios have been

attracted, with the encouragement of unit trust groups, to the idea of exchanging their portfolios for units in an established trust. This gives them all the advantages of unit trust investment, including a much wider spread than in their own portfolio and complete freedom from problems of management. Most of the leading unit trust groups operate such schemes and will take privately owned shares into their portfolios at a price higher than the bid price which the investor would obtain in the market. Those holdings which the trust managers do not wish to take over will be sold, but some groups pay the stock exchange commission on the sales. In all such schemes, the investor is usually receiving a higher consideration than would be obtainable on the sale of the portfolio in the market.

### Unitisation of investment companies

A number of unit trust groups will arrange special schemes whereby the shares in investment companies may be exchanged for unit trust holdings. Whereas the individual shareholdings may not have been readily saleable the units are, of course, marketable and any gain is not taxable until such time as units are sold.

### Linked Life Assurance

By far the most important single development in the unit trust movement has been the introduction over the years of 'linked' life assurance schemes which provide for the investment of life assurance premiums in unit trusts. It is a subject we can deal with more appropriately under the next chapter heading. The London & Edinburgh Insurance Company is usually credited with the introduction of the first equity linked policy because in 1957 that company brought out a scheme whereby life assurance premiums were invested not actually but notionally in the Unicorn Trust (then owned by the London & Edinburgh), and the policies were valued according to the value of the Unicorn units. In the twenty-year period which followed, unit linked life assurance grew enormously to a point today where investments through linked life assurance account for over one-quarter of all unit trust sales. The special advantages of unit linked life assurance to the managers are fourfold:

1 The contractual nature of most life assurance policies

provides a continuing flow of funds for investment, which as we have seen is so important to the unit trust movement.

2 Unit linked life policies can be sold by normal life assurance methods, thereby circumventing the statutory restraints, under the Prevention of Fraud (Investments) Act 1958, on unit trust advertising and marketing methods.

3 The permitted level of unit trust charges can be augmented by fees chargeable in the life office as distinct from the management company.

4 The investor receives the benefit of income tax relief on premiums paid under long term life assurance contracts – a good selling point.

The whole area of linked life assurance merits further consideration and it is a subject to which we will return later.

**Unit trusts for children**

Most unit trust groups operate schemes to encourage investment for the benefit of children and this can be done in various ways. In some cases a formal trust deed in standard form is used, normally providing for the invested sums to be set aside for the benefit of the child or children, the income of the fund being accumulated until the beneficiary comes of age. Such trusts tend to be a little inflexible, particularly in times of changing fiscal legislation, and most parents or other benefactors prefer to use the simple device of a designated account until such time as the child can have the units transferred into his or her own name.

**Exempt unit trusts**

A number of unit trust groups have introduced 'exempt' trusts for investment by pension funds and charities. Such institutions enjoy complete exemption from Income Tax and Capital Gains Tax and, by arrangement with the Inland Revenue, certain unit trusts are granted tax exemption on the basis that investment is restricted to tax exempt pension funds and charities. Among the clearing banks, Barclays Bank, Lloyds Bank and Midland Bank operate exempt trusts at the present time.

So much for the various plans and schemes which are now

common in the unit trust business. For the most part they have been designed to appeal to various sectors of the market and, as such, they have met with varying success. In the last analysis, however, a unit trust is judged by the quality of its investment performance. We have seen that in an authorised unit trust investment is restricted to quoted securities (with the occasional exception of a limited participation in unquoted stocks and shares), but even within such orthodox limits unit trust investment is not easy. We have said in an earlier chapter that investment success depends very largely on the ability to be liquid, or fully invested as the case may be, at the right time. In the unit trust world, rising stock markets tend to spark off rising sales of units. The investment managers often have substantial new monies coming in each week, which creates a degree of liquidity at a time when they would wish to be fully invested. The reverse is also true: on a falling market when managers would wish to maintain partial liquidity, they are seldom assisted by any new money coming in from unit trust sales other than the contractual premiums under monthly insurance plans.

In any case, it is rare for investment managers to take positive steps to go liquid to any major extent in unit trust portfolios. This is partly because of dealing costs and partly because the risk of being wrong is very considerable. Also some managers have the more philosophical view that they have been given money by the public to invest and not to hold in liquid form. The unit trust manager has a great responsibility. He has a duty to do his best in the management of the investors' money. He has no right to speculate with it nor to take undue risks, but he will be expected to bring an informed judgment to bear, not only as to the quality of individual investments but also in the timing of those investments, both as to entry into and withdrawal from the market. The investment manager is not expected to be a wizard, but he must exercise a very proper judgment, drawing on the best sources of information available to him.

Another area of difficulty for the investment manager is the choice of the number of holdings in the portfolio. There will have to be at least twenty stocks (because of the requirement already mentioned on page 77) and in time the portfolio will probably be built up to between fifty and 100 securities. In very

*'. . . positive steps to go liquid.'*

large trusts, the number will be even greater, as it will be in those specialist trusts investing in a wide range of small companies. As the number of holdings increases, so the management problems become greater. Partly for that reason and partly because individual successes or failures have less impact on the larger portfolios, one can normally expect a less volatile performance from the larger trusts. That is not to say that they do not perform so well in the long run. The widely accepted belief that small trusts perform better than larger ones is not easy to substantiate.

One of the most difficult areas is that of overseas investment. Under the Exchange Control Regulations in the United Kingdom, residents of the sterling area may purchase securities outside the sterling area only by means of investment currency, a 'pool' which in itself represents the sale of overseas securities by UK residents over the years. The cost of buying investment currency, i.e. the premium, varies considerably in relation to the widely varying demand for the very restricted pool of dollars. From the investment manager's point of view this means that the cost of buying foreign stocks can be very much above the listed price depending on the level of the investment premium. On the sale of the overseas securities, the premium is recovered, at the level of investment premium then obtaining.

The alternative is to invest overseas by means of a 'back-to-back' loan. Unlike investment trusts, unit trusts may not borrow money for the purpose of 'gearing up' the fund, but they may borrow currency for the purchase of overseas securities provided that the sterling equivalent of the sum borrowed is deposited with a bank in the UK. The Bank of England require such foreign loans to be covered by foreign securities to the extent of 115 per cent, the margin of 15 per cent having to be provided by the purchase of foreign securities through the premium dollar pool. As time goes by the additional 15 per cent may be covered by an appreciation in the value of the loan portfolio, but if for any reason the value of the securities falls below the 115 per cent level, further securities have to be purchased with investment currency to top up the cover. Thus, whether overseas securities are purchased with premium currency or by means of a back-to-back loan, additional hazards are introduced into the art of investment. A fall on, say, Wall

Street would quite often be accompanied by a fall in the level of investment premium with the result that securities purchased with investment currency would not only suffer a fall in their stock market price, but the recoverable premium on the purchase of the shares would also be reduced. There would also be an exchange risk, either way, as between the dollar and sterling. If alternatively the securities had been purchased by the back-to-back method, the cost of topping up the necessary cover on a falling market through the investment currency pool could be enormous. In addition, if the currency rate moves adversely it will also be necessary to top up the sterling deposit, and indeed a few unit trusts ran into difficulties for these very reasons.

Thus unit trust investment has its hazards. We have said in an earlier chapter that investment in unit trusts is suitable only for those who wish to commit part of their savings to equity investment and who understand that stock market prices can be very volatile. As a vehicle for investment in equities, unit trusts offer the following very real advantages:

1 It is possible to get a greater spread of risk than is normally available to the private investor.

2 Unit trusts enjoy the advantage of day-to-day management by those who are knowledgeable in investment matters.

3 The annual management charges are effectively allowed for tax within the fund, which would not be possible if an investor paid someone to manage his own portfolio.

4 Dealing costs are proportionately lower.

5 The investor has one investment instead of many and thus the administrative problems of dealing with dividend counterfoils, Income Tax certificates and allotment letters, etc. are reduced.

6 All subjective considerations are removed – the choice of shares and the degree of liquidity is left to the much more objective decision of the investment manager.

## The Unit Trust Association

Nowadays most of the unit trust groups are members of the Unit Trust Association, set up in 1959 as the Association of

Unit Trust Managers, to monitor standards throughout the movement. The objects of the Association are:

1 to uphold standards of unit trust practice, to protect the interests of unitholders and to maintain the good name of the unit trust industry;

2 to provide on behalf of its members an agreed channel of communication and representation to government departments and other authorities on matters relating to unit trusts;

3 to act in co-operation with other organisations on matters connected with investment protection.

It is doubtful indeed whether the saver is wise to embark on a regular unit trust saving scheme until he has first set aside his 'contingency reserve' in bank savings account, National Savings Certificates, building societies or the like. This still leaves a very big market for the sale of units. The number of existing unitholders is believed to be $1\frac{1}{4}$ million. This undoubtedly includes some of the 2 million or so private investors who are believed to have invested directly in the stock market in this country. The potential market is very considerable and consists of that part of the adult population who have a few hundred pounds to spare for investment in the industrial and commercial life of the community, having first set aside their safe and accessible nest egg as already proposed. In terms of regular saving out of income, we may say that the market consists of all those people who can afford, say, £10 a month for equity investment for themselves or their children. In recent times, however, the burden of inflation and taxation has fallen heavily on many who would otherwise be unit trust investors and in many homes there can be little enough to spare for stock market investment after meeting living costs, mortgage payments and life assurance premiums.

The tendency has been for the clearing banks to regard the market for their unit trusts as being limited to their own customers. This must be so to a considerable degree, but it is not entirely borne out by experience. (In the case of the Unicorn Trusts, which did not have their origin in the banking world, it was quite common to find on a random check of applications long after the group's acquisition by Barclays Bank that 60 per cent or more of cheques received for the purchase of units were drawn on other banks.) For practical purposes, however, we can say that the market for the clearing bank unit trusts is among the 15 million customers of the clearing banks. The market for unit-linked life assurance is very much wider including as it does quite a proportion of investors who do not have accounts with the clearing banks. We shall look at this more closely in the next chapter.

Like all the unit trust groups, the bank-controlled groups have recourse to extensive newspaper advertising. It may be thought that the very existence of extensive branch networks is sufficient for the marketing of units without heavy expenditure on advertising, but this is not the case. It is a combination of the two which is most effective, but this can make the whole operation very expensive. We have spoken already of the varying attitudes of bank managers to the question of unit trust investment. We hope never to see again the euphoria of the early 1970s which led to a lot of disappointment for investors generally and for some bank customers. It will be equally sad, however, if branch managers react too far in the other direction, taking a jaundiced view of everything to do with unit trusts. It is a pity that, unlike most products, unit trusts sell best when they are most expensive. Hence the advantage which we have already mentioned of regular systematic investment. Viewed sensibly and with a proper caution by bank managers and customers alike, unit trusts will remain for as long as we can see a highly desirable and commendable form of investment for customers with investable funds.

**Profitability**

In the 'bull' market in the early 1970s some of the unit trust groups made handsome profits. New money was pouring into unit trusts and at one point in 1972 the Unicorn Group, the largest of the bank unit trust groups, was receiving new money for investment at a sustained level of approximately £2 million per week. The stock market was high and this in itself meant that unit trust fees, which are on an *ad valorem* basis, were also high. It was the high noon of unit trusts in this country. In more recent years, the position has been quite different. Not only have market levels been lower, but potential unit trust investors are more conscious of the perils of falling markets and net investment in the industry has diminished. In fact, during 1978 unit trust sales rose by 42 per cent to a record figure of £530 million, but in real terms this was substantially lower than the previous record figure in 1972. Most significant of all, the costs of administration have risen astronomically. The business is labour-intensive and salary costs have more than doubled in recent years. The unit trust companies have also been particularly hit by the increase in costs for postage and stationery.

The pricing structure in the UK unit trust movement is a strange one. It is probably the only area of free enterprise where the level of charges is controlled completely by the Government through the Department of Trade. The charges in each unit trust are laid down in the trust deed, but these cannot exceed the maximum level authorised by the Department of Trade rules. Under those rules, the maximum charge exigible by the unit trust management company over a twenty-year period is 13¼ per cent of the value of the units in issue. Only two categories of fee are permitted. The first of these is the Initial Charge which may not exceed 5 per cent of the new monies invested in a trust. The other source of income is the Annual Charge which may not exceed ½ per cent of the funds under management. Thus, in order not to exceed the permitted maximum of 13¼ per cent over twenty years, the combination of fees is mainly an Initial Fee of 3¼ per cent and Annual Fees of ½ per cent, or an Initial Fee of 5 per cent and Annual Fees of ⅜ per cent. Out of these fees, the managers must pay all costs including the charges of the trustees and the auditors. The anomaly, if it be one, is that the permitted charges are related precisely to the value of the trust portfolios, but stock market values have not nearly risen in line with inflation. The Unit Trust Association has made representations to the Department of Trade in an endeavour to secure higher charges and greater flexibility in the system of charges, but so far without success. The structure of unit trust charges was recently reviewed by the Price Commission at the request of the Department of Trade, but the Commission rejected the case for higher charges largely on the basis that profit margins were adequate. In any case the problem is a difficult one. Even with Department of Trade approval, the only ways in which the fees could be increased in the 393 existing unit trusts in this country would be by an enabling Act of Parliament (which is not even a remote possibility) or by the agreement of the unitholders in each trust – a costly business with a far from certain outcome.

Why then did the banks enter this field? First of all, it must be acknowledged that the inordinate rise in costs was not foreseen. Early profit forecasts were soon exceeded and it seemed that the in-house unit trusts were set fair, not only to meet a very real investment need of bank customers but to make a very satisfactory contribution to profits. Even though profits are now hard earned, we may well see a return, at least in part, to the profitability of earlier days given a new pricing structure, if this be possible, and a stronger stock market.

Even if the more glamorous profits have gone for good, the management of unit trusts must be seen as a legitimate and logical extention of the asset management function. Mr F. W. Holder wrote in 1969 of the entry of Lloyds Bank into the unit trust movement, '. . . there are many thousands of bank customers of moderate means who would be prepared to entrust a few hundreds or a few thousands of pounds to their bank for investment in stocks and shares and wish to be relieved of the task of selection and the paperwork involved in owning a number of separate securities in their own names'.[1] That is still true today. It is a natural role for the all-purpose bank – to help their customers to put their money to work.

## Unauthorised trusts

Only trusts which satisfy the Department of Trade regulations will receive their authorisation. If for example a unit trust did not have an independent trustee, authorisation would not be possible. Equally, if the scale of charges did not conform to the rules, or if the portfolio was to include assets outside the statutory declaration of 'securities', no authorisation would be possible. There is nothing unlawful or reprehensible about unauthorised trusts as such. They exist in a number of insurance companies as part of the life fund and have also been set up internally in one or two other investment houses. They suffer from the disability that, being unauthorised, they do not satisfy the Prevention of Fraud (Investments) Act 1958 and so it would be an offence under the Act to invite public subscription for the units or to issue circulars or even to hold circulars calculated to induce investment in the unit trust. In the ordinary way, therefore, property unit trusts can be offered to the public only via the vehicle of a property bond, i.e. a life assurance policy. One bank, Barclays Bank, operates an unauthorised unit trust investing in property for the benefit of the bank's private investment clients, but this is possible only under an exempting clause in the Act which permits circulars as between trustee and beneficiary.

A more important exception to the general rule is that of property unit trusts for pension funds and charities. In the last ten years, a number of unit trusts have been set up with the express purpose of enabling pension funds and to a lesser degree, charities, to invest in property and, under their discretionary powers, the Department of Trade have permitted the issue of prospectuses to approved pension funds and registered charities. This exception was no doubt thought to be socially desirable, but more particularly it was possible because the managing bodies of such institutions are deemed to be experienced business people. There are now 33 pension fund property unit trusts in existence, managing folios to a total value of approximately £1,100 million. In most instances, these have been promoted by merchant banks in co-operation with leading firms of surveyors, but in one or two cases the clearing banks have played a leading role as trustee, or even as managing trustee.

Unit trusts designed for more esoteric forms of investment, such as antiques, works of art, commodities, wine, gold coins or whatever, are not remotely likely to receive authorisation even for a sophisticated market such as pension funds. It is possible for such trusts to be set up off-shore but for that reason alone, whatever the content of the portfolio, authorisation in this country would be impossible and the marketing of the fund would be proscribed by the very stringent provisions of the Act.

In all the circumstances, it is not surprising that entrepreneurs turned increasingly to a more traditional investment vehicle – the life assurance policy. As we shall see, it offers greater investment flexibility, a more advantageous fee structure and comparative freedom from statutory constraints.

## Reference

1 F. W. Holder: 'The Banks and the Unit Trusts'. *The Banker*, April 1969.

CHAPTER 7

# Life Assurance

At first sight, this must seem an unusual chapter heading in any book on bank services. Years ago it would have been unthinkable that the clearing banks should become involved in the business of insurance, or that the big insurance companies would move into banking. And yet, to a modest degree, that is what has happened. At least one large insurance company, the Norwich Union Life Insurance Society, now conducts a subsidiary banking operation and one or more other companies have taken powers to do so, whilst a number of the clearing banks are now involved in life assurance activities. Here we must distinguish between the provision of life assurance cover – the underwriting process – and the business of insurance broking. The British banks are engaged in both activities, but first let us look at the extent to which they are involved as writers of life assurance, leaving the broking role to a later chapter.

A second distinction we must make is between life assurance and general insurance. The terminological distinction between the two words 'assurance' and 'insurance' is a feature of the United Kingdom market, but has become somewhat blurred over the years and is probably no longer material. The theory was that one 'assured' against things which were bound to happen and 'insured' against contingencies or possibilities. Hence one assured against death, but insured against fire, theft and accident. However, the words do not matter: the essential point is that the banks are engaged in life assurance, but not at this point of time in the business of underwriting general insurance risks. As brokers, however, they are engaged in life and general business across-the-board.

None of the banks entered the life assurance field because they necessarily wished to be involved in the provision of life assurance *per se*. The writing of life contracts developed directly out of the banks' unit trust business in the form of linked life assurance, such as we have described.

The first move lay with Martins Bank, who on the acquisition of the Unicorn Group in 1967 also acquired control of Griffin Life Assurance Company, a newly created subsidiary of the London and Edinburgh Insurance Company designed for the purpose of issuing unit linked life policies. Shortly afterwards, Lloyds Bank announced that they would issue unit linked life policies through a newly formed subsidiary of the Royal Insurance Company. On 1 September 1967, the Westminster Hambro Unit Trust Group introduced a linked life policy, the insurance being provided by the Commercial Union Assurance Company and in 1971 Williams & Glyn's Bank launched their 'Nest Egg Plan' – a ten-year life assurance policy with Provident Mutual Life Assurance Association, linked to a deposit in Williams & Glyn's Bank. Thus, at one stage, only Martins Bank and then Barclays Bank were engaged as principals in life assurance business, but a few years later, in October 1975, Lloyds Bank introduced its own unit linked bonds through its own captive subsidiary, Beehive Life Assurance Company. In February 1976, Midland Bank announced its ten-year savings plan – to be sold over the bank counters – an insured savings scheme with Greville Insurance.

So it is that the banks are to a degree engaged in the business of 'linked' life assurance. The Scott Committee, which published its Report in April 1973, defined linked life assurance as:

'All life assurance and annuity contracts, the benefits of which are calculated in whole or in part by reference to the value of, or the income from, specified assets or groups of assets or by reference to movements in a share price or other index, whether or not subject to deductions in respect of tax or expenses.'[1]

Such policies were originally linked to authorised unit trusts so that on maturity or surrender of the policy, the value would be the value of the underlying units. It is equally possible, however, for the policy to be linked to units in a separate fund in the insurance company's life fund or, as the definition allows, linked to some other assets or index. The essential thing is that the value of the policy at any one time is calculable by reference to a formula and the amount payable under the policy whether on death, maturity or surrender, is ascertainable by reference to that formula. In contrast, the amount payable by a life office on a conventional 'with profits' policy would be a pre-determined fixed sum (the sum assured) plus any bonus or bonuses declared by the directors of the company at their discretion.

We may summarise the main differences between conventional 'with profits' policies and linked policies as follows:

1 In the case of a linked policy, its value at any one time will depend on the value of the underlying assets: the value of a conventional policy will depend on the proportion of profits allocated to the policy by the company from time to time.

2 The value of a linked policy, whether on surrender, maturity or death, may thus be subject to very wide fluctuations depending on the values of the shares or property or other assets to which the policy is linked: the benefits under a conventional 'with profits' policy will always be a fixed pre-determined sum (or in the case of surrender, a sum calculated according to a pre-determined formula) plus bonuses which have been declared.

3 Holders of linked policies will receive details of the assets to which their policies are linked, including current valuations at least once a year: holders of conventional policies receive no such details because their policies are not related to specific, identifiable assets (although they will of course receive details of bonuses added to their policies).

There will no doubt be differing opinions for many years as to the relative merits of 'conventional' and 'linked' life assurance. When the first linked life policies were introduced in 1957, by the London and Edinburgh Insurance Company in co-operation with the Unicorn Group, they were regarded by many as a matter of passing interest, but today approximately one-third of all new life assurance annual premiums for new sums assured are related to policies which are linked in one way or another. There is no doubt a section of the public who like to know that their policies are linked to particular assets and indeed to have some say in the choice of those assets. Equally, they count it a benefit to receive regular reports on the underlying assets. Some people like to know that the values of their policies are linked directly to the long-term performance of the economy and therefore of the stock markets or other markets, and to have the opportunity if they so wish of cashing in on their policies when market levels are high. To put it at its lowest, a linked life policy provides the investor with the opportunity of participating in the growth of definable assets, usually through unit trusts, with the benefit of tax relief on his contributions (subject to certain statutory requirements) and with a measure of life assurance for extra protection. These considerations are important to the bank manager and others in the front line, and it would not be appropriate, for example, to sell a customer a linked life assurance product when a conventional policy, and perhaps a particular type of conventional policy, is more suited to the customer's needs.

There are those who consider that linked life assurance is merely an extension of unit trust investment (as indeed it was in its original concept) and that it should not be governed by insurance law, but brought very firmly under the investment law of this country which means the various Companies Acts and more particularly the Prevention of Fraud (Investments) Act. With one dissenting voice, the Scott Committee came to the very clear view that 'there is no fundamental difference between linked and other policies: the distinction in the method used to calculate the benefits payable seems to us to be a matter more of form than of substance'.

This is perhaps a good point to consider the nature of life assurance business generally. As far as is known, the earliest form of life assurance was that practised by the Greeks in connection with their burial societies. The Romans too had a system of payment on death for the benefit of dependants and they are also credited with the development of marine insurance. (Other forms of commercial insurance had in fact existed from Babylonian days.) It seems that life assurance had its origins not so much in the desire to provide for dependants, but more in two other areas of human concern – the fear of not having a decent burial and the wish to protect personal fortunes. The desire to provide for burial found expression in the mutual societies of the mediaeval guilds and it is significant that even in modern times it was the fear of ending up in a pauper's grave which probably more than anything led to the massive growth of industrial insurance in this country. The commercial insurance of life – the real beginning of our life assurance business – had its origin in the golden age of exploration when the life of a ship's captain would be insured along with the ship and its cargo. The policy would last for the period of the voyage and seldom for more than a year. Thus our first life assurance policies were what we would call today term assurance – cover against the eventuality of death during a stated period. By the end of the seventeenth century a number of societies had developed providing life cover and annuity schemes but, as every lawyer knows, life assurance was looked upon as something of a gamble and it was difficult to distinguish between the life contract and an outright wager, as the punters of the day placed their bets on the expectation of life of leading soldiers and politicians. It was the Life Assurance Act of 1774 which required the proposer to have an 'insurable interest' in the life of the assured. From that point on, life assurance developed alongside the more traditional forms of insurance and throughout the nineteenth century in the aftermath of the Industrial Revolution, the insurance societies mushroomed. In 1854 the Prudential Assurance Company was formed to meet the increasing need for industrial assurance and in time became the largest life office not only in this country but in the world in terms of sums assured. By the end of 1977, the total premium income of the life offices in this country was £4,200 million, representing a very substantial proportion of personal savings. The total life assurance funds in this country at the end of 1975 were approximately £35 billion. During 1978, new annual premiums for life assurance in the United Kingdom rose by 28 per cent from £1.05 billion to £1.35 billion.

There are various categories of life assurance and they may be summarised as follows:

1 Whole life assurance – the sum assured is payable only on the death of the life assured.

2 Endowment assurance – the sum assured is payable on death or at the end of an agreed term, whichever comes first.

*'Golden age of exploration.'*

(Both these types of assurance may be (a) 'with profits', which means that in return for a higher premium the benefits will include a share of the profits of the company over and above the pre-determined sum or (b) 'without profits', which means that the benefits under the policy are as stated without further additions. Also, either category of life policy, i.e. whole life or endowment, may be 'conventional' or 'linked' as we have already described.)

3 Term assurance – the sum assured is payable only in the event of death during a specified period.

4. Convertible term assurance – this is similar to term assurance, but carries the option to convert to an endowment policy at any time during the term without further medical examination.

5. Mortgage protection assurance – this covers the life of a mortgage loan and the sum assured reduces in line with the capital sum outstanding on the mortgage over the years.

6. Children's assurance – this may be on the life of the parent or an endowment policy on the child's life.

7 Personal accident and sickness insurance – there are a great variety of such schemes available.

8 Immediate annuity – a regular annual or half-yearly payment commencing forthwith in return for a capital sum.

9 Deferred annuity – an annuity starting at some date in the future.

10 Annuity certain – an annuity scheme which provides a specific number of payments to be made regardless of the death of the annuitant.

11 Reversionary annuity – normally an annuity payable to the survivor of two persons, e.g. husband and wife.

12 Personal pension plan – a form of saving by life assurance with special tax benefits to secure a pension (deferred annuity) on retirement, with or without a lump sum benefit.

13 Pension schemes – in addition to individual retirement schemes, there are group schemes for employees of particular

companies, the premiums being paid by way of contribution by the employers and possibly employees over the years to provide individual pensions on retirement.

At the present time, none of the banks is involved as underwriter in such a wide range of insurance contracts, but as we shall see the banks as insurance brokers deal with the whole field of insurance, so that even at local branch level some understanding of the terminology and nature of the various contracts is necessary.

In its traditional form, life assurance is a matter of protection – protection against (or provision for) the costs of death (as in the case of burial policies) or the financial losses occasioned by death (as for example the need to provide for a family on the death of the bread-winner). For the most part, the life offices still emphasise the element of 'cover' in life assurance. In the last fifty years or so, however, life assurance has become additionally a method of saving and investment. This has been encouraged in the advertisements of the life offices and the public have been quick to respond. It was a natural and commendable development. If a sum of money is to be payable on the death of the insured, it is a small step for him to contract that it shall be paid to him at the end of a fixed period of years if he is still alive. As a means of building up a nest egg for the future, life assurance imposes a discipline on the saver which in most cases is reasonably painless. The opportunity to save in this way accounts on average for approximately 3 per cent of gross national product in the United Kingdom, i.e. at a higher level than in any other EEC country and higher than in the United States, Canada or Japan. In terms of personal saving, life assurance remains the largest single force in the country.

If life assurance has become a vehicle for savings and investment, so unit funds have become, for reasons we have mentioned, vehicles for life assurance. We have said that the banks did not seek to go into life assurance for its own sake, but they are very much there, albeit by force of circumstance. Although the banks' life assurance business is almost entirely linked life assurance, they are nevertheless in life business. That is the name of the game and the banks are bound by the rules of the game. They are governed by the Insurance Acts in all matters, including for example the capital structure of their subsidiary life companies, the methods of selling, the solvency rules and the appointment of actuaries.

We have referred to the distinctions between conventional life policies and linked policies, the principal distinguishing feature of a linked policy being that it is related to identifiable assets in the life fund. Thus, an equity linked life policy would be related to a particular unit trust and a property policy, usually called a property bond, would be related or linked to a particular portfolio of properties in the life fund. In the late 1960s, however, 'managed' bonds were introduced by the unit trust groups and the conventional life offices. The essence of such a bond is that the nature of the underlying assets may be changed, usually at the discretion of the life company, so that there may be switching among ordinary stocks, gilt-edged securities, properties and certain other securities. So it is that in the case of a managed bond the underlying assets are as amorphous as the life fund behind a conventional policy, blurring still further the differences between the two types of life assurance.

The linked life assurance products sold by the banks from, as it were, their own shelves fall into the following broad categories:

Equity linked policies;

Property linked policies;

Policies linked to gilt-edged and other fixed interest stocks, usually known as gilt bonds;

Policies linked to building society shares or deposits;

Policies linked to deposits in the money market, usually known as money bonds;

Policies linked to a mixed fund of varying assets, usually referred to as managed bonds.

In all these several categories of policies there will usually be:

(a) single premium policies where the premium will be a single lump sum. In such cases the life assurance cover will be little if any more than the amount of the investment. It is essentially an investment product—not sold for life assurance as such.

(b) multiple premium policies where the premiums are normally paid monthly as with conventional life assurance and the policies are sold on their merits for life assurance purposes. These policies may be either:
(i) whole of life – the proceeds are payable only on death or earlier surrender, there will be a minimum sum payable on death (the sum assured), but beyond that the proceeds will depend on the performance of the underlying assets; or
(ii) endowment – as with conventional policies already described, with the difference that the fixed sum assured will usually be smaller, the proceeds depending on the performance of the underlying assets in the market.

The linked life offices also provide personal pension plans as described elsewhere in this book (see p. 137), but the capital sum available at retirement to purchase the deferred annuity will depend on the value of the underlying assets at that date, and if the principal markets should be exceptionally depressed at that time, it may be appropriate to defer retirement in anticipation of a recovery in the value of the assets.

The life assurance products of the clearing banks are sold (a) over the bank counters; (b) by sales representatives; (c) by insurance brokers; and (d) by direct advertisement. Let us consider these in turn.

(a) **Counter sales:** The branch network of the clearing banks is usually the subject of envy on the part of other business houses. Well spread and well situated throughout the country, the branches are obviously a major force in the marketing of bank services. At the same time, however, they are costly to maintain and a good many branches do not earn their keep from banking business as such. The selling of many of the services described in these pages can make a useful contribution to branch profits, not merely because of the physical location of the branch, which is obviously important, but because of the captive market which every branch manager has amongst his customers. This applies particularly to the selling of life assurance and indeed many branch managers are familiar with the art from the days when they were allowed to sell insurance as agents for their own account. Here, however, we have a problem. All the British banks are engaged in insurance broking, whether through subsidiary companies or departments, as we shall discuss in the next chapter, and all the bank branches act as agents for those broking activities. It is the duty of an insurance broker to survey the market in relation to the needs of his client and to offer the insurance contract which is most suitable for the purpose. Those banks which additionally have their own subsidiary life offices are, therefore, acting in a dual role. They are both underwriters *and* brokers in the life assurance business. This is an anomalous situation and one which is not easily resolved. Indeed, it may not be possible to resolve it. Although the broking and underwriting activities of the major banks are conducted in separate parts of the group structure and, as it were, go their own ways without conflict, there is a confluence of the separate streams at branch level. How does the branch manager fulfil the role of broker if there is an overriding consideration to sell the products from his own shelf? Equally, how does the bank develop its life assurance business if on each occasion of a 'sale' the manager has to fulfil the role of broker and test the market for the best product? Some of the banks pursue only a passive role in the marketing of their own life assurance contracts and to that extent the problem is eased, although the risk of conflict still remains. Others take the view that they have products available for customers who seek them, but beyond that as brokers they are willing to research the market to meet their customers' needs. One or two banks take the view that these linked life assurance products are no more than a vehicle for equity or property savings and investment and that if a customer needs life assurance for its own sake, it is a matter for the broking department. The problem will remain, however, so long as the banks are acting as both principal and agent in relation to the same merchandise in the same market.

(b) **Sales representatives:** One hesitates to mention the exceedingly trite and rather boring dictum that insurance is not bought but sold. Certainly it is true of life assurance. Proposers for life assurance do not beat a path to the doors of the life offices, possibly because life assurance, rather like making a will, has been associated in people's minds with death. Perhaps people need the friendly if sometimes persuasive help of the salesman in order to concentrate their minds and come to a point of decision. Whatever the reason, the development of life assurance business has depended for the most part in this country, as well as in the United States and probably in all countries, on active selling by agents and representatives.

Although linked life assurance is sold widely by direct selling methods, only one bank life office, Barclays Life Assurance Company, has set up an organisation for the purpose. Apart from the early months of training, the representatives are paid entirely on a commission basis and the more successful ones achieve a handsome level of remuneration. In such a situation there must be risks of abuse, hard-selling, undue influence or misrepresentation or, at its lowest, the risk of giving offence to a reluctant audience. But this is true of all selling organisations and it is inevitably the over-zealous or the unconscientious who bring the rest into disrepute. In this country there is a tendency to disparage the role of the salesman. In some vague way he is regarded as surplus to requirements, a kind of parasite living on the backs of more legitimate occupations and existing by the unworthy pastime of selling people things they do not want. Traditionally, the commercial travellers were second only to mothers-in-law as fodder for music hall comedians. But this is unfair. Selling is a worthy occupation – and indeed for many it is a vocation. We are all engaged in selling: parsons and politicians, barristers and bankers, doctors and dentists, we are all engaged in purveying ideas or ideals, theories or solutions or, in the nicest way of course, ourselves. If an insurance representative does not have a good product to sell, he and his company will soon know. If he has a good product to sell he may take a pride in it, knowing as he does that insurance, and life assurance in particular, has brought more help and comfort to people than many of the tangible things of life and very often at a time when it was most needed.

If at times there be abuse, the life offices are their own best critics and the best guardians of their own standards. Bad selling methods only rebound on the company. Hard-selling and over-selling result in an undue level of forfeitures, which are not necessarily profitable to the insurer and in any case, in time, operate against the company's good name. The discontinuance rates in the field of linked life assurance are in fact lower than in the area of industrial assurance. It is perhaps not surprising that the Scott Report considered that the responsible salesman is performing a socially valuable function and that 'we received no evidence of widespread malpractice in the selling of life assurance, but we recognise that opportunities for it exist.'[2]

The sales representatives, numbering over 300, in the one clearing bank subsidiary which has such an organisation, are highly trained and highly disciplined. After an early spell of criticisms and misunderstandings, not least from the bank managers themselves, occasioned in part by the over-enthusiasm of some of the representatives, the organisation settled down into a highly elite team and complaints from any source dwindled almost to nothing. No cold canvassing is allowed on domestic premises, a 'cold' call being one made without any previous arrangement or introduction. Indeed, such calls when they were allowed years ago were usually unproductive. The salesman likes to have an introduction to his 'prospect'. Nowadays, introductions flow steadily from bank branches to the insurance representatives. This results in a sharing of commission between the bank branch and the representative, but in the long run it makes better use of the representative's time. The experience so far is that more than half of the total business taken on to their books by the sales force is on the introduction of the bank branches.

In the early days of in-house insurance selling, bankers and customers alike found it difficult to accept that the business should be 'sold' so directly, on the basis that the representative was rewarded wholly in commission. Nowadays, that view has mellowed, partly because all banks are having to go out and sell their services in one way or another and partly because it is recognised and remembered that life assurance has traditionally been sold on a commission basis. In fact, who more than the bank managers of earlier years had occasion to be grateful that it was so?

Recognising the dangers of over-selling, the Scott Committee made a number of recommendations which were subsequently reflected in the Insurance Companies (Amendment) Act 1973 (now consolidated in the Insurance Companies Act 1974). They are these:

1 The Secretary of State may make regulations as to the form and contents of insurance advertisements.[3]

2 It is now an offence to issue misleading sales material.[4]

3 The insurer must issue to the proposer a statutory notice in a prescribed form at or before the time the contract is entered into.[5]

4 A proposer may serve a notice of cancellation on the insurer within ten days of receiving the statutory notice, or on the earliest day that he knows that the contract has been entered into or the first or only premium paid.[6] (This is the so-called cooling off period.)

5 In the case of linked life policies, regulations may be made restricting the type of property to which such policies may be linked and regulating the manner and frequency of valuations.[7] Regulations may also be made in relation to the information which is to be supplied to policyholders as to the value of the benefits.

(c) **Sales through brokers:** There are believed to be approximately 9,000 insurance brokers in the United Kingdom operating throughout the entire spectrum of insurance business. Traditionally, however, brokers have not been a major force in the sale of life business nor indeed of personal assurance in general, but they account for the lion's share of the market for commercial business and a very large proportion, probably 90 per cent, of pensions business. It was perhaps appropriate that insurance brokers should apply their skills at the more sophisticated end of the market, but, be that as it may, most life assurance (including all industrial life assurance) is sold direct by the companies concerned, either by mail order or to a much greater degree by their own selling organisations of representatives and agents.

Against that traditional background it is perhaps not surprising that the banks have made little impact on insurance brokers with the life business of the banking subsidiaries. In any case, there are many brokers who did not welcome the entry of the banks into insurance broking, as is discussed in the next chapter, and they see no reason why they should assist in the development of the banks' underwriting business. Furthermore, the fee structure of the life policies from the banks' subsidiaries do not permit of substantial commissions and in many instances it is possible for brokers to obtain higher commissions for selling the life contracts of other companies. There is also the point that insurance brokers in the life field are usually, but not always, conditioned by the nature of their training to conventional life assurance. Whatever the reasons, efforts to sell bank life policies through insurance brokers have not been successful and, so far as one can tell, are unlikely to be.

Even the banks' own broking subsidiaries are way behind other outlets in the sale of the banks' own policies. This may be partly a natural caution in recommending one's own product (although we usually believe that our own products are the best), but more likely it stems from the brokers' preoccupation with conventional life assurance and an unwillingness to admit that linked life assurance may in some circumstances be equally or even more appropriate. However, it is no doubt best that the banking brokers should take a distant view of the group's in-house products – the more they bring them into the foreground, the more the element of conflict is emphasised.

(d) **Sales by advertisement:** Advertising is not in general a cost-effective method of selling life assurance. It is not a subject fit for 'instant' selling and a television advertisement today will not produce a queue at the local life office tomorrow. People like to think about life assurance, they like to talk about it and they probably like to be seduced into buying it. It is not a case of love at first sight, certainly not a marriage by proxy – the overtures have to be face-to-face. Nevertheless, advertising, whether press or television, is usually necessary to establish the name and image of a company and its products. A representative standing on the doorstep with a well-known name in his bag is probably half way to a sale. Probably the success of the Prudential Assurance Company will never be matched – 'the man from the Prudential', as familiar in placard and press as on the doorstep. A perfect combination. However, it may be argued that good wine needs no bush and that bank subsidiaries do not need to build up their own separate image or identity. The parent's name is all that matters. Indeed, it ought to be so, but there is a credibility gap. The diverse nature of many bank services and the extent of their departure from traditional banking calls for an educational process, in which advertising can help. If a clearing bank moves into life assurance, it is a short-cut to tell the world by press publicity. It is also quite a good way of reminding the managers and staff.

So-called 'coupon' advertising has its place in life assurance. It enables the 'prospect' to indicate his or her interest and provides a lead to be followed up by the representative. In other cases, an application form may be appropriate, but usually this would apply only to the more modest sums assured where medical examination could be dispensed with and where the underwriters can condense the necessary requirements into a few well-chosen questions in the confined space of a newspaper application. A lengthy application form, particularly for life assurance, would be counter-productive.

The advertising of linked life assurance is often similar in form and content (with obvious differences) to unit trust advertising. To the investor, a single premium life policy, usually referred to as a bond, is (quite rightly) an investment with life assurance attached. So it is that during times of stock market optimism, advertisements for life assurance bonds can be as productive as those for unit trusts. They can produce the same 'cash with order' type of response. They can be monitored for immediate cost effectiveness and when confidence is high, the weekend takings can be considerable. However, it is not a good example of life assurance advertising and in any case, it may be a long time before unit trust and bond advertising rides as high as during the euphoric months of 1972.

## Profitability

We have said that to the extent that the banks are involved in life assurance business, it was as a corollary to their unit trust investment business and they almost certainly did not regard life assurance as a profitable venture in itself. Used as a simple vehicle for selling unit trusts, a life company is barely profitable; but in those cases where a variety of linked contracts are being sold, including managed bonds and policies linked to internal funds, there is more profit potential than there is at present in direct unit trust business. It is a truism that in the first ten years or so of a life office's activity, there is little if any profit for the shareholders. During the years of relatively fast growth a life office experiences what is usually called 'new business strain' – this is a reflection of the high initial costs of writing life policies involving the training of staff, advertising and the payment of commissions to representatives and agents. The principal source of growth of a life company stems from surpluses in the life fund. They in turn arise for the most part from favourable mortality experience and more particularly good investment performance. In the case of linked life assurance, however, the benefit of the investment performance accrues to the policy-holders so that the sources of profit to the shareholders are virtually (a) favourable mortality experience, (b) certain taxation benefits and (c) any surplus of fixed fees over expenses. (Indeed the control of expenses in times of inflation can be one of the major items in determining a life company's results.) On the annual valuation of the life fund's assets and liabilities by the company's actuary, a surplus or deficiency will be disclosed. Only when any surplus has grown to a size when it can with safety be transferred to the general fund of the company, is it available for distribution to policyholders by way of bonuses or to the shareholders as profit. In the long run the rewards can be considerable, but it is a long haul.

In the case of the banking groups, the advantages of being in the life assurance business, even to a limited degree, are not entirely those of direct profit. As we have seen, linked life assurance provides a source of investment into the bank unit trust groups, but also makes its contribution to the concept of total financial management. Approximately 70 per cent of all life assurance in this country is taken out by what is sometimes patronisingly called the artisan class. In a later chapter we shall consider the importance of the so-called socio-economic groupings in relation to bank marketing. The point at the moment is that a very large proportion of persons seeking, or being persuaded to accept, life assurance are not among the 15 million or so customers of the clearing banks. In many cases, therefore, on the sale of life assurance the banks have the opportunity of insisting on the payment of premiums by bankers' order which in turn usually results in the opening of a new account with their own bank. It is not necessarily profitable banking. It widens the net of the bank and perhaps there is something in the character of a proposer for life assurance that marks him out as a careful, prudent chap who over the years ought to make a responsible bank customer. There is also the point that if banks seek ways and means of consolidating customer relationships, there is much to be said for a life policy taken out with the banking group. By its nature, it fits well with the 'cradle to the grave' concept of bank services. It does not follow that 'where my life assurance is, there shall my bank account be also', but like executorship business, life assurance has that long term quality which tends to keep the customer in the family.

What then are the risks to bank or customer? The normal 'risk' of life assurance, that is to say premature death, is oddly enough hardly a risk at all. So carefully and cautiously are the risks balanced by the actuary and so reliable is the record of human experience as expressed in the expectation of life tables that the so-called mortality risk is more of a certainty than a risk. Not necessarily so, however, is the matter of investment risks. Even if all the lives assured come to an end obligingly in accordance with the tables, the amount payable on death (the sum assured) depends upon whether the investment performance of the invested premiums over the years has come up to the arithmetical expectations of the actuary. In times of catastrophic stock market performance, as in 1929 and 1973–74, the calculations are upset and in general the longer the life office has been established and the greater its reserves, the better it will be able to weather the storm. A well-managed life office will match its assets and liabilities and not enter into guarantees which it can not keep.

The failure of a number of life assurance companies in the early 1970s arose not so much from disappointing investment performance, but from the failure of the companies to match their assets to their liabilities, both as to the quantum of those liabilities and the time scale. The sad story of guaranteed income bonds is outside the scope of this book, but it flowed almost entirely from the failure to match liabilities.

From a banker's point of view, there is also the risk of damage to customer relations if a policy taken out for investment purposes, and particularly a single premium policy, fails to come up to the customer's expectations. However cautious the advertisements and explanatory leaflets, if a customer has taken out a single premium policy with a bank group in expectation of a particular investment return and finds when he or she has to 'surrender' the policy for some particular purpose that their nest egg has diminished by two-thirds of its original value (which was in fact the case with some of the single premium policies taken out at the top of the stock market), the cherished banker/customer relationship begins to look a bit dented. On balance, however, life assurance customers are satisfied customers. They have acquired a degree of security and protection and embarked on a worthwhile programme of saving. They may also have the consolation that although the insurance company or bank cannot be responsible for the vagaries of the stock market, it is extremely unlikely that any large banking group would stand aside, or be able to stand aside, and see its subsidiary life office fail to meet its obligations.

Proposers for life assurance and existing policy-holders have received an added degree of protection under the insurance legislation of recent years, the main provisions of which are set out on pages 103 and 104.

Furthermore, in July 1977 the Life Offices Association and the Associated Scottish Life Offices issued a statement which, although not mandatory in itself, was accepted by the members of the two societies as an authoritative indication of insurance practice. The statement was also accepted by the linked life assurance group. The following are the main sections of the statement:

## 1 Claims

*(a) An insurer will not unreasonably reject a claim. (However, fraud or deception will, and negligence or non-disclosure or misrepresentation of a material fact may, result in adjustment or constitute grounds for rejection.) In particular, an insurer will not reject a claim on grounds of non-disclosure or misrepresentation of a matter that was outside the knowledge of the proposer.*

*(b) Under any conditions regarding a time limit for notification of a claim, the claimant will not be asked to do more than report a claim and subsequent developments as soon as reasonably possible.*

## 2 Proposal forms

*(a) If the proposal form calls for the disclosure of material facts a statement should be included in the declaration, or prominently*

*displayed elsewhere on the form or in the document of which it forms part:*

*(i) drawing attention to the consequences of a failure to disclose all material facts and explaining that these are facts that an insurer would regard as likely to influence the assessment and acceptance of a proposal;*

*(ii) warning that if the signatory is in any doubt about whether certain facts are material, these facts should be disclosed.*

*(b) Those matters which insurers have commonly found to be material should be the subject of clear questions in proposal forms.*

*(c) Insurers should avoid asking questions which would require knowledge beyond that which the signatory could reasonably be expected to possess.*

*(d) The proposal form or a supporting document should include a statement that a copy of the policy form or of the policy conditions is available on request.*

*(e) A copy of the proposal should be made available to the policy-holder when an insurer raises an issue under that proposal – information not relevant to that issue being deleted where necessary to preserve confidentiality.*

**3 Policies and accompanying documents**

*Life assurance policies or accompanying documents should indicate:*

*(a) the circumstances in which interest would accrue after the assurance has matured; and*

*(b) whether or not there are rights to surrender values in the contract and, if so, what those rights are.*

(Note: *The appropriate sales literature should endeavour to impress on proposers that whole life or endowment assurance is intended to be a long-term contract and that surrender values, especially in the early years, are frequently less than the total premiums paid.)*

**4 Commencement**

*Any changes to insurance documents will be made as and when they need to be reprinted, but the statement will apply in the meantime.*

The statement (and one issued earlier relating to non-life

insurance policies) was drawn up at the request of the Government in return for the exemption of insurance contracts from the Unfair Contract Terms Bill then before Parliament.

**Banking and insurance**

The two industries of banking and insurance are to a degree in competition with each other for personal savings. To the extent that banks were the traditional custodians of personal savings, we may say that the insurance companies have challenged the banks rather than the other way round. As we have seen, the banks' share of personal savings has decreased noticeably over the last twenty-five years, a period in which there has been a marked increase in the insurance companies' share of the savings market. To some extent the trend was reversed during the period of high interest rates since 1969.

We may say that the points of similarity between banks and insurance companies are:

(a) They are both in the market for personal savings although, as we have said, insurance companies are in the longer-term savings market, whereas bank deposits are traditionally the home of short-term savings.

(b) In both cases those savings are 'invested' in government, industry or commerce whether through the traditional markets or, in the case of the banks, by way of overdrafts and loans.

(c) Both act as channels to direct personal savings into the commercial sector.

(d) The marketing skills and commercial judgments are similar, but not of course identical.

There are, however, essential differences between the functions of banks and insurance companies, viz:

(a) Life assurance saving is contractual: bank saving is *ad hoc*.

(b) Insurance contracts are long-term: bank deposits are repayable on demand or short notice.

(c) Insurance companies invest their premiums whereas banks lend a proportion of their deposits, the skill of the investor being different from that of the lender.

(d) The risk-taking decisions of insurance companies tend to be centralised: the risk-taking decisions of bankers are widely diffused.

We may care to reflect on the probability and desirability, or otherwise, of a major coming together of banking and insurance. It is something which, at least in theory, could have happened during the bank merger period of the 1960s. It would still be legally possible in this country, but quite impossible under the anti-trust laws in the United States. In fact, such a merger in this country could lead to difficulties for the associates in the United States of the merging bank and insurance company. Would it be politically acceptable in this country? Would such a merger be seen as such a concentration of financial power as to invoke political opposition, at least in some quarters? On the other hand, might the coming together of the banking and insurance functions help to simplify and rationalise the marketing of financial services in the High Street? Might it not also produce a better use of management resources? Might the concentration of financial resources facilitate both the investment and lending function in the development of capital projects at home and abroad? In a few words, might it conceivably lead to an integration of financial services in the market, an availability of resources for industry and, for the shareholder, a better return on resources employed? The questions are purely rhetorical.

## References

1 'Linked Life Assurance': Report of the Committee on Property Bonds and Equity Linked Life Assurance [Chairman: Sir Hilary Scott], Cmnd. 5281. HMSO, 1973.
2 Ibid.
3 Insurance Companies Act 1974, s. 62(1).
4 Ibid, s. 63.
5 Ibid, s. 65.
6 Ibid, s. 66 and s. 67.
7 Ibid, s. 68.

CHAPTER 8

# Insurance Broking

In an article in the *Financial Times* on 15 March 1976, the insurance correspondent, Eric Short, wrote, 'Over the past few years insurance has come out of the shadows of several centuries. The public is now much better aware of how the industry functions. The insurance brokers – the middle men – are no longer the faceless men of old.'

We have already said that there are 9,000 or so insurance brokers in the United Kingdom. Whether or not they are 'faceless', as Mr Short says, is perhaps not very important. What is important is that the public are becoming more aware of insurance brokers and beginning to appreciate a little of the role they play in the business world. Insurance broking is not difficult to define. The broker's task is to meet the insurance needs of his client by obtaining cover in the market, having first researched the market to ascertain the most appropriate contract for the purpose. The 'most appropriate' is not necessarily the cheapest, although cost may well be a major factor. The good broker will look for the best all-round solution to his client's insurance needs and the answer may well lie in a combination of cost, the standing of the insurance company, past performance, flexibility and the customer's own subjective considerations.

It is perhaps anomalous that although the broker speaks of 'his client' and he is deemed to act for 'his client', he is paid by the insurance company with whom he does the business. There have been one or two attempts to change this situation, but it is a time-honoured custom in this country and one which is not likely to be changed easily.

Until 1976 there were four insurance broking bodies in the United Kingdom – the Association of Insurance Brokers, the Corporation of Insurance Brokers, the Federation of Insurance Brokers and Lloyd's Insurance Brokers Association. Approximately 3,000 brokers were members of one or other of these associations, the remaining 6,000 not being members of any broking association. The insurance broking bodies have been concerned in recent years about the ease with which anyone can profess to be an insurance broker, the carelessness of some brokers in dealing with the administrative aspects of insurance, certain unacceptable methods of selling insurance, the tendency of some brokers to place insurance where commission rates are highest and the general difficulty of applying any test of quality which the public could learn to understand and accept. In 1975 the Secretary of State for Trade invited the four principal insurance broking bodies to put forward proposals for supervision of the profession and this was done. The four bodies formed the British Insurance Brokers' Council (now the British Insurance Brokers' Association) as a step towards the formation of a professional institute, and the Council developed a dialogue with the Government, resulting in a number of developments to which we will refer in a moment.

We have said that it is easy to define an insurance broker, but it is not so easy to arrive at a definition which separates the men from the boys or the sheep from the goats. The European Economic Commission defines insurance brokers (in language characteristic of the Commission's directives) as:

'Persons who, acting with complete freedom as to their choice of undertaking, bring together, with a view to the insurance or re-insurance of risks, persons seeking insurance or re-insurance and insurance and re-insurance undertakings, carry out work preparatory to the conclusion of contracts of insurance or re-insurance and, where appropriate, assist in the administration and performance of such contracts, in particular in the event of a claim.'

Although the British Insurance Brokers' Council accepted this definition, it is difficult to see that it throws much light on the situation. One of the problems is that throughout insurance business there are a number of 'intermediaries' who place insurance on behalf of a client, but would not pass the test as a 'broker' because they would not have, nor claim to have, the skill of a broker; they would not in many cases have conducted any research in the market for the particular insurance in question and they would not undertake any administrative or negotiating responsibility on behalf of the client. In many cases, they would not have that 'freedom as to their choice of undertaking' mentioned in the EEC definition.

In the consultative document issued by the British Insurance Broker's Council in August 1976, the tripartite division of the insurance broking profession was described. The three broad areas are:

1 international insurance broking where brokers play a leading part in maintaining London's importance as the largest international insurance centre;

2 commercial insurance broking which consists mainly of servicing the insurance needs of industry and commerce in this country, a sophisticated area requiring great expertise; and

3 personal insurance broking – the great majority of smaller insurance broking firms or one-man businesses throughout the country seeking to meet the insurance needs of private individuals.

These broad areas are not mutually exclusive nor, is it always a matter of size. It is a loose functional division reflecting the historical development and varying skills of the different firms.

There is another line of demarcation in the insurance broking profession. This is the one which is drawn very clearly between Lloyd's brokers and the rest. It is no doubt a matter of general knowledge that the world famous corporation of Lloyd's had its origin in Mr Lloyd's coffee house in 1688, and from that modest beginning over a period of 300 years Lloyd's has become the world centre for shipping insurance. It is often said that anything can be insured through Lloyd's and although this is not true, it is very nearly so. The essential feature of Lloyd's is that, as in its earliest days, the insurance risk still rests on the individual underwriters personally. Membership of Lloyd's includes the underwriters who, as we have said, carry the insurance risk and the brokers who make the market. There are also brokers who are not members as such, but are subscribers. The underwriters cannot do business

'From a modest beginning . . .'

in the market place themselves. They rely entirely on the brokers who bring to them the insurance needs of their clients. The underwriters operate in syndicates specialising in one or other sector of the insurance market. A close understanding is developed between brokers and underwriters, the brokers with their world-wide network placing their clients' business with the underwriters depending on the nature of the risk. The risks covered at Lloyd's comprise virtually every type of insurance except life. All the major insurance brokers in this country are represented at Lloyd's.

Out of the 9,000 or so insurance brokers in this country, some 280 are Lloyd's brokers, i.e. they are members of the Lloyd's Insurance Brokers' Association. A Lloyd's broker does not place business exclusively with Lloyd's. It is his duty to his client to place the business on best terms in the market and a Lloyd's broker will often place business with insurance companies in this country or overseas.

The top two dozen or so insurance broking companies account for nearly 60 per cent of the total broking market, but the remaining business is well spread. Insurance brokers as a whole deal with approximately one-half of all non-life insurance business in the United Kingdom, between 30 per cent and 50 per cent of life business and up to 90 per cent of pensions business. On a rough approximation, it is thought that the value of premium income of all the insurers in this country, including Lloyd's, is of the order of £12,000 million, of which insurance brokers produce some £7,250 million.[1] Insurance broking in total is big business.

One may say also that insurance broking is a socially desirable business. If insurance brokers did not exist, they would have to be created. How else could the uninitiated seeking to cover an insurable risk find his way through the maze of insurance possibilities on the market or indeed, in many cases, know where to start. Of course there are the good and the bad. A major London broker placing a multi-million pound insurance contract with underwriters throughout the world displays a professionalism unsurpassed in other walks of life. At the other end of the scale, there are those whose main concern is a quick commission, who are not qualified even by experience and who are no more than intermediaries between one or two insurance companies and the public.

Insurance brokers also play a major role in their contribution to the invisible earnings of the United Kingdom. The total premium income from overseas obtained by insurance brokers in 1974 was estimated to be £1,350 million.[2]

Let us come then to the involvement of the clearing banks in the business of insurance broking. As with many other services described here, insurance broking has little if anything to do with banking. However generous one might be in the definition of the banking function, it would not include the placing of insurance business. Like most of the newer services it is a banking appendage. The move of the clearing banks into insurance broking is a feature of the last ten years or so. Nevertheless, it was not unknown before that. If one looks outside the United Kingdom, the placing of insurance for customers was probably one of the oldest of the banking-related services. For example, many years ago some of the constituent banks of Barclays DCO had their own insurance departments; the National Bank of South Africa placed insurance business with Bray Gibb & Co. (now Stewart Wrightson), the Colonial Bank placed business with Sedgwick Forbes and the Anglo Egyptian Bank placed customers' insurance through the Marine Insurance Company (subsequently part of the Royal Insurance Group). When the three banks amalgamated to form Barclays Bank (Dominion, Colonial & Overseas) in 1925, an insurance department was set up under the head office inspector, later to become the insurance manager. The department was not a broker as we know the term today, but was an intermediary for the placing of insurance in connection with financial operations conducted by the bank on behalf of customers. Marine insurance would include rice, wheat and grain cargoes and apparently the 'ship of the desert' was not excluded because insurance was taken out regularly for approximately £1½ million of silver which crossed the Sudan every month on the backs of camels. It was the proud boast those days that the bank 'never lost a shilling', which means no doubt that the insurers also lost nothing. Other contracts also placed with the Marine Insurance Company included the entire tin ore production of West Africa from the moment of its mining until its arrival at Liverpool. Insurance contracts for gold, diamonds, ground nuts, growing crops and wool on sheeps' backs were all placed by the old insurance department.

Coming nearer home it was the National Westminster Bank which first moved in a major way into insurance broking in this country. Before the merger, the Westminster Bank had been operating a small insurance department since 1928, which was expanded in 1961–62 when the decision was taken to discontinue managers' agencies. Thereafter, this department developed rapidly and acquired corporate status in 1973 with the formation of the present insurance broking company, National Westminster Insurance Services.

In February 1970, Barclays Bank, which had not hitherto had an insurance department in this country, announced the formation of Barclays Insurance Services Company to 'act as brokers to the Group for all classes of insurance business'. Six years later Barclays Bank formed an additional company, a Lloyd's broking subsidiary, Barclays Insurance Brokers International, in order to place business for their customers with Lloyd's.

In 1971, Lloyds Bank set up its own centralised insurance department to provide 'a comprehensive insurance advisory service for its customers', but a few years later, in December 1977, followed the pattern of the other clearers in establishing a separate company, Lloyds Bank Insurance Services.

In 1971, Williams & Glyn's Bank incorporated a new wholly owned subsidiary, Williams & Glyn's Insurance Consultants, 'to provide insurance consultancy services and insurance broking', and in November 1972 the Midland Bank entered the field with its subsidiary, Midland Bank Insurance Services.

By 1976, it was estimated that the insurance departments or subsidiaries of the English and Scottish clearing banks were responsible for placing in the previous year no less than £750 million worth of life business in terms of sums assured. It is difficult to assess the proportion which this represents of the whole market – the banks' share is still small but increasingly significant and, in terms of commission earned, the total figure for the English and Scottish banks must be approaching £10 million per annum. The total premium income passing through the broking subsidiaries of the banks is now believed to exceed £100 million per annum.

It is interesting to reflect on the reasons advanced at the time for the banks' entry into the broking field. Those who know the ways of the British banks will not be surprised that it was not a quick, greedy decision to snatch a profit from some new enterprise to the detriment of others in the field. The prospect of a direct and overt profit seems to have been low down in the banks' thinking and in at least one bank the tentative suggestion of 'profit' was described as 'the cream on the cake'. Not surprisingly, however, the banks were thinking along similar lines and there were one or two common themes running through the deliberations of the time which together made up the rationale of the banks' decisions.

First, it was generally accepted that to set up a broking department or subsidiary company was a natural extension of the existing arrangements whereby bank managers placed insurance on behalf of customers.

Secondly, in most banks the branch managers were accustomed to retaining all or part of the commissions earned on customer insurances and the opportunity was seen for dispensing with this custom. It no doubt had its origin in country banking of former days when a local solicitor or other professional man would be the 'Agent' for the bank and agent for various insurance companies, as well as attending to his professional duties. Whatever the history of the matter, it was certainly an anomalous situation. It was perhaps the only instance where the bank manager, in the bank's time and in some cases using bank staff, could conduct what amounted to his own private business – and in a number of cases, particularly in the North of England, the annual commissions received by the manager exceeded his bank salary. It made it difficult to promote a man to another area and resulted in wide disparities of total remuneration quite unrelated to the purely banking duties. When the new departments or subsidiaries were set up, the agencies of the managers were acquired on the basis of one year's purchase of the annual commissions or some similar arrangement.

Thirdly, it was realised that to the extent that managers were selling insurance, they were acting in a professional field without having the necessary professional knowledge. No doubt in Westminster Bank the setting up of their insurance department helped to remedy this situation by providing a central source of advice and information. As financial life became more complicated, it must have been increasingly difficult for managers without central guidance to exercise a proper advisory role in matters of insurance.

Fourthly, there was perhaps an undefined awareness that the selling of insurance fitted in nicely with the marketing of other bank services. Mr Randle Manwaring, former Vice-Chairman, Midland Bank Insurance Services, has said that apart from a man's income 'the two most basic financial requirements of the individual are a bank account and some form of insurance cover'.[3] Certainly from a marketing point of view the two go nicely together. The bank manager is accustomed to talking with his customers about their personal financial affairs and the subject of insurance is a natural one to be raised, whether by customer or manager. In any case it is, as we have said above, a service which most managers were already accustomed to selling.

There were those, of course, who saw insurance broking as part of the concept of total financial management – another item on the shelf of the financial supermarket. (The author recalls that the corporate plan for the formation of Martins Bank Trust Company, designed to be a financial services conglomerate, included provision for insurance broking.) Perhaps, therefore, it does the banks an injustice to suggest that they did not necessarily see themselves embarking on the full-blooded business of insurance broking in all its aspects. In 1974, speaking at the World Insurance Conference, the author referred to the situation by saying that 'the banks espoused the business of broking partly in order to rationalise what was already happening and partly to augment their very comprehensive range of financial services. There was no particular wish to become "the biggest", no thought of putting anybody out of business, no desire to corner the market or to do other than take their place in a modest way in a highly respected profession.' These words which others have been kind enough to quote were probably an over-statement of the banks' intentions. It is doubtful whether they saw themselves as entering a new profession as such. But that in fact is what has happened. The banks are now in the business of broking in a big way and are well on the road to becoming among 'the biggest'.

All this could not easily have been foreseen at the time the decisions were taken. Barclays Bank, for example, in setting up Barclays Insurance Services Company for the domestic market, did not necessarily contemplate that within a few years they would be initiating their own firm of Lloyd's brokers, Barclays Insurance Brokers International, taking their group broking activities into a new dimension both at home and abroad. Even less could Midland Bank have realised in setting up their broking company that in due time, through the acquisition of Samuel Montagu, they would acquire the very large broking firm of Bland Payne. In January 1979, Midland Bank announced the sale of its interests in Bland Payne to Sedgwick Forbes, a merger which resulted in the now Sedgwick Forbes Bland Payne Group becoming the largest insurance broking operation in the UK.

The entry of the banks into insurance broking was not received with general acclaim. Although the larger broking companies did not see it as any sort of a threat to their business, the smaller and medium-sized firms naturally expressed concern at this new competition. The banks have facilities which smaller and more local organisations can never have. They have vast branch networks, occupy prime positions in the towns, they have central resources for research and information and, at local level, an unequalled opportunity for meeting the public for discussion of financial matters. Nevertheless, there is one aspect which could well favour the smaller professional broker. We have said that personal insurance, as distinct from commercial insurance, has not traditionally been placed to a large extent through brokers. Personal insurance has been sold predominantly through the insurance companies' own branch offices and their sales representatives. It has also been sold through intermediaries, including solicitors, accountants, garages, estate agents and building societies, and the industrial life companies have sold most of their business through their 'home service' agents. Banks, too, of course, were among the intermediaries selling personal insurance, particularly life assurance. The change on the banks' part from 'intermediary' to 'broker' merely switches the statistics from one column to another, but the very considerable increase in insurance broking business among the banks does mean that far more personal insurance is now coming through the broking sector and, perhaps more important, the public are becoming more aware of the role of insurance brokers, which in turn should lead to increased business all round.

Criticism of the banks came in one or two unexpected ways.

One anonymous writer in the *Policyholder Insurance Journal* suggested that 'The trouble seems to be that they (the banks) were not able or willing to equip themselves with strong enough false teeth to chew what they hoped to bite off!' [4] The complaint was that the service from the banks was inefficient and that in many cases the banks were leaving it to the insurance companies to handle many of the details which in the ordinary way would be done by the broker. There may have been grounds for this type of criticism and inevitably in the early days of the banks' broking activities there were teething troubles. Today, however, the banks pride themselves on having very substantial broking organisations with extensive facilities, management in depth and the ability to provide a speedy and efficient service throughout the country.

Another, at first surprising, criticism of the banks was that they would use their knowledge of their customers' affairs to attract business from existing broking connections. One suggestion was that the banks examined the standing orders of their customers to identify existing insurance contracts so as to offer alternative policies, or at least a switch of the existing ones to the banks' agencies. There may have been such cases of over-enthusiasm on the part of individual managers, but in general it was made clear by the banks that their branches were not to take advantage of their special position to the detriment of other brokers, many of whom were in any case good friends and customers of the banks.

Another criticism was that banks would make the granting of overdraft facilities conditional on the taking out of life assurance, and indeed other insurances, through the bank. No such pressure would be permitted. The question of insurance may often arise in the course of negotiations for a banking facility, but the customer is absolutely free to place his insurance business as he pleases. Fortunately, most bank managers cherish the traditional banker/customer relationship too much to risk offence by an over-weaning ambition to build up their insurance book.

As for the customers of the banks, they appear to have welcomed the new broking services in so far as they have noticed at all this further extension of banking activity. They may not know what an insurance broker does and they may not think of the banks in that role, but if they have an insurance problem they no doubt find it convenient to raise it on the occasion of the next visit to the local branch. If customers see their banks as solvers of financial problems, the banks no doubt like it that way.

In varying degrees, the banks are now engaged in virtually every aspect of insurance broking. On the personal side, life business has tended to predominate partly because branch managers are accustomed to selling life assurance and partly no doubt because, as a vehicle for savings and investment, it is a kindred activity to the banks' more traditional roles. In the section on life assurance, we have listed the various forms of life contract and all these are undertaken by the banks' broking departments or companies.

The leading banks claim that there is no insurance that they will not undertake, including marine, aviation, fire, theft, motor, fidelity, public liability, livestock, insurance against the weather and insurance against the birth of twins.

Some of the major commercial contracts, particularly those of a specialist nature or involving an international spread of insurance, might be placed through the banks' Lloyd's broking subsidiaries. The rest will be handled in the centralised insurance departments, on the introduction of the local bank branches. Some of the simpler everyday insurance arrangements are handled on the spot at the bank branch. In this category are a number of 'pad' schemes (so called because the branch will have a pad of application forms), arranged by individual banks with particular insurance companies, or for such purposes as travel insurance and household insurance. Such package schemes cannot necessarily provide the best terms available on the market at a given time. The essence of the schemes is their simplicity and accessibility. On the whole, such schemes have not been popular and may not in all cases be continued.

The market for insurance is considerable. In the previous chapter we have referred to the life assurance market and now for a moment we can look at the total market for insurance in all its forms. In one sense, of course, it is unlimited because as life goes on new ventures are undertaken, new possessions acquired, new risks arise and new lives come into being. The British insurance market also enjoys the special position that the world is its market. The domestic market consists of every home and every business in the country. It is often said that most people are underinsured and, taking all insurance needs into account, this is probably true. The number of life policies in force in the United Kingdom at the end of 1977 was:

| | |
|---|---|
| ordinary life assurance | 19,200,000 |
| industrial life assurance | 60,900,000 |
| linked life assurance | 2,500,000 |
| | 82,600,00 |

[Source: The Life Offices Association]

There are approximately 40 million adults in the United Kingdom, but many of these will hold two or more policies. It is estimated that only two out of five people have a whole life policy and it is probable that no more than 60 per cent of the adult population have any life assurance at all. This estimate is supported by the results of a survey conducted in 1978, which found that 36 per cent of adults had no life assurance and that a substantial proportion of the remainder had policies for comparitively small sums assured (*The Psychology of Life Insurance*, Liberty Life Assurance Company).

Just over half the householders in the United Kingdom are owner-occupiers, the great majority buying their houses on building society mortgages for which insurance would be compulsory, but it is estimated that one-tenth of all owners do not have any insurance on the fabric of their properties. Even more remarkable is the fact that approximately 40 per cent of householders do not have any insurance on the contents of their properties.

The market for motor insurance has grown with the increased number of cars on the road – the average number of new vehicle registrations each month is now in excess of 150,000.

The market for insurance broking is *ipso facto* the market for insurance, with the proviso that the market for each individual broker is that part of the whole for which he has the expertise to give advice and the facilities to provide service. For the most part, it is an uninformed market. People do not know much about insurance, they are not always aware of the risks against which they may insure, they are not familiar with the choices open to them and they do not understand the small print. None of this will be remedied by high-pressure selling. What is needed is education (as indeed in most financial matters) and the insurance broking profession can play a valuable part in that. The broker has a responsibility to the insurance companies whose products he sells, because if he sells the wrong policy or fails in some way to service his client's needs it is usually the insurance company which comes into disrepute in the eyes of the client. The broker also has very clearly a responsibility to his client in the quality of the advice he gives, in the administration of the contract and the handling of any claim.

The market for the banks' insurance broking activities is primarily, as with many bank services, the existing customers of each bank. Again, as with most services, the focal point of the marketing effort is the local branch. The marketing methods include the distribution of explanatory leaflets, displays and presentations in the bank branches, discussions with customers as opportunity permits, and in support of all that a certain amount of advertising. The successful marketing effort that has been made along these lines is reflected in the considerable growth of the banks' broking business in only a few years.

The remuneration of an insurance broker comes primarily from commissions on the policies he sells. Lloyd's brokers also receive management fees from the syndicates for whom they act. The large broking companies also have substantial investment income and fees from sources outside their main broking activities. The profits from broking vary enormously from the one-man broker who ekes out a modest living to the very considerable profits of the big companies. However, for the banks entering this field it has not been an easy ride. Salary costs are high for qualified insurance officials and the administrative costs are high for servicing a nationwide network of branches. At branch level, the costs in terms of bank salaries and overhead charges in the collection and recording of premiums can be disproportionately high, particularly for the smaller items of business. It is doubtful whether there is any profit for the banks in handling small items of insurance over their counters, although there would be differing views as to what constituted 'small'. The position has been aggravated for all brokers by the change in the method of payment of commissions on life business. The traditional basis of calculation for the brokers' commission was 2 per cent on the sum assured. Thus, in the case of a life policy for £5,000, the broker would receive on completion of the contract commission of £100. Thereafter he would receive a small annual commission during the life of the policy. For some time the system had been the subject of criticism on the grounds that it encouraged the over-selling of policies, or in some cases the selling of wrong policies, in order to achieve the immediate commission. With effect from October 1976, the Life Offices Association and the Associated Scottish Life Offices brought in a new system of commission payment by their member companies. Under the new arrangements the commissions are calculated on the annual premiums instead of on the sum assured. In the case of endowment policies, the companies pay 2½ per cent of the annual premium multiplied by the number of years the premiums are payable, up to a maximum of 60 per cent of the first year's premium. In the case of whole life policies, a further 30 per cent of the total premiums can be paid in the second year, bringing the maximum commission to 90 per cent of the first year's premium. The revised arrangements render it less immediately profitable to concentrate on the sale of whole life business and during the first year of the new arrangements there was a falling off in the proportion of whole life business sold through the broking market.

Overall, the growth in life business has continued and after a slightly sluggish period in 1977, new annual life assurance business in terms of premium income showed an upsurge of 27 per cent in the first nine months of 1978. This trend has been augmented in recent times by the boom in pensions business. The banks' involvement in pensions services is discussed in the next chapter. Suffice to say here that after a period of some years when pensions were a political football, the Social Security Pensions Act reached the Statute Book in 1975. The main effect of the Act is that with effect from April 1978 all employees were covered automatically by the government earnings-related pension scheme unless they had been contracted out and covered by the occupational pension scheme of their own employer. It has been estimated that approximately two-thirds of all the pension schemes in the country are insurance based, which means that the contributions paid by employer and employees are paid to an insurance company as premiums to provide pensions and a degree of life cover for the employees of that company. The remaining one-third of pension schemes are self-administered, funded schemes usually run by the companies themselves, the investments being held by trustees. It was perhaps natural that some of the life offices and specialist insurance brokers developed an expertise in pensions matters and some life offices, apart from offering insured schemes, also operate funded schemes for their company clients. The new legislation required careful examination of the pros and cons of contracting out of the government scheme. This resulted in an enormous demand for the consultancy services of life assurance brokers with a considerable upsurge in new business. To some extent the bank broking subsidiaries shared in this as is indicated in the following chapter.

Recent years have been a time of great change for the insurance broking profession, partly because of the advent of the banks as competitors, partly because of the new commission structure, partly because of the flurry of pensions business and partly because of the emphasis on consumerism and 'fair trading' throughout the whole of business life. We have already referred to the Consultative Document issued by the British Insurance Brokers' Council in 1976 in response to an invitation from the Secretary of State for Trade who asked the four insurance brokers' organisations to consider possible arrangements for a self-regulatory body to determine standards for brokers, to draw up a code of conduct and consider arrangements for controlling admission to the profession and maintaining discipline. The subsequent discussions culminated in the Insurance Brokers (Registration) Bill introduced by Mr John Page, MP, and supported by the government. The Bill became law on 29 July 1977. In broad outline the Act provides for the establishment of self-regulatory arrangements within the profession under the Insurance Brokers' Registration Council which was set up on 1 December 1977. Under the Act, the Council is required to maintain a register of insurance brokers and lays down the broad qualifications which the Council shall accept for registration. The Council is charged with the task of drawing up a code of conduct for insurance brokers and laying down the financial requirements to be met by registered brokers.

The Council is also required to set up a disciplinary committee to regulate the conduct of registered members and to have powers of erasing names from or restoring names to the register. Perhaps the most sweeping provision is that the Act provides for legal penalties against anyone who, not being registered under the Act, or any corporation which, not being enrolled under the Act, uses the style, title or description of 'insurance broker' or other related description.[5] Although the Act also confers powers on the Council to regulate the educational requirements and qualifying examinations of insurance brokers, it makes wide provision for the registration of those who are qualified by experience.

Thus in a swift and comparatively painless way, the profession of insurance broker moves into a new dimension. The coming together of the four professional bodies in the compilation of the Consultative Document and the excellent presentation of that document won the confidence of the Government and Parliament, and secured for the profession the right to regulate its own affairs with what would appear to be just enough statutory backing.

## References


1 Evidence of The British Insurance Brokers' Association to the Wilson Committee.

2 The British Insurance Brokers' Council: Consultative Document, August 1976.

3 R. Manwaring: 'Insurance and Banking: two sides of the same coin'. *The Banker*, March 1977.

4 *Policyholder Insurance Journal*, 4 February 1977.

5 Insurance Brokers (Registration) Act 1977, s. 22.

*'A pension for life.'*

CHAPTER 9

# Pensions Services

Pensions business is a phenomenon of our times. Probably no other single branch of financial activity in modern times has seen such mushroom development. Today, pension schemes in their various forms are almost certainly the largest source of new investment in the various financial assets of this country, and have certainly become the largest single category of investor on the Stock Exchange. Sir Harold Wilson, Chairman of the Committee to Review the Functioning of Financial Institutions, has remarked that pension fund investment might reach a point where the funds controlled both the affairs of British industry and the British economy. It is believed that the capital assets of pension funds stand at a figure of over £40 billion and new money flowing into pension schemes is of the order of £3 billion per annum.

Until comparatively recent years, occupational pensions, i.e. those paid by employers, were regarded as a matter of 'grace and favour'. Charles Lamb's 'Superannuated Man' who expressed 'surprise and gratitude' at receiving 'a pension for life to the amount of two-thirds of my accustomed salary – a magnificent offer!' may well have expressed the same surprise in quite recent years. Many retired persons alive today have no benefit from any occupational pension scheme. Indeed it is estimated that out of the total work force of some 23 million employees, only 11 million or so are in occupational pension schemes.

Only in very recent years and then only with a bit of a push from the circumstance of various government wage freezes have pensions been looked upon as part of the total remuneration package. The concept of pensions being 'deferred pay' used to be forcefully denied. In very few cases were pension schemes the subject of negotiation between the employer and employees, and seldom did trade unions show any interest in pensions, being much more concerned, understandably perhaps, with 'jam today'. One wonders whether there has ever been any major industrial dispute in the United Kingdom on the subject of pensions. Rather sadly, employee representation has been exclusively concerned with the working years, notwithstanding that it has been the retired employees, with or without pensions, who have borne much of the brunt of inflation. The lack of interest in occupational pensions is perhaps even more surprising in relation to the lengthening years of retirement occasioned partly by the lowering of retirement age and partly by greater longevity. It is not untypical for a man to work for forty years and to be retired for twenty. In the case of a woman, particularly if she happens to be a bank pensioner, it is perfectly possible that she will be as long a pensioner as she was on the active list.

It has also been a feature of our society that the clerical forms of employment have tended to be accompanied by pension rights, whereas manual labour has not. It was something special to have a job with a pension and the credit for leading the way with occupational pension schemes must go to the banks and insurance companies whose schemes have always been among the best that the legal and fiscal framework permitted. Despite the inadequacy and in some cases total absence of pension schemes, the emphasis on pensions in recent years has produced the upsurge in pensions business to which we have referred. A whole new dimension has been brought to the financial scene. New schemes have been formed and old ones re-designed. The pension funds of the large companies have grown to enormous proportions because of the effect of inflation on salaries and therefore on pension contributions. The development of the nationalised industries led to the formation of some of the biggest pension funds in the country.

The National Association of Pension Funds estimates that, whereas ten years or so ago only 2½ per cent of total wages and salaries in this country was paid into pension schemes, this proportion had increased by 1977 to 4½ per cent and was expected to become 5 per cent. Nevertheless, there was a considerable gap between the 'haves' and 'have-nots' and far too many people were retiring with no provision for their old age other than the retirement pension under the National Insurance Acts. It was left to government to breach the gap and both the major political parties sought to introduce schemes in the early 1970s. After a few years of political differences and therefore great uncertainty in the pensions field, a measure of agreement was reached with the passing of the Social Security Pensions Act introduced by the Labour Government in 1975. We have already said that with the coming into force of the Act in April 1978 all employed persons automatically come within the new government pension scheme unless, by agreement with their employers, they have been contracted out of the state scheme and included in a satisfactory private scheme.

We may classify all pension arrangements under the two general headings of the state scheme and private schemes.

## The State Scheme

This is by its nature outside the scope of this book and a brief note is included here merely as part of the general picture of pensions business. In broad terms the scheme provides that, in addition to the state pension which everyone will receive, those employees who are not contracted out of the scheme will receive an additional pension calculated by reference to their earnings. Thus there are two state pensions and it is customary to refer to the State Scheme. Here we are concerned, however, only with the scheme which provides an earnings-related pension. To the extent that an employee's earnings fall between a lower earnings limit (approximately the amount of the basic state pension) and an upper limit (approximately seven times the basic state pension) each year of earnings will qualify for an additional pension equivalent to $1\frac{1}{4}$ per cent of those earnings up to a maximum of twenty years. Thus, an employer who has contributed for twenty years will receive a pension equal to 25 per cent of his earnings within the prescribed limits, in addition to the basic state pension. Furthermore, the calculation of earnings for this purpose will be revalued at the date of retirement in order to bring the actual earnings figure in line with the growth in earnings generally. The state scheme provides for retirement at age sixty-five years for men and age sixty for women. The scheme also provides for a widow to receive a pension based on her husband's earnings and also on her own earnings if she has been a contributing employee. The total contributions to provide for the basic pension and the additonal pension are: from the employer – 10 per cent, and from the employee – 6½ per cent of earnings up to a maximum of £6,240 per annum.

The state scheme is subject to certain limitations, in particular that (a) there is no provision for a lump sum on retirement, (b) there is no provision for dependants other than widows and (c) no provision for early retirement.

On the other hand, the scheme provides for pensions to be adjusted in line with the cost of living so that there is protection against inflation.

If an employer contracted out of the state scheme, his own and his employees' contributions were reduced by 4½ per cent and 2½ per cent respectively. It was not possible to contract out of the state provisions for the basic pension, but an employer could contract out of that part of the scheme which provides the additional earnings-related pension, provided his private occupational pension scheme was approved by the Occupational Pensions Board. To be approved the occupational scheme would have to provide benefits at least equivalent to the minimum benefits under the state scheme.

It is estimated that as many as 11 million employees were contracted out of the state scheme, a much higher figure than originally estimated.

**Private schemes**

Private pension schemes may be considered under the following broad headings:

Insured schemes
Managed pension funds
Self-administered schemes
Individual pension arrangements
Personal pension plans.

The first four of these are schemes for employed persons including directors. The fifth category, personal pension plans, relates to self-employed persons.

We have already made referencc to the difference between

insurance schemes and those which are separately funded and self-administered. The more traditional insurance schemes are those where an insurance company agrees to underwrite certain pension benefits, which are fixed at the outset in relation to the premiums paid.

The second category, the managed pension fund, is of comparatively recent origin. It is normally a unit-linked insurance contract offered by a life assurance company, whereby the pension scheme participates in the investment performance of one of the life company's 'managed' funds. Such contracts are not insured schemes in the conventional sense in that they do not offer any guaranteed benefits other than provision for the purchase of an annuity when the pension becomes payable and, in some cases, a related life assurance benefit to cover death in active service. Such schemes are in the nature of a half-way house between a fully insured scheme and a self-administered scheme. They were introduced by life companies to meet the demand for participation in visible investment performance and are an extension of linked life assurance, which we have already discussed.

The third category is that of self-administered schemes. A company which wishes to retain the maximum control over its own pension matters will normally decide to have its own self-administered scheme, assuming that the amounts involved justify such a course. This will normally entail some degree of administrative costs, but this may be so even in the case of an insured scheme unless it is part of the arrangement that the insurance company will pay the individual pensions. Opinions vary on the relative merits of the various types of scheme, but in general the larger the amount of money involved the more economical it would be to manage the scheme internally as a separate fund. The relevant factors will be the number of employees, the size of the fund and the annual cash flow into the fund, the willingness of the company to underake the administrative responsibility and the ability of the company to provide or pay for the necessary investment expertise.

The main variations among occupational schemes, whether they be self-administered or insurance schemes, usually lie in the following areas:

some schemes are contributory on the part of members: other

schemes are non-contributory, the employer making the entire provision for pensions;

some schemes provide for pension units to be one-sixtieth of salary multiplied by the number of years of service: others use a less generous factor, say one-eightieth;

pensions are based in some cases on final salary, but in other cases on the average of the last three years' salary or some similar formula;

some schemes provide for retirement for men at sixty-five and women at sixty: others provide for retirement at lower ages;

some schemes make provision for dependants: others do not;

in some cases there is provision for the commutation of a part of the pension in return for a capital sum: some schemes have no such provision;

in some cases there is provision for a discretionary payment in the event of death in active service: in other cases this is not so.

Nowadays pension contributions, whether by the employer or the employee, are allowed in full for tax purposes and with some minor exceptions (e.g. development land tax and withholding tax on some foreign investments) pension funds enjoy complete freedom from tax on income and on capital gains. The taxation aspect of pension funds has been the subject of varying legislation over the years, going back to the Finance Act of 1918. The provisions of more recent Finance Acts are embodied in the New Code governing Inland Revenue approval of pension schemes. Since the passing of the Finance Act 1970, as amended the following year, all new schemes have had to satisfy the New Code and with effect from 1980 all schemes, old and new, will be brought within its provisions. These are principally:

retirement ages will normally be between sixty and seventy for men and between fifty-five and seventy for women;

the maximum pension will normally be forty-sixtieths of final salary, subject to a minimum of ten years' service;

maximum lump sum benefits will be equivalent to one-and-a-half times final salary, provided twenty years' service has been completed – in cases of less service, the permitted maximum will be proportionately lower;

the maximum pension payable to widows will be two-thirds of the employees' maximum pension;

the maximum lump sum payable in the event of death in active service will be four times the employee's salary plus a refund of any contributions he has paid.

Individual pension arrangements can now be made on quite a wide scale for directors and other senior executives where it is desired to provide supplementary benefits in addition to those available under the main scheme. The maximum benefits allowed for tax purposes listed above will still apply, but individual schemes permit of greater flexibility. There is for example no limit to the amount of contributions made by the employing company that would allow full tax benefits, with the result that the maximum pension benefits may be achieved over a shorter period of years. Prior to 1973, it was not possible for a director who held more than 5 per cent of the voting power of a company, which was director-controlled (i.e. where the directors held more than 50 per cent of the shares), to be a member of the company's pension scheme, nor was it possible for the company to take out a separate scheme on his behalf. With the passing of the Finance Act 1973, this rule was changed and it is now possible for such a 'controlling' director to join the company's scheme or to benefit from a separate individual pension arrangement.

In the case of controlling directors, such individual pension schemes enable substantial sums to be built up outside the company with complete freedom from Capital Transfer Tax, which would otherwise be payable on the director's death or other transfer of his interests in the company. The flexibility of the scheme also permits the company to make larger transfers in the more profitable years, thus reducing the company's Corporation Tax liability. Schemes of this kind are particularly attractive to family-controlled companies, but the Inland Revenue require an undertaking from the trustee of the fund that he will not agree to its winding up, other than in accordance with the terms of the trust deed.

The remaining category of pension provision is the personal pension plan. This terminology is usually applied in relation to people who are self-employed or partly self-employed. To the extent that a person is self-employed, up to 15 per cent of his or her income (after deducting allowable expenses) may be set aside in an approved pension scheme, whether an insurance scheme or an individual pension fund, with the benefit of full tax relief up to a maximum contribution of £3,000 per annum.[1] The contributor may elect to withdraw his pension at any time between the ages of sixty and seventy-five and to take part of his pension as a lump sum within the Inland Revenue rules. Employees who are in an existing pension scheme, but who undertake other private work in a self-employed capacity (e.g. consultants, lecturers and writers) may contribute to such personal pension plans from those earnings which would otherwise be non-pensionable.

Thus it is that pension schemes in their various forms have become something more than deferred remuneration or provision for old age. They have become one of the major means of saving in this country. To many people, the right to commute part of their pension gives them the one opportunity, with the exception of endowment assurance, to have a lump sum of their own to spend or not as they please. At the higher income levels, individual pension plans for the employed and self-employed have become major features of tax planning, perhaps the only remaining way of setting aside a tax-free fund out of profits or earnings which enjoy relief from tax at the highest rate.

The clearing banks in the United Kingdom have participated to a degree in the growth of pension fund business. The areas of their involvement are these:

**Trusteeship for pension schemes**

The nature of this function has already been dealt with in Chapter 4 on 'Corporate Trusteeships'. Although some companies appoint themselves or their senior officials as trustees of their pension schemes, this is not an ideal arrangement. The interests of a particular company are not necessarily identical with the interests of those employees past and present who are the members of the pension scheme. A company may go into liquidation, but the pension fund continues. A company may merge or be taken over, but the pension fund cannot, as such, be taken over, although there is provision in most modern pension fund deeds for the merging of pension funds where the need arises. In other cases, funds may be merged either, by agreement of the members, of if necessary by order of the Court. No act or default of the employer company can be allowed to vitiate the terms of the pension scheme without the approval of the members. It is desirable, therefore, that the trustees should be independent institutions of substance. The banks are well suited for this role, but do not in fact have a large share of this type of business. Many companies have no doubt hesitated to appoint banks or other outside trustees because they have preferred to retain the destinies of their pension funds within their own control. This, however, can give rise to conflict particularly if

(a) a company invests pension fund monies in ways which benefit the company, e.g. in premises leased to the company; or

(b) pension fund monies are invested in the company's own shares in order to retain a degree of control over the shareholdings; and particularly if

(c) a company seeks to use the pension fund voting power in a contested takeover situation.

It is desirable, therefore, that independent trustees of standing be appointed in order that these and other possible conflicts can be avoided.

It must be recognised, however, that the employer company has a very real interest in the well-being of the pension fund. If the assets of the fund become insufficient to meet the rising cost of pensions, the deficiency can become a burden to the employer. In the past, this burden has been assumed voluntarily by many companies in order to maintain the level of pensions. Good performance of a pension fund can therefore save a company a lot of money so that employers will seldom wish to relinquish altogether the control of the pension scheme. The need remains however for strong trustees.

## Investment management

This is the largest single source of pension fund business. The 1977 survey of occupational pension schemes, conducted by the National Association of Pension Funds, showed that out of a total of 881 pension schemes in the survey, 52 per cent were privately invested. All these, including all the larger funds in the country, require investment management. The options open to a company in the matter of the investment management of its pension fund are:

(a) to appoint a salaried manager to manage the fund,

(b) to appoint an independent advisor to assist the salaried officials, or

(c) to appoint an external investment manager such as stockbroker, merchant bank, actuary or clearing bank.

The choice very often depends on size. In smaller companies, the function of company secretary or a similar office will often be combined with that of pension fund manager. In the very large companies and nationalised industries, the company or nationalised board will appoint a salaried manager with the necessary staff to manage what in some cases will be a very large portfolio.

In the great majority of cases some outside help is sought on investment matters and traditionally the merchant banks have had the lion's share of this business, although stockbrokers too have had an increasing share of the investment management market for pension funds. The banks have not put much muscle into the marketing of their pensions services. In recent times, however, they have been much more in evidence in this vast arena of pensions business and one estimate is that they have an investment responsibility for approximately £2,000 million of pension funds money excluding their own staff schemes. Even so, it is not a large proportion of the whole.

One advantage of appointing an external investment advisor or investment manager is that it is easier to make a change if performance is not satisfactory. With the increase in emphasis on pension fund performance in modern times, it has become increasingly the practice to place investment management business on a competitive basis – competitive, that is to say, in terms of performance and not merely in terms of fees charged. The practice, hitherto more common in America, of dividing large funds among two or three investment managers has also become a little more widespread in this country. The theory is that investment managers will be judged by the performance they achieve with that part of the fund for which they have responsibility. It is not always a satisfactory arrangement. Keenness of competition and the fear of losing the account can lead to over-anxious management, seeking in some cases short-term performance at the expense of the long-term strength of the fund. It can also encourage over-activity in the portfolio, whereas a more cautious approach often produces better long term results.

The measurement of pension fund investment performance is a matter which has exercised the minds of experts over many years. Comparison of one fund with another is difficult. Between any two funds there may well be differing guidelines, quite different portfolio structure, differing proportions of new money in relation to existing funds and differences in the flow of money into and out of the fund. However, employers and trustees have become increasingly aware of the importance of performance and one or two institutions now provide performance tables based on data supplied by individual fund managers. Nowadays, most pension funds have very wide powers of investment. Historically, the investment clauses of pension trust deeds were very restricted. In many cases investment in equities was not permitted, but during the post-war years many deeds were widened to allow equity investment. Many funds, like the superannuation funds of local authorities, were restricted to the limited provisions of the Trustee Investments Act 1961. Some of the local authorities promoted their own Acts of Parliament to permit wider investment. From time to time most funds have taken the opportunity of widening their investment powers and many have powers which are now all-embracing.

### The provision of investment vehicles

Despite the wide powers now available to pension fund trustees, many funds cannot call on either the resources or the expertise to invest in a wide range of assets. We have seen in Chapter 6 that the Department of Trade permitted property unit trusts to be formed for the convenience of pension funds. One or two of the banks were involved in the promotion of such unit trusts. They offered the advantages, compared with direct property investment, that (a) investment could be in smaller amounts, (b) the units could be sold back to the unit trust managers, (c) the portfolio contained a spread of properties and (d) the management was in the hands of property experts.

Another vehicle introduced by unit trust companies for the benefit of pension funds was the exempt type of unit trust, which we have already mentioned in Chapter 6 (pages 81 and 82). Such funds enable pension funds, themselves exempt from taxation, to invest in tax-exempt unit trusts, thereby getting a wider spread of investments than might otherwise be possible.

**Pension fund structure and administration**

Pension funds are a changing scene. Many older funds have had to be brought up to date. Smaller funds have become large. Funds have become merged on takeover situations. Insured schemes have become self-administered funds. Benefits have been improved and, as we have said, investment powers widened. This evolutionary process has enabled the banks to draw on their experience of pensions matters and to advise on the structure of new or changing schemes in co-operation with consultant actuaries. Barclays Bank, in particular, introduced an advisory service for this purpose. All the banks are able to provide administrative services for pension funds and are able to relieve employers of the day-to-day chore of pensions management. Perhaps most of all there is a need for a computerised service which will provide employer companies with records of their employees' contributions and pension entitlements.

**Insurance schemes**

The insurance broking subsidiaries of all the banks advise their clients on group schemes for life assurance and pensions purposes and also market the personal pension plans for self-employed people, as outlined above.

So it is that the banks in total offer a very wide range of pensions services, but thus far the results have been disappointing. The clearing banks have not overtaken the merchant banks in obtaining investment business from pension funds; the specialist vehicles set up by the banks for pension fund investment have not on the whole grown so large or performed so well as those of other business houses; the advisory and management services have not been seized on by employer companies, many of whom have preferred to manage their own pension affairs; and the insurance broking arms of the banks have not as yet achieved a reputation as pensions consultants such as that enjoyed by some of the specialist broking firms.

Nevertheless, the market is enormous. The employed work force in the United Kingdom is in the order of 23 million. The total number of employers is not known, but in the mid-1970s there were 88,600 occupational pension schemes[2] (allowing for the fact that some employers might operate more than one scheme). Of these, 66,000 schemes had less than ten members.

It was calculated in 1972 that 35 per cent of all companies with less than 100 employees had no pension scheme, and that 27 per cent of all companies, regardless of size, had no scheme.[3]

It was also estimated in 1972 that 85 per cent of all pension schemes were insured schemes[4] and that one-half of all managed funds were conducted with insurance companies. Approximately 20 per cent of managed funds were found to be managed by merchant banks. Less than 4 per cent of all schemes were managed by other institutions, including the clearing banks.

So we can say that the total market for the banks' pensions services in all their forms consists of 88,600 or so occupational pension schemes (with approximately 11 million members) and 1½ million self-employed persons.[5] Despite the range of pensions services offered by the banks including trusteeships, administrative services, investment management in all its forms and various insurance services, the banks act in a trustee or investment role for only 350 or so pension funds with a total value of less than £2½ billion. It is surprising that the penetration of the market has been so modest, bearing in mind that over 90 per cent of all the employer companies in England have accounts with the six clearing banks. Thus, it would seem that the banks miss out on the largest business phenomenon of our time. Why is this? We can only say that the banks did not make a sufficiently determined onslaught on the market. Traditionally the banks had not been noted for their pension fund business and some image-building was necessary for them to be accepted as pensions experts. There were those who saw the scope for pensions business and its long-term advantages in the development of banking connections. In at least one bank a major national pension scheme was prepared in outline, with full knowledge of the authorities, to provide employees with a private enterprise national scheme as an alternative choice to the statutory proposals to be introduced by the then Conservative Government. However, the marketing and administrative arrangements for such a scheme would have strained the resources of even a major bank and it was difficult to see that the end result would have been profitable. In any event, the subsequent legislation introduced by the Labour Government left no room for a private national occupational scheme of the kind contemplated. The three areas where the banks might have made better progress were investment management for funded schemes, administration services for pension schemes and consultative work as brokers for insurance schemes. As we have seen, some modest progress was made with the growth of investment management business – and from the insurance side, the explosion in pensions business came at a time when the banks were organising themselves in the area of insurance broking. They were not equipped to compete in this highly specialist market with those firms who had led the field for many years in the designing and placing of insurance-based pension schemes.

After the upheaval of the new pensions legislation, the dust is now settling. All employed people are now covered by the state schemes or their own occupational scheme. As time goes by there will be further refinement and upgrading of existing schemes, but the market for new occupational schemes will be limited to those cases where companies decide to contract out of the state scheme and introduce their own occupational scheme, and those cases where employers decide to 'top up' the benefits under the state scheme by introducing their own supplementary scheme. In recent times, for example, Barclays Life Assurance Company have introduced an Executive Pension Plan designed for company directors and senior executives. There is also a very considerable market for private pension plans for self-employed people. We have referred above to the benefit of such plans – and the banks' insurance broking subsidiaries, as well as their in-house life offices, are well placed to offer personal pension plans to their self-employed customers. The great majority of self-employed people have no private pension arrangement and yet the tax savings are such that these schemes provide one of the best savings packages of our time.

The main area for the banks must remain, however, that of investment management. It is increasingly difficult for companies to manage their own invested funds. The breadth of knowledge now required of a fund manager is such that there is a shortage of such men and they are very expensive. Furthermore, an investment manager who hopes to compete in modern markets with worldwide investment powers needs back-up resources for research and distillation of investment data. There is also a degree of isolation about in-house investment managers which can make it difficult for them to anticipate market trends. To employ a man to manage a modest-sized pension fund of, say, £500,000 would cost approximately £25,000 annually, including his own salary, his pension, his secretary's salary and pension, and a modicum of assistance in the office. For managing the investments of a fund that size, a leading bank would charge approximately £2,500 and in some cases less. Even for a much larger fund of, say £5 million, when a bank's charge might be £25,000 per annum (but in fact is usually much less), the 'do-it-yourself' resources required by the employer company for that level of fund would be increased correspondingly. Some pension fund experts estimate that a fund would have to be of at least £50 million and probably as high as £100 million for it to be economical to employ its own investment staff.

We have referred to the scope of present-day pension fund investment. It includes equities and fixed interest stocks or bonds in all the major stock markets of the world; in addition many funds undertake property investment and property development in this country and overseas, and some funds undertake investments of a more entrepreneurial nature in North Sea oil, new and developing companies, commodities and works of art. Only the largest companies and nationalised industries can afford the resources to manage such diverse portfolios. A large number of pension funds are run by company officials who would not claim to be other than amateurs in investment matters. With the narrower investment powers of former years this was perhaps acceptable, but nowadays it is very much a matter for the professional. The large banks, with their day to day contact with the market, their considerable research facilities and their worldwide contacts, are better equipped than most to deal with the realities of present-day pension fund investment.

In a survey conducted in 1972[6] approximately one-quarter of all respondents among companies with pension schemes could think of no disadvantages of employing outside investment management. Strange as it may seem, 28 per cent (the largest single category) thought that there was 'too much risk' in employing outside management, but only 6 per cent thought it would be too expensive. Presumably the 28 per cent who thought there was too much risk considered that there was less risk if they did the job themselves. It would be strange if the clearing banks with their fuddy-duddy image of the past in matters of investment management, were now categorised along with other institutions as too risky. The sad thing is that many of the respondents to the survey, when thinking of 'outside investment management', would not have been thinking of the clearing banks at all. Indeed, of all those companies who thought it likely that they would change their investment management arrangements in future years, none envisaged changing to a clearing bank!

## References

1 Finance Act 1977.
2 Government Actuary's Report, 1975.
3 Opinion Research Centre: 'The Pension Fund Market'. 1972.
4 Ibid.
5 We should also include companies which do not have pension schemes.
6 As for 3 and 4 above.

CHAPTER 10

# Personal Advisory Services

'I have found,' said Mr Justice Salmon in the case of Woods v Martins Bank Limited,[1] 'that it is part of the defendant's business to advise customers and potential customers on financial matters of all kinds.' His lordship reached this conclusion having quoted at length from the Bank's published literature, which included such statements as 'You may consult your bank manager freely and seek his advice on all matters affecting your financial welfare' and 'We shall be delighted . . . to help you with your finances in every possible way . . .'. It was part of the Bank's defence in that case that it was no part of their business as bankers to advise on the particular type of transaction on which the claim for negligent advice was based, but his lordship found as a matter of fact rather than one of law that it was within the scope of the Bank's business, on the evidence of its own publications, to give advice on all financial matters.

To some extent the line taken by the Bank in that case typifies the slightly ambivalent attitude of the clearing banks over the years in the matter of giving advice. On the one hand, it is widely claimed in advertisements and elsewhere that bank managers will assist their customers and potential customers with advice on financial matters. On the other hand, the banks have been reluctant to formalise their role as advisors, and in some specific instances the bank is no more than a channel for the purpose of obtaining advice. This is well illustrated in the matter of investment advice, which we have already discussed in Chapter 5.

Even where banks adopted a clear advisory role, they were reluctant to charge for the advice given. This was no doubt partly because of the known unwillingness of the British public to pay for advice (it being a commodity which is given freely on all sides) and partly because of the assumption, almost certainly erroneous, that gratuitous advice was less likely to give rise to legal responsibility than advice given for a fee. On one occasion, National Westminster Bank caused a slight furore in the press by suggesting to their managers in a circular that in appropriate cases customers should be charged at the rate of £6 per hour for interviews. This, of course, had nothing to do with payment for advice. It was no more than a rationalising of the managers' time and an indication of a greater profit consciousness at a time when the true earnings of banks were newly exposed to the public.

In more recent years, any bashfulness on the subject of advice has faded and in a number of areas clearing banks overtly and for reward offer highly developed advisory services. In almost all these areas, however, it is not the bank manager who gives the advice, although it may come through him. It may even be arguable that the bank manager in person gives less advice today than in former years because of the increase in the number of specialist departments which now assume the advisory role.

Advice to customers falls into two main categories – personal advice to the individual, and business advice whether to an individual or to a corporate body. In this chapter we are concerned with personal advice to the private individual. There is considerable overlapping in the areas of advice, but for simplicity's sake we can list the main advisory services as follows:

Investment advice
Insurance advice
Taxation advice
Personal financial planning
Special categories of customer.

We have discussed investment advice in Chapter 5 and insurance advice by the banks as insurance brokers in Chapter 8. We come now to the role of the banks as taxation advisors.

**Taxation services**

The taxation service of a bank is something more than

'advisory'. It is a full agency service under which the bank, as agent for a customer, completes the taxation return for the year, computes the tax liability or repayment and settles the position with the Inland Revenue. In most cases, but not always, it is a continuing service and the bank will advise the customer on any aspect of his taxation affairs as the occasion arises throughout the year.

In the United Kingdom at the present time personal taxes may be payable under the following headings:

Income Tax, which, subject to the statutory allowances, is payable on all incomes earned and unearned;

Higher rate Income Tax, which is payable on incomes in excess of £8,000 per annum, on a graduated scale;

Investment Income Surcharge, which is payable on unearned income above £1,700 per annum;

Capital Gains Tax, payable on the disposal of capital assets, with some exceptions, where the capital gains exceed £1,000 in any one year;

Capital Transfer Tax, payable, subject to certain reliefs and exceptions, on the transfer of assets to another party whether in life or on death;

Development Land Tax, which, subject to the statutory exemptions, is payable on realised development gains.

Despite attempts at simplification, the taxation structure has become increasingly complicated over the years and people from all walks of life require help in the settlement of their tax positions. Even those who have the time and basic knowledge to deal with their own tax do not necessarily have sufficient acquaintance with the quirks of revenue law and practice. Most difficult of all is the task of keeping up to date with the system of rules which seldom remain the same for more than two years.

There are over 19 million tax payers (counting a married couple as one tax payer) in the United Kingdom. The great majority deal with their own tax affairs and never know whether with the right advice they might have achieved a worthwhile saving. Taxation advice is not cheap and

> 'Wise men affirm it is the English way
> Never to grumble till they come to pay.'[2]

As taxation has become more complicated and the need for advice has grown, so the training of tax experts has become more costly and the price of advice has increased. There are three main sources of taxation advice. First, there is the accountancy profession who have a natural and leading role in the provision of taxation services for their clients. Secondly, and a little less obvious, there are a large number of solicitors who deal with their clients' taxation affairs, taxation being very much a matter of law although the resultant computation of tax liabilities and the application of the rules is more particularly a financial matter. Thirdly, there are the banks. They have been in the business of taxation advice for nearly sixty years. It is a matter over which there has always been an uneasy relationship between the banks and the accountancy profession. As long ago as 1936 the Committee of London Clearing Bankers agreed with the Institute of Chartered accountants in England and Wales that they, the banks, would not advertise their taxation services other than to their customers and potential new customers. The banks stated that 'it was not their practice to solicit income tax work from those who are not their customers, although they occasionally agree to do such work upon request as the result of recommendation by a satisfied customer'.

The agreement is still honoured in its spirit, with perhaps occasional departures by the banks in their advertising. In general, however, the banks advertise their tax services only to their existing customers or as part of their more general advertising of services, and even when offering taxation help to an existing customer of the bank it is customary to say 'If you do not already have professional advice in connection with your tax affairs, we shall be pleased, etc. . . .'. Whatever the reason, the growth of the banks' taxation services has been very modest. Out of the 21 million or so tax payers in the country, the English clearing banks act for only 171,000.

The banks have not in general sought the taxation work of business customers. The argument is that if an individual is in business, it is necessary for accounts of his business to be prepared and this is properly the work of an accountant. There has been a departure from this to the extent that at least one bank has set up in recent times a special service to deal with the taxation affairs of business customers, including the preparation of accounts.

The susceptibilities of the accountancy profession are understandable. They are precluded by their own professional rules from advertising and it must be irritating to see the banks openly seeking taxation business on all fronts. On the other hand, in this over-taxed country there is enough business for everyone and the problem is not that of competition, but the fact that neither the banks nor the accountants can afford to provide taxation services except at a level of remuneration which at present the market will not bear. It is doubtful whether any of the banks make any profit from their taxation services, after allowing for a full allocation of overhead costs.

Most of the banks will offer an *ad hoc* advisory service where a customer needs immediate help but does not necessarily require a continuing service. In Barclays Bank this is known as the Tax Aid Service as distinct from the more comprehensive service. It has the advantage that costs can be kept to the minimum and a customer can be interviewed at a local branch, given assistance (for example with the completion of his income tax return), and charged an on-the-spot fee on an hourly basis.

In some instances, the banks provide a tax service to their customers without charge, provided that an interest-free deposit is maintained with the bank. This practice was taken up in recent times by the Institute of Chartered Accountants who were given an assurance by the Committee of London Clearing bankers that it is not the policy of the member banks to advertise, or otherwise offer, such a facility to customers who are professionally advised elsewhere.

To help a citizen with his taxation problems is a socially desirable thing. It is a sad commentary on our society that taxation has become so complicated that the ordinary man in the street cannot hope to understand it. It is particularly sad that the cost of paying those who can is prohibitive. One possible solution would lie in the allowing of tax fees as a deduction for income tax purposes, as is done in the United States. In the

UK such fees are allowed as accountancy charges for the purposes of business expenses, but the same relief is not allowed to the private individual.

From the standpoint of the banks, taxation work – even if it brings no profit – makes a very real contribution to the consolidation of banking business. It provides another point of contact with the customer and it is another area where lasting goodwill can be built up. It is a common cry of bank managers that they do not have as much time to meet their customers as they would like, particularly those who maintain credit accounts and do not therefore see their bank manager in connection with overdraft facilities. In such cases the contact maintained through the taxation service will be stronger than through the local banking branch. In many cases the taxation branch will know more about the customer's affairs than will the banking branch and thus will be able to advise him in some of the wider aspects of finance. In fact, contact with customers through the taxation departments is often one of the most successful in terms of the cross-selling of other bank services.

### Personal financial planning

It is nearly a quarter of a century since the distinguished banker Mr L. C. Mather wrote in the *Journal of The Institute of Bankers*:

'From time to time the wealthier type of private customer complains to his bank manager concerning the heavy burden of estate duty, and may seek advice in friendly manner as to what means are legally available to limit the likely liability of his estate in this respect for the benefit of his dependants. Let there be no doubt at the outset; it would be foolish of the manager to attempt to advise on such a complicated and delicate subject. To deal adequately with serious enquiries of this kind demands deep knowledge of an extensive and specialised branch of the law and it is no part of the duty of a bank manager to pretend to guide the customer through the complicated maze of estate duty, replete with legal pitfalls. But, before recommending the customer to discuss the problem with his solicitor, it is always helpful to have a general chat, carefully avoiding any suggestion of advice, nevertheless displaying a working knowledge of the salient principles at stake. To profess ignorance or disinterest would be contrary to the tenets of our business, particularly in view of the publicity accorded in recent years to several aspects of the matter in the financial press.'

Mr Mather's words illustrate yet again the nature of the tightrope walked by bank managers in the matter of giving advice. 'Display a working knowledge', says Mr Mather, but avoid 'any suggestion of advice'. At branch level, those words are still valid. The difference is that nowadays the bank manager can refer his customer to some other part of the group where the most detailed financial planning advice will be available.

Financial planning for wealthier customers is often referred to as estate planning. (The author first came across this term in the United States in 1966, when the best-seller among non-fiction for the month of June was a massive tome with the improbable title of *How to Avoid Probate*, selling at $15.) It is the organisation of one's financial affairs to the best advantage according to one's personal philosophy. Generally, estate planning is concerned with the conservation of capital by minimising taxation.

In former years, the trustee departments of the banks would quite often prepare 'estate duty savings schemes' for beneficiaries of trusts or, on occasions, for customers of the bank. They helped a lot of families to save a lot of money in estate duty. The amounts involved in such schemes were usually considerable and those giving the advice were conscious of the risks involved. Always the advice was hedged in by provisos and disclaimers, but in at least one case the accidental omission of a few words led to a very substantial claim in later years. The first bank to introduce a formal estate planning service was Martins Bank. This was subsequently adopted by Barclays Bank and all the clearing banks in varying ways will now assist customers with advice on the arrangement of their affairs.

The true estate plan must be comprehensive. It must take account of the basic thinking and needs of the customer and must take into account all aspects of his financial circumstances. It is usually a very impressive document running perhaps to twenty or thirty pages and setting out in fine detail the customer's present position with the various alternative courses open to him. In the course of eight years, Barclays Bank, for example, have prepared estate plans for over 1,000 customers. It is a rich man's service. The fees can be substantial, often running into four figures, but the costs are high and there is no direct profit. There is some spin-off to other services and, here again, an opportunity for creating goodwill. It is a platform for displaying the sheer professionalism of the trustee departments: a person who is impressed with the quality of the advice in his lifetime will be more inclined to entrust the bank with the management of his affairs on death.

The banks' principal competitors in this field are life assurance brokers and a small number of highly specialised financial counsellors. Some large insurance brokers were in fact the forerunners in this field, but not surprisingly their schemes often tend to be insurance orientated whereas the banks would claim that their planning services embrace the wider aspects of finance, including taxation planning and investment planning. Perhaps only the banks can draw together such a cross-section of financial expertise under one roof and perhaps only the banks can afford to maintain what is very much a luxury service.

What then of financial planning for the man of modest means? Midland Bank Trust Company, for example, offers a financial planning service to individuals whatever their means, but no written report is prepared, the advice being given entirely by word of mouth. So far only Barclays Bank have attempted a comprehensive report service for the middle classes and this, the 'Money Doctor Service', received almost universal acclaim in the press. The applicant for the service is invited to complete a questionnaire about his financial affairs and in due time he receives from the Money Doctor Department a comprehensive survey of his finances with recommendations for improvement. The financial affairs of most people fall into a limited number of defined categories. They are, for example:

(a) savings and investment;
(b) provision for contingencies, e.g. insurance;
(c) provision for the family, e.g. education, family trusts;
(d) pension arrangements and provision for retirement; and
(e) testamentary arrangments.

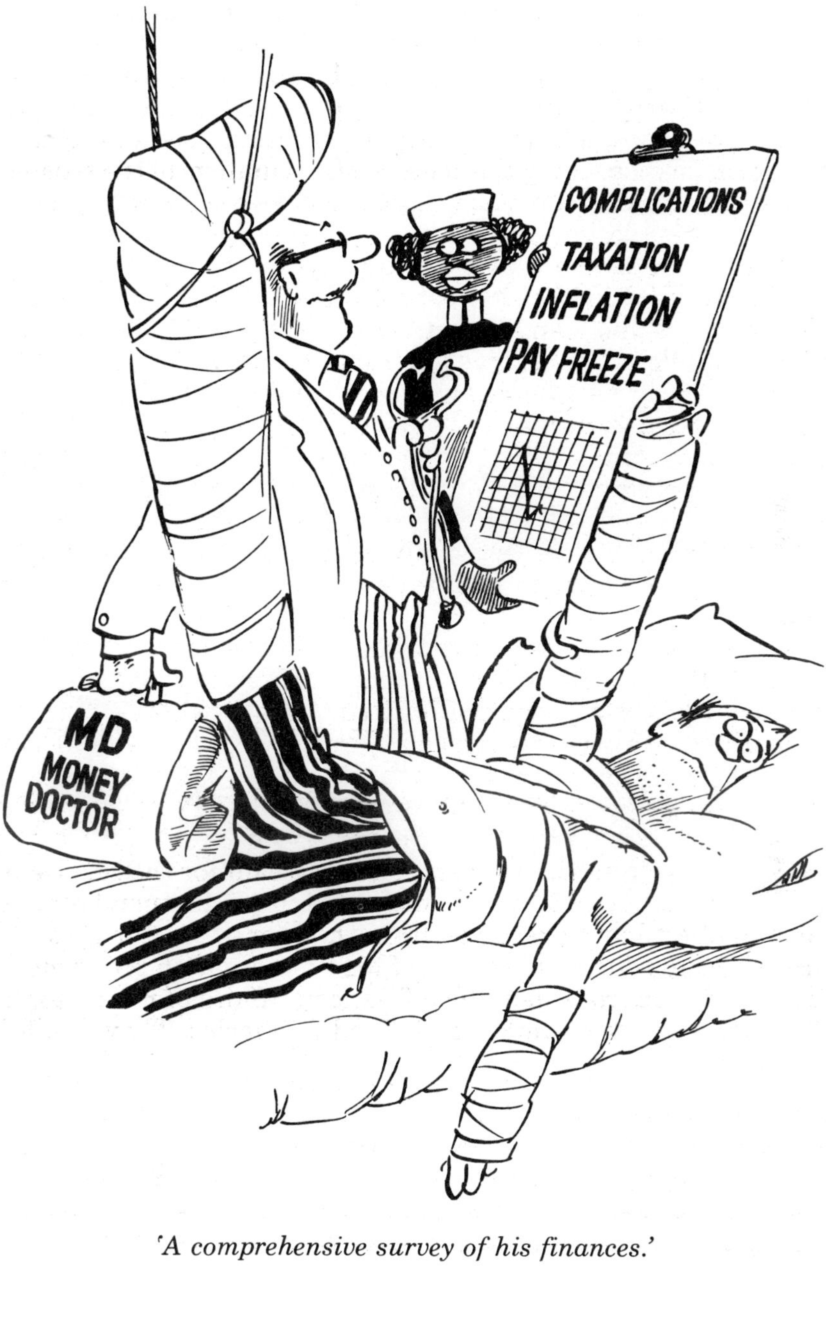


*'A comprehensive survey of his finances.'*

These are matters on which everyone needs help and advice at some time, and the Money Doctor Service seeks to provide the answer. That there was a need for such a service was borne out by the initial flood of applications, but it transpired that many of these came from people of substantial means who really needed more expensive estate planning advice. The main problem with any service of this nature is the cost of providing it. As we have said elsewhere, the effect of inflation on bank salaries was dramatic and so today it is impossible to provide a middle-of-the-road planning service on the lines of Money Doctor at less than an average fee of approximately £60. Although one may point out that this is merely the cost of having a car serviced or carrying out some modest repairs to one's house, the same obstacle is there – that people are generally reluctant to pay for advice.

There remain one or two specialist schemes for particular categories of customer, the principal of which are perhaps the advisory schemes run by Barclays Bank and Midland Bank, for two of the leading football pool promoters. It was the Littlewoods Organisation which approached Martins Bank some eighteen years ago with the request that a senior official of the Bank be given full-time responsibility for advising Littlewoods prize winners. The scheme has worked well ever since. In the case of the larger amounts, an advisory committee is set up for each winner, the committee consisting of a trust official and a nominated solicitor and stockbroker, together with the local bank manager and a representative of the Pools organisation. The winners do not have to accept the assistance of either the committee or the Bank, but usually they elect to do so. On behalf of the pools organisation, the Bank maintains contact with the winners on a regular basis over the years and at times the financial service becomes almost a pastoral function. In more recent years, Midland Bank Trust Company have established a similar service on behalf of Vernons Pools.

There are of course other categories of people for whom the banks' advisory services are particularly appropriate. There are those in receipt of substantial inheritances, those who receive large capital sums on the sale of a business and others who find themselves in possession of unaccustomed wealth, perhaps as the result of a court order or a compensation award. In many ways such cases are straightforward. The greater difficulty lies in providing a continuing, economic, advisory service for the man in the street. Most people will no doubt continue to obtain financial advice in pub or club, or from their banker or broker on an *ad hoc* basis. Perhaps this is good enough. On the other hand, it seems a pity that there is no comprehensive source of information and advice on personal financial matters to which people of all walks of life can turn, knowing that they will receive reliable, comprehensive and up-to-date answers at a price they can afford.

## References

1 Woods v Martins Bank Ltd and Another (1958) 3 All.E.R. at page 174.
2 D. Defoe: 'Britannia'.
3 L. C. Mather: 'A Practical Approach to the Problem of Saving Estate Duty'. *Journal of The Institute of Bankers*, March 1954.

*'. . . giving advice to kings.'*

CHAPTER 11

# Merchant Banking

Lord Denning's dictum that banks are easier to recognise than to define (see p. 1) might have been applied with even greater force to merchant banks. Merchant banks and merchant banking are almost impossible to define. Indeed, to quote the late Sir Edward Reid, the term merchant bank 'is sometimes applied to banks who are not merchants, sometimes to merchants who are not banks and sometimes to houses who are neither merchants nor banks'.[1] There is no doubt that the title 'merchant banker' still has glamorous overtones. It conjures visions of power and influence, giving advice to kings and being in the confidence of governments. Even in these down-to-earth days the name has a cachet and a mystique which is uncommon in other professions. The merchant bankers are the princes of the financial world. Nor is this reputation undeserved. The history of the old merchant banks makes fascinating reading. Not without good reason were the six Great Powers of Europe in the late nineteenth century listed as England, France, Russia, Austria, Prussia and Baring Brothers.[2] Nor is it all in the past. Among the modern merchant banks, it has been said of the rise of S. G. Warburg & Co. that 'there has been nothing like it this century'.[3] The student who wishes to know more of merchant banking history will find pleasure in Richard Kellett's entertaining and well-researched book *The Merchant Banking Arena*, but here we must concern ourselves with more functional matters.

What then is merchant banking? The term has its origin in the merchanting activities of the late eighteenth and early nineteenth centuries when trade between countries would be financed by bills of exchange drawn on the principal merchanting houses. At that point, the merchants were merely financing their own trading activities. As international trade grew and other lesser-known names wished to import goods from abroad, the established merchants 'lent their names' to the newcomers by agreeing to accept bills of exchange on their behalf. The 'accepting house' would charge a commission for this service and thus there grew up the business of accepting bills to finance the trade not merely of themselves, but of others. Acceptance business thus became and to a degree always has been the hallmark of the true merchant bank. The acceptance 'credit' was primarily a means of financing international trade until the 1930s, but the use of acceptance credits for domestic business was given an impetus by the Macmillan Report in 1931. The Macmillan Committee recommended that commercial bills be used more widely as a means of financing domestic trade and either for this reason or because of the falling-off in foreign trade and the difficulties of a number of countries, bills of exchange became more widely used as a means of financing domestic trade. Although bank overdrafts were comparatively cheap by present-day standards, it was cheaper still to finance current transactions by means of acceptance credits. Thus bill finance became and still remains a valuable alternative source of finance for the shorter term transactions of industry in this country. Seventeen of the leading merchant banks constitute the Accepting Houses Committee, which acts as the regulatory and disciplinary body and also the principal mouthpiece of the merchant banks in this country.

The second historical characteristic of the merchant banks was the raising of capital for foreign governments. In many cases, the merchants had been trading in the countries concerned and had gained the confidence of the governments and other authorities in those countries. So it was that they were entrusted with the issuing of bonds in the London market. Originally the interest on such bond issues would be payable in foreign currency, but in 1818 Nathan Rothschild, the founder of N. M. Rothschild & Sons, floated the first foreign loans carrying interest in sterling and as Mr Kellett tells us, within two years of the Battle of Waterloo, Rothschild 'had floated £7 million of loans in London for four Continental governments, the Austrian, Prussian, Russian and the defeated French'.[4] In the next 100 years or so, despite the interruption of the First World War, loan after loan was to be raised in London for foreign governments. Hambros Bank made thirteen issues of loans for continental governments in the three years 1926–28; Morgan Grenfell & Co. handled six issues in those years; and Barings dealt with twelve, all of them for various countries around the world.

As with acceptance credits, it was international business which preceded the developments in the domestic market. During the spate of foreign government loans, there had been very few issues for industry in this country. The foreign bond business ceased with the failure of international currencies and the lack of international confidence. Those years – the 1930s – were to see the gradual move of British industry into a new dimension partly from growth within and partly from mergers. New capital was required and the merchant banks with their vast experience were on hand, both with expert advice and the machinery for capital issues. Thus the second principal ingredient of merchant banking became and still is the raising of capital through the issue of stock or bonds. This business, however, was not by any means the preserve of the merchant banks. Some of the leading stockbrokers have a long tradition of issuing work, and there are many firms with no tradition of commercial credit business which have undertaken issuing work. The regulatory body is The Issuing Houses Association, with 56 members.

Thus there are accepting houses and issuing houses, and most of the leading merchant banks are in both categories. Together they make up the merchant banking scene. That is not nearly, however, the sum total of their business. Some retain their original merchanting activities and all have moved into new financial activities. The scope of those activities was well summed up in the evidence of the Accepting Houses Committee to the Radcliffe Committee,[5] which may be paraphrased as follows:

The granting of acceptance credits is a business which all have in common.

Many of the members act as issuing houses.

All conduct banking accounts in one form or another for customers at home and abroad.

All handle stock exchange business on their customers' behalf.

Most of them manage investments for private customers, pension funds, colleges and charities.

Several members have an active trustee business.

Several conduct registration work for companies.

Three are prominent in the bullion market.

Several are active dealers in foreign exchange.

Several handle insurance business.

Two run merchanting companies.

One owns subsidiary companies in the production and marketing of timber and one trades in rubber.

One is prominent in the London Coffee Market.

We may also add that acceptance houses and issuing houses manage investment trust companies, unit trusts, life assurance companies, pensions consultancy services and almost every other legitimate form of financial activity.

Two particular characteristics are usually attributed to merchant bankers. They are (a) their entrepreneurial instinct, which is borne out in many ways – at one time by their merchanting activities and their handling of government loans, which in the early days they would take on to their own books in full before placing them with the public, usually at a large profit; and (b) their adaptability, borne out not only by the catholic nature of their present-day activities, but by their ability to adjust to changing circumstances over the years. The perfect example is their invention of the eurodollar (or eurocurrency) – the making of a market which enabled the principal currencies of the world to be used outside their countries of origin.

It has not all been plain sailing for the merchant banks and not all have survived. Perhaps the most dramatic moment was the weekend of November 1890 when the great house of Barings could not meet its commitments and the governor of the Bank of England swiftly and secretly mounted a rescue operation with the aid of the joint stock banks and the private banks, and with some help from Russia and France – surely the first 'lifeboat' operation the City had seen. For all the merchant banks there were good times and bad and for the most part they have survived by virtue of their own great resilience. Out of the thirty largest merchant banks, no less than twenty-five were incorporated before the end of the last century. Barings, the oldest, goes back over 200 years to 1772, and Rothschilds, Schröder Wagg and Brandts can look back on over 170 years of history. Perhaps their greatest growth period was in the late 1950s and early 1960s, with the enormous increase in public issues and the growth of the eurodollar markets. In March 1963, Mr C. Gordon Tether, the Lombard columnist of the *Financial Times*, was able to write, 'The past five to ten years have seen the merchant banks fully restored to their glory'.

It is in the last twenty years or so that the merchant banks and issuing houses, and others who enjoy neither title, have moved into the field of corporate advice and with it the attendant business of 'bids and deals'. This is something of a 'chicken and egg' development, but for the most part these services grew out of the issuing side of the business which in itself, as we have already noted, was dominated in the earlier years by stockbrokers. The issuing of capital on behalf of a company which is quoted or to be quoted calls for a combination of functions, principally (a) advice, (b) investigation, (c) documentation and (d) financial muscle or placing power. The accountants to the issue will carry out the necessary investigations in their field and the solicitors will attend to the documentation. The advice on the issue and the underwriting of it – indeed the whole responsibility for the issue – rests on the issuing house, which may be a stockbroker or merchant banker or other type of issuing house, or a combination of these. The advisory and issuing role are inseparable and as more and more companies have turned to merchant banks to handle their capital issues, largely because of their placing power, merchant banks have in turn developed their corporate advice departments. It was natural that those companies which were not seeking new capital but seeking advice on the development of their business, or a merger, or an acquisition or defence to a bid, should turn to the merchant banks for advice. Ideally, the advisory relationship should be a continuing one, but this has not always been the case in this country. This is partly because industrial companies turn to their advisors on an *ad hoc* basis in the kind of situations we have mentioned and the merchant banks in many cases have been less interested in a continuing advisory role than in handling the first public flotation and subsequent capital issues for their client. In some instances, particularly contested takeover bids, companies would choose their merchant banks rather as one might choose defence counsel, and some banks acquired reputations not unlike those of eminent defence lawyers of former days. Some companies would change their merchant banker advisers at intervals and this inhibited the creation of a continuing advisory relationship. Nevertheless, there are many merchant banks who have had a number of their clients for very many years and have a close working knowledge of their clients' affairs.

It was the traditional view of the clearing banks that merchant banking was a role apart from the mainstream of domestic banking. This view was partly in recognition of the entrepreneurial nature of merchant banking; partly because of the equity participation by some merchant banks which did not seem to fit in comfortably with the lending function of the clearers; and partly because of the advisory function of the merchant banks – a role which was thought to be better exercised objectively, aside from the everyday banker-customer relationship, particularly in contested and possibly contentious situations. On the other hand, there were those in the clearing banks who disagreed with this view. It seemed to them that for many years they would nurse a particular account, giving help in good times and bad, only to find that when the fledgling company left the comparative seclusion of its unquoted status to seek a stock exchange listing, the pickings in the form of large fees and a certain amount of financial kudos would go to a merchant bank. In fact, long before that stage was reached many companies would be seeking an institutional investor, perhaps to relieve the estate duty position, and the clearing bank would have no alternative but to introduce its customer to a merchant bank that could place the shares. It seemed at times that the clearing banks were losing not only the opportunity of equity participation, with its anticipated growth, but also the prospect of substantial fees for the issuing work (fees which could exceed the net banking profit on the account over many years) and the opportunity of a continuing advisory relationship.

In the event, in a comparatively short period of time, all the clearing banks moved into the business of merchant banking and it is the extent of their involvement which we must now consider. Out of the long list of merchant banking activities which we have mentioned there are many which the clearing banks already traditionally undertook, e.g. acceptance credits, export finance, investment management, share registration and foreign exchange dealing. Some 'newer' activities which overlapped with those of merchant banks included unit trust management, insurance broking, pensions advice and linked life assurance. When, therefore, we speak of the clearing banks' entry into merchant banking we are contemplating a mere handful of non-traditional activities, viz:

medium-term lending (and here it is a matter of emphasis or degree, because medium-term loans were not unknown to the banks in bygone years);

new issues;

equity participation in developing companies; and

corporate finance advice.

It is generally accepted that the first move towards merchant banking came when, in 1965, Westminster Bank issued a debenture stock for Tecalemit Limited, the first occasion in modern times on which a clearing bank had brought an issue to the market. This was seen by Westminster Bank as a natural development of their banker-customer relationship, but it was the subject of a certain amount of criticism at the time. Nevertheless, by 1969 some six companies were brought to the market by Westminster Bank. In 1967 Midland Bank acquired a one-third interest in Samuel Montagu & Co. 'to give Midland's customers immediate access to Samuel Montagu's skills'. It was a major step for a clearing bank to take and the then Governor of the Bank of England made it clear that the further acquisition of accepting houses by the clearing banks would not have the approval of the authorities. Thus, in this twilight period, the banks moved tentatively into merchant banking activities by the development of their own subsidiaries.

In the same year, 1967, Glyn Mills entered the issuing house field with the handling of an issue on behalf of Beatson Clark & Co., indicating that more issues were in the pipeline and that they had built up a team of ex-merchant bankers for the purpose.

Perhaps the most energetic move into merchant banking was that of the National Westminster Group which in 1969 announced that one of their small subsidiaries, County Bank (a subsidiary of the District Bank and thus part of the National Westminster Group), would undertake merchant banking. Over the next seven years, County Bank was to become twelfth in the batting order of merchant banks in terms of the number of clients, and towards the end of that period they were to achieve a client growth rate greater than that of any other merchant bank.

Barclays approached merchant banking rather more diffidently. Their subsidiary, Barclays Bank (London & International), was developed as a deposit-taking and medium-term lending institution and gradually over a period of a few years a merchant banking team was built up. In the early 1970s Barclays Bank Trust Company handled three issues through their investment department, but it was primarily a caretaker operation until such time as the merchant banking side had been established. In the Chairman's address to stockholders for 1972 it was stated that Barclays Bank (London & International) 'has also entered into the field of merchant banking' – a modest way to describe such an important decision. It was not until 1975 that the new name, Barclays Merchant Bank, was adopted.

Meanwhile, following a change of attitude on the part of the Bank of England, Midland Bank had acquired the remainder of the equity of Samuel Montagu and thus became the first clearing bank – and still remains the only clearing bank – to own one of the old-established merchant banking houses.

Lloyds Bank, like Barclays Bank and National Westminster Bank, chose to develop 'from within' and in December 1972 set up a special corporate services operation to develop its merchant banking activities.

The merchant banking activities of the Bank of Scotland were centred on the Bank of Scotland Finance Company set up in 1968. Although this originated as a deposit-taking institution, similar to the finance house subsidiaries of the English banks, it moved into the business of commercial lending and, through its subsidiary companies, engaged in leasing, investment banking and related operations. As the corporate advice side was developed, the Bank moved more positively into a merchant banking role and became the largest of the Scottish 'merchant banks'. In 1977 the business of the finance company was transferred to the British Linen Bank, which has thus become the merchant banking arm of the group. The British Linen Bank, which was merged with the Bank of Scotland in 1971, holds a Royal Charter going back to 1746 and its entrepreneurial traditions of those days fit in well with its modern role of merchant banking.

Thus the banks came by varying routes to the business of merchant banking and their choice of vehicles was perhaps typical of the empirical approach of the British banks.

In the late 1960s all the banks had set up or made use of existing subsidiary companies in order to compete for larger deposits and also operate in the eurocurrency markets. Because of the official liquidity constraints and the agreement on interest rates, it was not possible to operate in this way through the parent banks. Thus, these 'bidding subsidiaries' competed for the deposits of large customers, deploying the funds in the market and moving gradually into the business of medium-term lending. A few years later, with the new freedom to compete, the subsidiaries were no longer necessary for the original purpose as outlined by the banks in their evidence to the Wilson Committee:

'After the introduction of Competition and Credit Control in 1971, the clearing bank parents were free to bid for deposits and the original rationale for the bidding subsidiaries disappeared. The function of bidding for deposits from branch customers was in most cases transferred to the parent bank, and eurocurrency business for the most part either to the parent or to an international subsidiary. But given the specialist expertise that had been built up in sterling medium-term lending and sterling "wholesale" money market dealing, the banks found it convenient to keep the bidding subsidiaries in being for one or both of these purposes.'[6]

It was natural to use these subsidiaries for the wider range of merchant banking activities which the banks embraced, but there is little uniformity in the final pattern. Barclays Bank, for example, linked together the functions of medium-term lending, corporate advice and the role of an issuing house, but deliberately kept portfolio management separate from their merchant banking function. Lloyds Bank retained investment work and corporate finance in the parent bank, but continued to use its subsidiary, Lloyds Associated Banking Company, in a deposit-taking and term lending role. In the case of the National Westminster Group, County Bank has three divisions, viz. corporate advice, finance and investment, the last division having responsibility for the unit trusts of the group as well as pension fund management. In the case of the Midland Bank Group, their merchant banking subsidiary, Samuel Montagu & Co., embraces not only the traditional merchant banking business but investment and unit trust management (through Drayton Montagu Portfolio Management).

The structural differences of large businesses are often a matter of historical accident (and sometimes a matter of personal susceptibilities). Discussion of structure and organisation can sometimes be a rather barren matter and it is not our purpose to pursue the subject here. For those who would like to compare the differing organisations of the principal banks in relation to the services described in this book, the Table which accompanied the clearing banks' evidence to the Wilson Committee is reproduced in Appendix C (see p. 310).

We have already said that if one leaves aside those various activities which were already undertaken by the clearing banks in varying degrees, the only new functions which they assumed under the heading of merchant banking were corporate advice, company issues and equity participation. Although the first two are inseparable in everyday life, we shall deal here only with the work of an issuing house, leaving the wider aspects of corporate advice to be dealt with in Chapter 13 on business advice generally.

The work of an issuing house is to supervise the issue of a company's stock or shares. This may be the first public issue of an hitherto 'private' company which is seeking a stock exchange quotation or it may be a further issue of stock (a 'rights' issue) to existing shareholders. It may be an issue of ordinary stock or of loan stock, or a variation of either. It may be a public issue or a private placing.

The issuing house which brings a company to the market has a great responsibility. It must be satisfied that the company is one for which a public quotation would be appropriate. This is partly a matter of assets size, turnover, past profitability and profit forecasts, but it is more than that. The issuing house is putting its name to a venture in which the public at large are being invited to participate. The issuing house must therefore satisfy itself as to the standing and business integrity of the company, the nature and value of its contracts, the quality of the management, the adequacy of its records, its labour relations record, its marketing strength and virtually every aspect of the business relevant to its long-term stability. For a stock exchange quotation is a long-term matter – it is not for birds of passage. In all this the issuing house will work closely with the firm of accountants – usually known as the reporting accountants, whose report will accompany the offer documents – and with the firm of solicitors responsible for the documentation of the issue. The issuing house will also work closely with the stockbrokers to the issue and one of the major decisions will be that of the issue price. This will be fixed at the last moment and will reflect the general state of, and expectation in, the market, and indeed the economy at large; the size and standing of the company in question; the market view of that particular sector; the level of interest rates; dividend expectations and the dividend cover of the company concerned; and every factor large or small which may affect the price of the shares when issued. Then there are the imponderables, including the public awareness of a company before it comes to the market. Companies like Pilkingtons and Christie's were household names before they became public companies. In the case of Penguin Books, the remarkable over-subscription was attributed to the success of *Lady Chatterley's Lover*. The issuing house has a responsibility to the proprietors of the company, as much as to the new shareholders, to pitch the price at or around the right level. The new shareholders will not wish to see the share price sinking to a serious discount within a few weeks of the issue. Conversely, if the shares move to a substantial premium, no matter how much this may please the 'stags', the proprietors will know that their shares were introduced to the market at too low a value.

There was a time when smaller, thrusting businesses considered that they had 'arrived' when they were ready for, and accepted for, a stock exchange quotation. That is probably less so today and perhaps some of the smaller and medium sized companies, usually family businesses, are more inclined to cling to the comparative seclusion of having a small number of shareholders, notwithstanding that there is no exemption nowdays from publication of the accounts. There will always be cases, however, where a market quotation will be desirable, assuming a company satisfies all the criteria. In some cases, large shareholdings in a family company will be in private hands and to 'go public' may be the most satisfactory way of exchanging a proportion of the shares for cash as well as ensuring the future marketability of the shares which are retained. Perhaps even more typical is the successful company which needs resources for expansion on a scale which would only be obtainable if it widened its shareholder base by going public.

In recent years, there have been comparatively few cases of new companies coming to the market. This may be because of an increasing reluctance to accept the exposure which accompanies the sacrifice of private company status – exposure to press comment, possible 'interference' from institutional shareholders and greater disclosure in the published accounts. Another more immediate reason for the fall in new share issues is the high volatility of the stock market which has been a feature of recent years.

Traditionally, British companies have sought to finance expansion from their own resources backed by bank lending. At one time, up to 70 per cent of industry's additional capital needs in the course of a year would be met from retained profits. In more recent years, the pressure on profits from taxation and recession has reduced the availability of profits for expansion. There has been a steady flow, however, of 'rights' issues – so called because the shareholders are given the right to subscribe for new shares and in 1978, new capital raised in this way amounted to £969 million, an increase of 25 per cent on the figures of the two previous years. It is part of the issuing house's role to assist with the raising of capital in this way and to handle the 'rights' issue.

Wherever there is a cash subscription for shares, it is necessary for a bank to receive the applications and the accompanying cheques. This is the role of the 'receiving banker': usually part of a clearing bank group because of the need to deal with large volumes of cheques through the clearing system. In the case of a popular public issue where the offer is heavily oversubscribed, the volume of funds handled by the receiving banker may be very large indeed and the value to the bank of these balances, albeit short term, may be very substantial.

Although the fees for issuing work can be considerable, the fall in the number of issues has reduced the level of contribution from this source to merchant banking profits.

All the merchant banks have their differing traditions and philosophies and have tended to specialise in particular fields. Some have concentrated on corporate advice, others on equity participation, others on international issues, notably of eurobonds, and others have made their name in mergers or 'bids and deals'. What then is the particular characteristic of the merchant banking affiliates of the clearing banks? Like all merchant banks, they handle capital issues, they conduct marriage bureaux for companies seeking merger situations, they act in mergers and acquisitions and defend companies from takeover bids, but principally they are involved in corporate advice, as discussed in Chapter 13.

Perhaps the two features which characterise the merchant banking arms of the clearing banks are (i) the links with company customers, many of whom at one time or another will be eligible for the corporate advisory services and (ii) the vast resources of the banks which enable the merchant bank subsidiaries to back up their advisory services with financial help, particularly in the area of medium-term loans.

It would probably be generally agreed that there is little or no profit in corporate advice as such. Where this leads, however, either to equity participation or loan financing, or both, the rewards can be very considerable. So far, the clearing bank groups have sought but little equity participation in their clients, although County Bank have participated in some seventy or so equity situations and no doubt more will follow. Seldom does such a stake exceed 5 per cent and rarely would the clearing bank expect to have any representation on the client's board of directors. It is well known that the German banks have substantial stakes in the industrial life of their country, but this arose from the special situation after the First World War when the support of the banks was needed to get industry going again. In fact, it has been suggested that the extent of this investment tends to be exaggerated and that the German banks exercise a far greater influence through share proxies held for their customers. There is little, if any, counterpart of that situation in this country, and no apparent inclination on the part of the clearing banks to have anything but modest equity participation in their company customers. Indeed, they would argue that the roles of lender and shareholder are not always compatible and that, in any case, the functions should be kept apart.

A number of merchant banks will assist with the equity funding of new or emergent companies – usually referred to as venture capital. Their requirements are stringent, however, and they consider that there is a dearth of good projects. Seed capital is short for new projects and on the whole the clearing banks have not seen this as an area for their involvement. Nevertheless, County Bank, Barclays Merchant Bank (through their subsidiary company, Barclays Development Capital), Samuel Montagu (through their subsidiary, Midland Montagu Industrial Finance) and the National and Commercial Banking Group (through National and Commercial Development Capital) are all providers of development finance and keep a look-out for interesting and potentially profitable situations in which to participate.

The converging roles of clearing banker and merchant banker caused a certain amount of speculation on the possibility of conflict. For example, the role of an issuing house can fit in uncomfortably with that of investment manager if there is any temptation or persuasion to support an issue from the portfolios under the bank's management. Even greater is the risk of conflict if the merchant bank is dealing for its own account in shares held in a fiduciary role in its portfolio department, or again, if in a contested bid situation the merchant bank can command blocks of votes through its fiduciary portfolios. In fact, all merchant banks have resolved this problem by segregating their investment management activities from the corporate advice area – and even where, in a leading clearing bank group, the two activities are under one roof, strict separation is maintained and there is no question of disclosure or discussion in these areas of possible conflict.

Another field of possible conflict among the clearing banks is the contested takeover where the in-house merchant bank might be opposing, strongly and publicly, a bid by a customer of its parent bank for the customer of another bank. Thus County

Bank might be defending, say, a Lloyds Bank customer against a bid from a National Westminster Bank customer. When one recalls the bitterness of some public takeover battles, one can appreciate the risk of some lasting resentment. However, the merchant bankers among the clearers affirm that they see their role as doing the best for their client, of whatever bank, and that all concerned, winners or losers, respect their special position.

Yet another kind of conflict is the competition between the merchant bank and other parts of the banking group for customer business. This may apply to a degree where the domestic bank and the merchant bank are offering comparable services, for example, medium-term loans. It may also arise in another way. The merchant banks pride themselves on high-level personal contact with their clients and indeed, this is essential if they are to maintain a proper advisory role. As that contact is strengthened, it is possible that the link with the domestic bank, whether it be at local manager, regional director or general manager level, may be weakened. With the modern tendency for account executives in the clearing banks to deal with the business of the larger companies, this could possibly conflict with the merchant banker's idea of being *the* corporate advisor. However, if it is a problem, the banks will no doubt resolve it with their customary resilience.

The merchant bankers among the clearing banks consider, no doubt very rightly, that they have something special to offer. By training, many of them being accountants and lawyers, they tend to have a more analytical approach than the traditional bank manager. Also they pride themselves on their ability to give a quick answer. By training and temperament, the merchant banker tends to be a different animal from the clearing banker, but there seems no good reason why they should not live together and hunt together very successfully.

## References

1 Sir Edward Reid: 'The Role of the Merchant Banks Today' – being the Presidential Address to The Institute of Bankers, 15 May 1963.

2 P. H. Emden: *Money Powers of Europe in the Nineteenth and Twentieth Centuries*. Sampson Low, 1946.

3 R. Kellett: *The Merchant Banking Arena.* Macmillan, 1967.
4 Op. cit.
4 Report of the Committee on the Working of the Monetary System [Chairman: Lord Radcliffe], Cmnd. 827 HMSO, 1959.
6 Committee of London Clearing Bankers: *The London Clearing Banks – Evidence to the (Wilson) Committee to review the Functioning of Financial Institutions.* Longman, 1978.

CHAPTER 12

# Share Registration

One of the comparatively backroom services of the commercial banks has assumed considerable proportions in recent years. It is share registration work or, more correctly, the function exercised by banks and others as company registrars.

It is a requirement of company law[1] that every company shall keep a register of its members and that the register will contain the names and addresses of the members, a statement of the shares held by each member, distinguishing each share by its number so long as it has one, and the amount paid or agreed to be considered as paid on the shares of each member. The register must also show the date on which each person was entered as a member and the date on which any person ceases to be a member.

The Companies Act also requires the register of a company to be kept either in a bound book or in such other form as may be adequate to guard against falsification[2]. Under a recent Act of Parliament[3], there is provision for company registers to be kept 'otherwise than in a legible form so long as the recording is capable of being reproduced in a legible form'. The Act is to come into force on a day to be appointed by the Secretary of State and its purpose is to permit company registers to be stored on computers.

The term 'Registrar' has no legal definition, nor are there any precise duties of a registrar laid down in the Companies Acts. It is the person or institution appointed by the directors to maintain the register of the company and to see that the company's legal obligations in that respect are fulfilled. In practical terms, the registrar of a company maintains the list of

*'. . . otherwise than in a legible form . . .'*

stockholders and shareholders with their addresses and individual stock and share holdings, he issues certificates, registers transfers, attends to the payment of dividends and, in effect, supervises the mailing list of shareholders for the purpose of despatching notices and reports to members.

There are approximately 2,000 companies whose shares are quoted on the London Stock Exchange. Many of these are small companies with, say, a few hundred shareholders, and the secretary or other official of the company will normally deal with the company registration work. For larger companies, however, the duties of a registrar can be an immense chore and it becomes a matter of decision whether or not the company maintains its own registration department or contracts the work out to a professional registrar.

There are eight or so major registration services operating in England, handling approximately 12 million shareholder accounts out of a total market of about 20 million. Five of these are clearing bank registrars who handle 7 million or so individual shareholder accounts. There is a continuing trend for business to be concentrated in the hands of these service registrars, the largest of which handles nearly 3 million shareholder accounts, involving the registration of ¾ million transfers a year – some 12½ per cent of the Stock Exchange company business. The number of transfers registered each year will of course vary with market activity.

The banks, then, exercise a very major role in the business of share registration, and although there are 900 or so company registrars (including companies which maintain their own registers) acting for companies listed on the London Stock Exchange, approximately 30 per cent of all shareholding accounts are administered by the registration departments of the clearing banks.

Although company registrarships may seem to be among the banks' less glamorous activities, it is in fact a highly professional service involving minute attention to detail. There is a high routine content in the work associated with the maintenance of company registers which in the past required the employment of large numbers of staff, but as the operation on a large scale lends itself to computer applications, it is now far less labour intensive. In the past, it was not unknown for some of the smaller registration companies to run into difficulties because of the sheer weight of administrative routine. It is a service which the large financial organisations, such as the banks, are well equipped to provide. The work involved may be summarised as follows:

**The maintenance of the register of members**

A large company may have over 100,000 shareholders, although a more typical figure would be in the region of 30,000–60,000 shareholders. The majority of companies, however, have fewer than 5,000 shareholders and may have even less than 2,000. As shares are bought and sold, the transfer forms are registered and in the case of partial sales, the transfer forms have to be 'certified'. It has been established that approximately 50 per cent (by volume) of all share transfers on the London Stock Exchange are handled by the ten largest registrars, including the Bank of England and ICI who keep their own registers.

Apart from such voluntary transfers, there are transfers on death involving the registration of death certificates and grants of probate. Changes of name on marriage have to be registered, as do other documents affecting the transfer of and title to shares, for example powers of attorney and court orders.

On average, there is some activity each year in connection with 25 per cent or so of total shareholdings. A large bank may have an average of 3,000 share transfers to deal with each day. In a typical day, they would deal also with over 150 deaths of shareholders, 600 or more changes of address and 700 or so new dividend mandates.

**Preparation of share certificates**

Share certificates in the United Kingdom come in all shapes and sizes and traditionally have been completed by manual means. In more recent times, a process has been developed for the printing out of share certificates by computer. These must bear the company seal, but the majority of companies' articles of association permit the affixing of the seal without signatures or with signatures affixed by mechanical means. In many cases a facsimile of the common seal is held by the service registrar for this purpose but, as opinion is divided over the legality of such an operation, the opportunity has been taken in the recent Stock Exchange (Completion of Bargains) Act 1976 (Section 2) to authorise companies to use a separate seal for the purpose of sealing certificates. This is a facsimile of the common seal with the addition of the word 'securities'.

## Enquiries from shareholders, stockbrokers and others

A considerable amount of time is involved in dealing with written enquiries concerning a register. For example, National Westminster Bank deals with over 2,000 enquiries a week relating to the registers of over 300 listed companies and local authorities. These may be received either in the form of correspondence or by telephone and largely relate to the current and historical holdings of shareholders and to matters associated with the payment of dividends, e.g. regarding tax credit figures and requests for duplicate dividend tax vouchers.

## Dividend and interest payments

The registrarship service includes the preparation and despatch of all dividend and interest payments on behalf of the company or authority for which the registrar acts. In the case of the bank registrars, the usual procedure is for the bank to open dividend accounts for payment of the warrants, the total cost of the dividend being covered in one payment from the company. Dividends may also be paid by means of the mandated dividends system which routes dividends direct to the shareholders' banking accounts. Considerable savings in postage costs can be obtained by the use of this system. Thus it is that a registrar handling, say, 500,000 shareholder accounts might operate at any one time as many as 300–350 current banking accounts, to deal with the dividend and interest payments for various companies and various classes of share.

## Company communications

The statutory requirements relating to the maintenance of a company's register must of necessity include the addresses of members to facilitate the despatching of notices of meetings, annual reports and accounts and other documents of title to the shareholders concerned.

## Statutory returns

It is a duty of the company secretary to make the statutory returns, but it often falls to the registrar to provide the necessary information. In particular, the registrar will prepare the annual return required under Section 124 of the Companies Act 1948, which is a list of past and present members of the company with addresses and certain other statutory information regarding transactions in the shares. In other cases, the registrar will assist the secretary in the preparation of such returns as 'Notice of change of directors or secretaries in their particulars', pursuant to Section 200 of the Companies Act 1948 and 'Notice of change of situation of registered office', pursuant to Section 23(3) of the Companies Act 1976.

**Company meetings**
The registrar frequently deals with assessing the proxy votes returned through the post for annual or extraordinary general meetings. At meetings of companies, the registrar will often be required to assist the company secretary in checking the names of shareholders against the attendance sheets and in the conduct of a poll.

**Transfer audit**
It is usual in the case of the registrar services provided by the clearing banks to provide a continuing internal audit, in some cases through the Inspection Department of the bank, thus avoiding the time and expense of a transfer audit by the company's accountants.

So much for the role of the registrar. From the standpoint of the client companies, there are considerable advantages in having this large volume of work taken over by a bank or other registrar company. The charges made by the banks, however, have seldom if ever caught up with rising costs and for the most part company registration work has been for the banks a loss-making activity. In earlier times, the level of charges was almost certainly fixed too low as the banks sought to compete for this type of business. It was and presumably still is a matter of prestige to have the bank's name on virtually every communication sent out to scores of thousands of shareholders by a large company. It was also considered, as with many bank services, that the registrar service would consolidate the existing banking connection.

These assumptions need examination and perhaps qualification. It is not untypical for the registrar's department of a clearing bank to run at a substantial loss. At no time have there been adequate compensating profits. The prestige value of an administrative service of this kind is probably minimal. In terms of its advertising value, the level of losses can make it very expensive. Furthermore, it must be doubtful whether the provision of a registrar service for a particular company is very material in relation to the obtaining, retaining or losing of that company's account. Admittedly as with many bank services, it is another point of contact with the bank's customers. It is another way in which a bank can extend its influence. If a bank registration department handles, say, 1 million accounts, 3 or 4 million communications are going out each year bearing the bank's name. Each bank must evaluate these intangible benefits for itself. Even if registration services were to break even after a full allocation of costs, there are risks and responsibilities which remain unquantified and the resources employed in these services are very considerable.

Among the banks, the charges for registration work vary quite a lot, depending on the size of register and the number of transfers handled. There is normally a fee per shareholder account and an additional charge if the volume of transfers processed is abnormally high. The charge per account for the smaller company is normally substantially higher than that for the larger company where economies in volumes may be obtained – the tariff is also influenced by the overall size of the individual bank registration business, and the relationship of a particular company with its banker may also have a bearing on the tariff.

A number of companies, including some very large ones, still maintain their own registers because they prefer to keep these under their own control. The banks would suggest, however, that there are savings to be made even for the largest companies by transferring the registration work to a bank, and that all relevant information from the registers is still readily available to the directors and officers of the company. This was apparently acknowledged in recent times by a company with 140,000 or so shareholders, which was pleased with the economies achieved by transferring the register to a clearing bank. From the banks' point of view, profitability remains a problem, although the position is better if one takes into account the earnings from handling new issues.

Work of this nature, largely done nowadays with the aid of computers, can well be based in low-cost areas and in recent years the four major banks have moved their registration departments out of London – Barclays Bank to Knutsford, Lloyds Bank to Goring-by-Sea, Midland Bank to Sheffield and National Westminster Bank to Bristol.

Although by this means it is possible to stem the tide of rising costs, there is the additional problem that company registers are getting smaller in numbers of shareholders. As mentioned elsewhere, the proportion of private shareholders has diminished considerably in recent years and, in a few cases, companies have been known to encourage holders of small numbers of shares to sell their holdings. In some companies the numbers of shareholders on the register have diminished quite substantially in the last few years. From a profitability point of view, with fees on a per account basis, a high volume of work is essential to achieve maximum economies, although where market conditions are favourable, contributions from capital issues augment the earnings. Although the combined effect of rising costs and diminishing registers will be passed on to the companies concerned, it will inevitably be a continuing struggle. Nevertheless, the banks will no doubt continue to provide this most valuable service.

At the time of writing, there is a new development affecting the business of company registration work. This is the proposed new Stock Exchange centralised settlement system known as Talisman, which is designed to come into effect in March 1979. In essence, this is a central pooling system for the purchase and sale of quoted securities and it is anticipated that 90 per cent of London stock market settlements will be channelled through Talisman by the year end. It is a feature of the new system that stock will be delivered by the vendor in advance of settlement and will be held temporarily by the Stock Exchange nominee company, SEPON, pending transfer to the new owner. There will thus be a lacuna in the title chain, for it is a matter of legal argument whether or not stock held by SEPON is in the ownership of the vendor, the purchaser under the contract or indeed, of SEPON itself. The problem, if such it be, will no doubt be resolved in due time, but the new arrangements are of course relevant to the role of the professional registrar and may well be welcomed by registrars as a move towards greater speed and efficiency of stock settlements. It will be interesting to see how the system develops.

## References

1 Companies Act 1948, s. 110.
2 Ibid, s. 436.
3 Stock Exchange (Completion of Bargains) Act 1976, s. 3.

*'. . . according to the size of the concern.'*

CHAPTER 13

# Business Advisory Services

There are approximately 9,000 public companies in the United Kingdom, 2,019 of which were quoted on the Stock Exchange in September 1977. Of these quoted companies, 1,186 have individual market capitalisation of less than £5 million.[1] There are in addition just under 300,000 private companies. Even those substantial figures do not of course constitute the entire business life of the country. Although we are no longer a nation of shopkeepers, a considerable amount of business is conducted by private individuals and partnerships. The total number of private people and partnerships assessed for income tax on trading profits in the year 1972–73 was just over 2·4 million.[2] It has been estimated that between one-sixth and one-fifth of business assets (excluding the public sector) are owned by private companies and private individuals.[3]

All businesses, large and small, require advice at one time or another and the availability of advice has tended to vary according to the size of the concern. Large companies have traditionally had access to the merchant banks and leading firms of accountants, and from their own resources they have been able to marshal and distil all the available advice. Smaller firms and those in the middle range have not in general known where to turn for guidance on the more sophisticated aspects of modern business, nor indeed could the comparatively small number of experts in the corporate advice field have coped with such a large demand.

The problem of smaller businesses was considered in great depth by the Bolton Committee on Small Firms. Among a large number of far-ranging recommendations, the Committee made the following comment:

'We hope, however, that the Clearing Banks will consider whether they could further improve their services to the small businessman in two particular respects. First, if it were possible for the banks to impose as a normal condition for the grant of an overdraft to a firm the production of regular cash-flow statements, or the employment of adequate estimating and budgetary systems, and if such disciplines, valuable in their own right, came to be recognised as being helpful for obtaining bank finance, the efficiency of small firms might be much increased. We do not suggest that a control system should be insisted on as a kind of bureaucratic formality, but rather that the bank manager might be able to improve the efficiency of his customers, in their interests and his own. He could also help them by pointing out the benefits of regular attention to certain simple indices of the health of a business – the profit/sales ratio, the debtor/sales ratio, the stocks/turnover ratio, return on capital employed and so on. In this way he would give powerful support to the efforts of the accountant in improving the performance and hence the overall viability of the small firm sector. Second, the bank manager should be ideally placed to advise small businessmen on the availability, the cost and the advantages of different forms of finance, in cases where an overdraft facility is not the appropriate kind of finance for the purpose in mind. The Clearing Banks have represented to us that their branch managers are already providing advice of this kind, especially as regards the facilities offered by the Banks' own subsidiary and associated companies, and we do not doubt that many branch managers now go to considerable trouble to keep themselves informed about the terms on which other financial institutions are prepared to do business with small firms. Nevertheless we have repeatedly been told by the specialist finance institutions that the quality of the advice on available sources of finance given to most small firms by their bank managers is poor. The same was said, often with greater force, of accountants. Certainly the strong prejudice of many small businessmen against any form of borrowing other than by overdraft, and their ignorance of the terms on which it is likely to be possible, suggest that there is great scope for improvement in the advice they receive on financial matters.'[4]

At a later point, on the subject of sources of finance, the Committee reported:

'We have found that small firms have suffered and still suffer a number of genuine disabilities, by comparison with larger firms, in seeking finance from external sources.'[5]

A number of the banks saw in the Bolton Report a new challenge and an opportunity to do some good for themselves and their customers. In his Chairman's Address to the stockholders of Barclays Bank in 1972, Sir John Thomson said:

'The ordinary customer will require sympathetic and skilful understanding of his needs and frequent quick decisions. The Bolton Report on Small Firms has a special message for us because we see it as placing firmly on the shoulders of the branch manager this task of servicing a most important sector of the economy. Local staff, having adopted a project, are also in the best position to keep an eye on future progress. There has been criticism that banks have been too slow in diagnosing problems before it is too late to save their customers from complete failure, resulting in dire trouble for owners, employees and creditors. It has not always proved advisable for bank managers to have been the first to intervene because such intrusion has been resented and the business taken to a competitor. On recovery, a valuable account will have been lost. Many remedies have been prescribed, but it is important that we should train our staff not to be slaves of historical statistics of past performance but truly to understand cash flow and the assessment of future prospects. Any such assessment must involve close contact and exchange of information with customers.'

The following year Barclays Bank announced its new Business Advisory Service.* In a preparatory six months' period a team of managers had been set up 'able to investigate and find solutions to financial planning and control problems which face their customers and to advise on and help instal management accounting systems'. In due time the service was extended to every district of the bank.

It was stated at the time that this was the first occasion a

* At the time of writing, Barclays report that 7,500 companies have had the assistance of their Business Advisory Service.

major bank had drawn together its various services for the purpose of advising smaller companies. Barclays Bank provide the service free to customers of the bank, but make an appropriate charge for non-customers.

In 1971, Midland Bank had in fact organised its Finance Management Service designed not specifically for small customers, but for corporate customers generally. Sir Archibald Forbes, Chairman of Midland Bank, said in his Statement to Shareholders in 1972:

'Early last year we set up a Finance Management Service with which customers can discuss the whole range of their financial requirements and determine the most appropriate methods of meeting them. The officials of this Service are thoroughly versed in the more specialised activities of the Group, including for example not only the various lending facilities and outlets for surplus funds, but also insurance, the provision of equity finance and the introductions to such activities as mergers and flotations. The part played by this Service will surely become increasingly important as the financial problems of our customers become more and more complex. The Service will, we think, be found of particular value to medium sized and small business undertakings which are often handicapped by lack of knowledge of the range of financial facilities available to them. This was emphasised in the Report of the Committee of Inquiry on Small Firms presented last year.'

Although only Midland Bank and Barclays Bank formalised their advisory services in the wake of the Bolton Report in this way, all the banks would now claim to give financial advice to their business customers in one way or another. Lloyds Bank have set up a business advisory service and also advertise the services of their Trust Division to assist family businesses with taxation, insurance and pension problems. In other cases, the advisory services are an extension of the existing merchant banking function. In the case of Midland Bank, the finance management service has been absorbed within the bank's Corporate Finance Division.

What then is the sum and substance of the advice offered by the clearing banks to their business customers? In the first place it must be seen as a very recent development. We have already commented on the reluctance of banks to give advice and until a few years ago it would have been unthinkable that any bank should presume to tell its customers how to run their businesses. Bank managers at local level would assist in a variety of comparatively minor ways. Certainly some small businesses would lean quite heavily on their bank managers, but it is no disparagement to say that few if any managers were equipped to give advice at other than a very unsophisticated level.

Even up to the present time, a large number of proprietors of businesses do not consult their bank managers on business matters. A recent survey of twenty-three London branches, which provided banking facilities to over 8,000 small firms, showed that 45 per cent of the owner-managers had not conferred with their branch managers during the previous year.[6] The survey also showed that in the case of firms without borrowing facilities, over 60 per cent of the owner-managers had not conferred with their bank managers during the year. Of those who had any discussion with their banks, understandably as high a proportion as 94 per cent were seeking advice on borrowing and 72 per cent on the economy generally. On the more detailed aspects of the customer firm's business, only 56 per cent had discussion with their banks on the subject of debtors, 45 per cent on taxation matters, 45 per cent on inventories, 24 per cent on budgeting and as few as 4 per cent on such subjects as leasing and factoring. Out of the total of only 45 per cent who conferred at all with their banks, only 8 per cent discussed the investment of surplus cash. Perhaps an even more telling comment from the survey was that 'there was a wide range of opinion among the bank managers concerned as to the subjects on which they should be advising'.

It would never be possible, nor necessarily desirable, to train bank managers throughout the country in modern business techniques to a point where they could advise all sorts and conditions of customers. Bank managers have their own branch business to run and they cannot all become business consultants. So it is that the banks chose the obvious course of training small teams of chosen officials to run their advisory services.

Nevertheless, as Mr Timothy Bevan, Deputy Chairman of Barclays Bank, said in his address to the Institute of Bankers' 1978 Cambridge Seminar:

'It is difficult to see the branch manager ever being totally supplanted by the small business adviser or any other non-line specialist.'

Mr Bevan went on to stress the need for selected bank staff to be given appropriate training in business advisory matters before progressing in the normal way into branch management.

To go into the 'business' of business advice was a major, unprecedented step – a complete departure from banking as such but nevertheless an activity which fits well enough with the basic business of the lending of money. It was yet another example of the ways in which the banks can respond to pressures or suggestions from outside their ranks – in this case from the Bolton Committee. However, we can say that the clearing banks are prepared to help in an advisory way anyone large or small engaged in a legitimate business activity. The type of problem, the nature of the advice and the infrastructure within each banking group will vary very largely according to the size of the firm in question. (We were taught in our youth that a firm was a partnership and a company was a limited company. The distinction has much to commend it, but has long since gone by the board.)

Any dividing line between large companies and small ones must necessarily be an arbitrary one. The Research Unit set up by the Bolton Committee of Inquiry into Small Businesses defined 'small' at different levels according to different types of business. In the case of manufacturing industries, for example, any company with assets of less than £250,000 and a turnover of less than £1 million would be classified as 'small'. It would be meaningless to say that large companies are those which have a public quotation and 'small' companies are those which do not. On the other hand, quoted companies and those companies which hope for a quotation in the foreseeable future are, as our American friends say, in a different ball game. The scene changes very considerably with the transition from 'private' to 'public' and even more so when 'public' is accompanied by an official listing on the Stock Exchange. There is another reason for this differentiation between the public and the private company. The business of corporate advice began with merchant banks and in general, a merchant bank would not seek an advisory role for an unquoted corporate client unless there was some prospect of leading that client along the road to a public quotation. Merchant banks were entrepreneurs and their interest in giving corporate advice was not altruistic. They would give their support to an up and coming, well-managed company, taking or placing a share of the equity and possibly taking a seat on the board, in order to enjoy one day the substantial fees for bringing the company to the market and, more particularly, a handsome return on their investment which would then be in a marketable form.

There is another difference in the nature of the advisory function depending on the size of the business. A large company engaging a merchant bank as corporate advisor would be entering into a continuing relationship until such time as it might change to another advisor. In the case of a clearing bank advising a small business, this would normally be a once-for-all operation (with a follow-up arrangement if required) and although naturally the banker-customer relationship would continue, the bank would not assume a continuing consultative role. However, these are peripheral matters. The point is that for one reason or another a company customer seeking advice will be dealth with either by the bank's merchant banking operation, or by a special business advisory team, depending on the size of the company and the nature of the problem.

For a publicly quoted company, the merchant bank will often be required to advise on such matters as:

the capital structure of the company including the sources of available capital, and the pros and cons of equity capital and long-term debt;

dividend policy;

investment appraisal and cost-benefit analyses;

merger or take-over possibilities;

management of liquid resources;

development of overseas business and import and export financing.

For a company approaching public status the bank will advise on:

overall strategy;

profit planning;

constitution of the board;

the general structure and organisation of the company;

the raising of capital and the placing or offering for sale of shares to the public.

Turning to smaller companies, we may quote from the evidence of the clearing banks to the Wilson Committee:

'The clearing banks are the main, and in many cases the only, point of contact with the financial system for the $1\frac{1}{4}$ million businesses in the country believed to meet the Bolton Committee's definition of a small firm . . . small firms still contribute about 20 per cent of Gross National Product and provide employment for about 6 million people or 30 per cent of the working population.'[7]

And in a later paragraph:

'One of the most important features of the development of the clearing banks over the past 20 years has been the increasing range of facilities available through their branch outlets to meet the needs of smaller businesses at each successive stage of their development.'[8]

Because of the great diversity and range of activity of smaller companies, there is almost an infinite variety of subjects on which the banks might be called upon to advise. Only when the bank's representative has made an initial survey will the problem areas be identified. The student of these matters will wish to know something of the areas covered by the advisory services and they include in particular the following:

Philosophy and objectives: overall business strategy, long-term and short-term planning, the setting of targets, the communication of objectives and performance measurement;

Budgeting: the importance of budgeting in relation to corporate objectives, budgeting assumptions and the quantifying of variable factors, the monitoring of progress and analysis of variations;

Costing: the choice of a costing system, the setting up of records, the application of standard costing, marginal costing or absorption costing techniques, contract costing and estimating and allocation of overheads;

Pricing policy: methods of fixing product prices, market data, elasticity of demand and price sensitivity generally;

Credit control: the terms of trade, the credit-worthiness of customers, the efficiency of debt collection, the bad debt experience and the suitability for factoring or invoice discounting;

Cash flow: the importance of cash flow forecasting, relationship to the budget, performance monitoring and reporting of variances;

Stock control: determination of stock levels, liaison with production units and sales force, stock recording methods, methods of perpetual stock valuation, stock insurance and valuation of work in progress;

Management control: management information and management accounting systems to facilitate day-to-day control of the business;

Bookkeeping and financial accounting: the choice of system, electronic aids, audit procedures and preparation of accounts;

Use of resources: the management of assets and liabilities, better utilisation of assets, return on resources employed and methods of productivity measurement;

Financing: possible sources of finance, increase in capital, gearing or medium-term loan finance, sale and leaseback of property, factoring, leasing or bill discounting;

Import/export business: methods of financing, market information, choice of agents and distributors, export credit guarantees and international factoring.

No list is exhaustive, but these examples will serve to show the breadth of the business advice now available from the clearing banks. In many ways, these matters are a natural extension of the more modest role played by the traditional bank manager on the review of a customer's overdraft. But the bank manager was never expected to be an expert in business methods and indeed such expertise can only be concentrated at any one time in a comparative handful of specialists, as has now been done in the banks.

Why should the banks have taken on this extra responsibility? The answer does not lie in terms of an immediate profit because such services are costly to provide and in many cases are given without charge. The benefits to the banks may be summarised thus:

1 A successful customer is a more valuable customer and so the banks hope to reap the long-term benefit from the advice they give. At its lowest, the bank's lending risk will be reduced – at its highest, the banks will share in the growth prospects of an increasing number of successful customers.

2 The banker-customer relationship is strengthened because the customer receives from his bank, probably without charge, a service which is not readily available elsewhere.

3 The investigation in depth of a customer's business provides the bank with opportunities of offering a wide range of services, e.g. medium-term loans, leasing and factoring, insurance, pensions and family trusts.

4 The advisory services can be a means of securing new accounts.

5 The bank is seen to be offering a highly professional service in the whole field of business administration, which in itself encourages confidence in that banking group – it is seen as – a bank which understands business problems.

In total, the banks will now assist their customers or potential customers in virtually every aspect of financial and business life. In some cases, they run a 'marriage bureau' for companies seeking to merge. In other instances, they will advise on marketing techniques, factory layout or deployment of the labour force – all matters beyond the cognisance of the clearing banks until recent years. In many cases, they are using the language of techniques which were foreign to the banks themselves only a few years ago. Until comparatively recent times, no major bank had an adequate costing system; none of them was marketing-minded nor knew much about their markets; corporate strategy, management by objectives and performance measurement were as foreign to British banks a decade ago as they are to many of the businesses to whom they are introducing these matters today. That is not a matter for cynicism and certainly not a subject for reproach. If anything, it is yet another indication of the quite remarkable resilience and adaptability of our massive banking institutions.

There is one area of 'advice' which should more correctly be called 'information'. That is the provision of economic and business data on almost every developed country and every sector of business throughout the world. The economic information services of the banks are impressive and perhaps far too few customers have recourse to them. The importance of such data has taken on a special significance in relation to the European Economic Community. The clearing banks now have up-to-date information on file relating to all relevant aspects, legal and fiscal, of business in the Common Market countries. Anyone with an interest in overseas countries – whether as importers or exporters, members of trade missions, executives taking jobs abroad, lecturers, writers and schoolboy essayists – now has the opportunity of tapping, through their banks, the reservoirs of information on overseas countries. And it is all free.

## References


1 Evidence of The Stock Exchange to the (Wilson) Committee to Review the Functioning of Financial Institutions: Evidence on the Financing of Industry and Trade – Vol. 3. HMSO, 1978.

2 Inland Revenue. Statistics. HMSO, 1976.

3 Research Report No. 4 of the (Bolton) Committee of Inquiry on Small Firms. HMSO, 1971.

4 Report of the Committee of Inquiry on Small Firms [Chairman: J. E. Bolton], Cmnd. 4811. HMSO, 1971. para. 10.14.

5 Ibid, para. 12.98.

6 R. D. Back: 'The Branch Manager as an Adviser to Small Firms'. *Journal of The Institute of Bankers*, December 1977.

7 Committee of London Clearing Bankers: 'The London Clearing Banks' – Evidence to the (Wilson) Committee to Review the Functioning of Financial Institutions. Longman, 1978. para. 9.1.

8 Ibid, para. 9.20.

CHAPTER 14

# Leasing

In English law, the word 'leasing' is historically associated with land, i.e. freehold and leasehold property. Thus, a freeholder may grant a 'term of years' to a lessee and a lessee or leaseholder may grant a shorter term of years (or sub-lease) to his lessee. Until comparatively recent times, the terminology of leasing was not applied to movable property. One's goods and chattels might be hired, loaned, bailed, chartered or borrowed – but not leased. Even the Oxford English Dictionary does not contemplate the possibility of anything but land being leased, apart from the occasional exception such as the wartime expedient of 'lease-lend', which was in any case an Americanism.

Here, however, we are concerned with the modern use of the word in relation to the leasing of goods and equipment. In fact, it is not all that new. Whatever terminology may have been used, we are told that the leasing or lending of one's goods for the benefit of other people goes back at least 5,000 years. In the Sumerian cities of Southern Mesopotamia, where all land was deemed to be owned by the local deity, the ruler-priest would 'lease out' seed to the villagers for the next year's crop. Indeed, all down the ages there have been instances of the goods of one person being used by arrangement in the business of another. Perhaps the chartering of ships is as good an example as any. More particularly, we might mention the hiring of railway wagons in the last century – the origin of much of our hire purchase business in this country (see p. 234), but nevertheless more akin to leasing in its concept.

The business of leasing as it is in the United Kingdom today had its impetus in the United States in the post-war years. The opening up of subsidiaries of American companies in this country brought with it an awareness of leasing facilities and leasing transactions were entered into by the merchant banks and finance houses. This applied particularly in the late 1960s when the more traditional methods of finance were restricted by government policy. Although there were some difficult years to follow, particularly during the liquidity crisis of the early 1970s, the eventual development of leasing activities among the subsidiaries of the clearing banks brought a great upsurge in business and an awareness of the advantages of leasing contracts.

What is leasing? In its simplest form it is the use of an asset which belongs to somebody else. In more precise terms, it is a contractual arrangement under which one party, in return for an agreed rent, uses a capital asset owned by another party. Such capital assets are usually business plant and machinery or other forms of equipment and, as we shall see, embrace a great variety of items.

Leasing is based on the quite fundamental concept that one does not have to own an asset in order to enjoy the benefit of it. This has been accepted readily enough over the years in such matters as the renting of houses and more recently the hiring of television sets, but only recently has it been applied on a large scale to business activity. There are obvious examples of course of businesses which have benefited from their investment in fixed assets over the years. Some businesses have made substantial capital profits from the sale of assets, or have been able to improve the look of their balance sheets by the revaluation of assets. In countless instances, a strong asset base has enabled businesses to borrow for working capital and development purposes. But the reverse is also true. Some businesses would have traded more profitably if their capital had not been locked up in fixed assets and in many cases the proprietors have seen their capital assets, often of a specialist or purpose-designed nature, depreciate over the years. In the main, the profitability of a business lies in the use to which the resources are put. It is the use, not necessarily the ownership, which matters. Once a business decision, i.e. the investment appraisal, has been made on some new venture, the choice of purchasing or leasing is partly a matter of arithmetic, partly a question of the availability of capital and partly a question of whether or not there is a case for taking finance outside the balance sheet.

It follows that to run an airline one does not need to own the aircraft, to carry oil one does not need to own a tanker, to computerise a business one may lease the hardware, to equip an office one may lease the desks and chairs. The same applies, albeit for different reasons, to non-profit making bodies. To equip a school a local authority may lease the furniture; a hospital may lease its beds. There are psychological barriers to leasing. The successful business man likes to feel that he owns the plant and machinery around him and even in large companies there is a pride in the possession of assets. To quote from one survey: 'Perhaps we are old fashioned, but we prefer to own what we use.'[1] The same survey showed that the usual method of acquisition of assets by British industry was still by purchase; 83 per cent of companies had bought more than two-thirds of their assets outright. Perhaps more significant was the fact that, in the short space of time that leasing has been available in the United Kingdom, 45 per cent of companies had made use of financial leasing arrangements and the figure would be in excess of this if one included operating leases (which we shall come to in a moment) and various forms of hire purchase.

It must be doubtful whether leasing would have gained ground in this country so rapidly were it not for the special taxation provisions relating to the purchase of business assets. Certainly the capital allowances introduced by the 1971 Finance Act gave a considerable impetus to leasing in the United Kingdom. Exponents of leasing argue with some justification that the advantages of leasing do not depend on the special tax concessions. The same generous benefits are not available in most other European countries and yet leasing in those countries continues to flourish. On the other hand, any major reduction in the taxation benefits in this country would almost certainly be a set-back to the leasing companies.

Until 1971, the taxation allowances on the purchase of capital assets were roughly in line with the standard methods of annual depreciation. Under the 1971 Finance Act, however, 60 per cent of the cost of acquisition of a business asset was treated as a 'capital allowance', deductible for tax purposes in the year

*'... psychological barriers to leasing.'*

of acquisition or carried forward at the discretion of the tax payer, in whole or in part, against future profits. In the following year, the taxation relief was extended to 100 per cent of the acquisition costs of business assets. Different rules apply to motor cars. In many cases, however, companies will not have in the year of acquisition sufficient taxable profits to take advantage of the full capital allowances. They may not be sufficiently sure of future profits to take advantage of capital allowances carried forward, and in any case in times of inflation, the real value of those allowances must diminish. In the case of non-commercial corporations, such as local authorities and charities, the capital allowances are in any case meaningless because there are no taxable profits as such. Nevertheless, in all such cases there is benefit to be gained by the leasing of assets. The leasing company becomes the purchaser and becomes entitled to the capital allowances. Assuming that the leasing company has taxable profits to take advantage of the capital allowances, the benefit of the allowances will be passed on to the lessee company in the rental terms. Thus the lessee obtains indirectly the benefit of capital allowances which might not otherwise have been available in that year or indeed at all.

In certain parts of the country, development grants are available in addition to the full capital allowances and the leasing company may obtain the benefit of these provided that they are to be used by the lessee company in the designated area. The benefit of the grants will be passed on to the lessee in the rental terms.

It is the essence of a leasing contract that the equipment remains in the ownership of the lessor and, in this respect, leasing differs from hire purchase. Under a hire purchase contract, there is provision for the goods to be acquired by the hirer under the terms of the contract at the end of the contract period. If a leasing contract contained such a provision, it would result in a deferred purchase by the lessee, the capital allowances would be lost to the leasing company and would revert to the lessee.

We have already said that, for a leasing company to secure the capital allowances and pass these on by way of reduction in the rental costs to the lessee, the leasing company must have sufficient taxable profits. This has meant that for the most part only large groups with taxable profits from other activities can undertake major leasing transactions on competitive terms. As we shall see, this is one of the reasons why the major banks were well equipped to enter the leasing field.

Although the tax allowances are a legitimate feature of the leasing business, the Inland Revenue will not permit a capital allowance to be claimed if the contract is not a bona fide leasing transaction and has been entered into merely for the purpose of securing allowances which would not otherwise be obtained. This will apply also if the vendor and the purchaser are connected with each other.[2]

So much for the taxation aspects. Despite the importance of the tax allowances, leasing should not be regarded purely as a means of securing a taxation advantage. It is a legitimate and important method of financing the purchase of capital assets and should be regarded as an alternative, or indeed additional, source of finance. A company in a growth situation may well be short of working capital and the position could be aggravated by the additional purchase of fixed assets. The leasing of those assets will leave the working capital position unimpaired and if indeed it is a question of replacing existing assets, the working capital position can be improved by the sale of the old ones and the leasing of the new ones. In any case, the cash outflow on the purchase of assets can be an unwelcome burden and leasing provides a means of spreading the cost over a number of years. If the investment appraisal has been worked correctly, the additional income earned by the new assets should of course outweigh the leasing rental and, to that extent, a leasing contract may be regarded as self-liquidating.

Another important feature of leasing as a source of finance is that it covers the full cost of the equipment to be purchased. Most forms of finance would require a margin of security in favour of the lender, particularly in the case of depreciating assets. In the case of a leasing operation, however, ownership remains with the lessor whose 'security' is automatically increased as each rental payment is made but, as mentioned below, the depreciation of an asset may exceed the rental payments, particularly in the early stages of a contract.

Another way in which leasing contrasts with the more traditional forms of finance is that it 'stands on its own feet'. A leasing contract can be viewed as a single transaction outside the normal balance sheet situation of the company. Other forms of finance, for example equity financing, long-term debt, medium-term loans and bank overdrafts, are all absorbed in the overall financial situation of the company and are only as safe as the overall performance of the company permits. A leasing contract, however, is an independent transaction outside the asset and liability structure of the company. The leased assets belong to the lessor and are not, for example, available to the general creditors of the company, and the 'liability' is not of a capital nature but rather a revenue obligation to meet rentals as they fall due. Thus, a company in a strained capital situation but with a good cash flow and good growth prospects might, with advantage, turn to a leasing situation to finance further developments.

The fact that a leasing transaction does not appear in a company's balance sheet has been the subject of criticism. The Companies Act 1967 (s. 11(3), schedule 1) requires a company to show in its profit and loss account 'the amount, if material, charged to revenue in respect of sums payable in respect of the hire of plant and machinery'. Some accountants have maintained that obligations under leases should be 'capitalised' and shown in a company's balance sheet. Purists would argue, however, that the leased assets belong to the lessor and that the rental outgoings are no different from any other annual revenue item. A standard accounting practice will no doubt emerge in time, probably based on the recommendation of the accounting bodies' joint Accounting Standards Committee. Whatever the outcome in terms of accounting procedures, lenders of money to companies or other corporate bodies will no doubt, as a matter of prudence, take into account any leasing commitment when assessing the overall financial strength of the customer.

Apart from these characteristics of leasing as an additional source of finance, there is the advantage that it facilitates the budgeting process. Capital costs are spread evenly over the years, uncertainties are removed, peaks of expenditure smoothed out and all in all there is introduced into the budgeting process a degree of certainty and stability, which smaller companies in particular will welcome.

Lastly, leasing arrangements are exceedingly flexible and contracts are increasingly tailor-made to suit the needs of the client company. The leading leasing companies will usually structure the rental arrangements to suit the anticipated cash flow of the lessee and, wherever possible, the terms of the agreement will take into account the characteristics of the industry and the special situation of the lessee.

There are two broad categories of leasing situations. These are (a) finance leases and (b) operating leases. It is the first of these, finance leasing, with which we are principally concerned here. It is the essence of a finance lease that the lessor has no commercial interest in the transaction other than as a supplier of finance. The lessor pays for the equipment and thereafter remains throughout the owner of it. The rental paid by the lessee will cover the capital cost of the equipment, the lessor's expenses, interest on the money and the lessor's margin of profit. Under the leasing contract, there will normally be a primary period, possibly up to five years except for very big contracts when the period may be longer, within which the entire costs of the lessor will be recovered. There will then be provision for the contract to be continued into the secondary and sometimes indefinite period at a nominal rental level. Under such a contract, the lessor is not concerned with the servicing of the equipment nor, after the primary period, is he so interested in its value or in problems of obsolescence. He will be concerned, however, to ensure that the primary period does not exceed the useful life of the asset. The primary period is the period of risk. It is during that time that the lessor still has substantial funds outstanding under the contract and in the event of the failure of the lessee, the lessor must look to the sale value of the asset to recoup his losses.

A typical finance lease will include:

(a) a schedule of the equipment to be leased;

(b) an undertaking by the lessee to pay when due the rent provided for in the agreement;

(c) undertakings by the lessee to keep the equipment in good repair, to keep it insured to its full replacement value and to allow the lessor access for inspection of the equipment;

(d) provision for termination of the agreement in the event of default;

(e) provision that the equipment shall remain movable

property in the ownership of the lessor, notwithstanding that it may be affixed to any land or buildings; and

(f) an indemnity in favour of the lessor against any claim by a third party arising out of the condition or use of the equipment.

Although a lessor owns the leased equipment and to that extent may be looked upon as a secured lender, there are financial risks attaching to leasing. The day after new equipment has been purchased it has only a secondhand value. It has been installed in the lessee's business, perhaps adapted to his use, and if subjected to even the minimum wear and tear the saleable value may be considerably less than the purchase price. The leasing arrangement will normally have started on the payment of the first month's rent and it is quite likely that the depreciation of the asset will exceed the rental paid for the early part of the primary period. In the case of very large contracts, the shortfall could be considerable. The lessee is concerned, therefore, not so much with the value of the leased assets, but with the credit-worthiness of the lessee. He will not normally enter into a leasing contract with a company which is not well-established and which does not have a good record of credit-worthiness and a cash flow forecast which will support the rental payments.

The other main category, known as operating leasing, is undertaken mainly by manufacturers and suppliers, or agents on their behalf, as a means of developing the market for their equipment. It is a form of contract particularly suitable to specialised or highly technical equipment, such as computers. It is a convenience to the lessee to be relieved of such problems as maintenance and servicing, the risks of obsolescence and occasional needs for upgrading the equipment. On the replacement of the leased equipment, the lessor will where appropriate make some allowance for the value of the replaced items. As we have said, this is not strictly a financing operation, but in some cases the leasing houses will finance the manufacturer on a sale and leaseback basis, the manufacturer then sub-leasing the equipment to his customer on an operating lease basis.

As already mentioned, leasing was not developed in the United Kingdom until the early 1960s and only gained momentum with the period of credit restriction in 1967–69. A number of the leading finance houses set up leasing operations as an alternative to the more traditional forms of finance and it was, as it were, through the back door of the finance houses that the clearing banks entered the field. In 1958, the then National Provincial Bank had acquired the North Central Wagon and Finance Company, the oldest surviving hire purchase business in the country (see p. 234). In the same year, Westminster Bank had acquired a 20 per cent interest in the Mercantile Credit Company as had Martins Bank. In his Annual Statement for that year, Lord Aldenham, Chairman of Westminster Bank, referred to the purchase of the interest in Mercantile Credit 'after careful consideration of the desirability of obtaining a participation in the field of hire purchase finance, about which we are wholly satisfied'. In May 1958, Barclays acquired a 25 per cent interest in the largest finance house, United Dominion Trust. The interest of Midland Bank in Forward Trust and the joint venture of Lloyds Bank and the Royal Bank of Scotland in Lloyds & Scottish completed the involvement of the clearing banks in finance company business. Thus, the banks were into instalment finance (as we shall discuss in Chapter 16), but not necessarily into leasing as such. Barclays Bank developed its own leasing activities using the re-structured Barclays Export Finance Company for the purpose; Midland became involved in leasing through Forward Leasing, Midland Bank Finance Corporation and Samuel Montagu & Company, and in 1974 these activities were rationalised to create Midland Montagu Leasing; Lloyds Bank formed a new subsidiary in 1973, Lloyds Leasing, notwithstanding its interest in Lloyds & Scottish; National Westminster Group, having disposed of its interest in Mercantile Credit in 1972, concentrated its leasing activities in Lombard North Central, itself an amalgamation of North Central Finance and Lombard Banking. When Barclays Bank ultimately disposed of their interest in United Dominion Trust and acquired the entire share capital of Mercantile Credit, the combined leasing activities of Barclays Bank and Mercantile Credit were concentrated in Barclays Mercantile Industrial Finance, which is now the largest leasing house in the country. At present, nine of the ten largest leasing companies are owned, or controlled, by the principal banks.

The National and Commercial Banking Group are involved in leasing operations partly through their 39 per cent interest in Lloyds & Scottish via the Royal Bank of Scotland, partly through Royal Bank Leasing, partly through Williams & Glyn's Leasing Company and partly through St Margaret's Leasing.

In addition to their in-house leasing operations, a number of the banks have combined to form Airlease International to finance the re-equipping of the world's airlines and shipping lines, and have set up Omnium Leasing for the purpose of leasing a complete oil refinery. Lloyds Bank (in conjunction with British Aerospace) operate Lloyds Associated Air Leasing for the purchase of British aircraft for leasing to airline operators. Midland Bank also has a joint venture with I.C.L. for leasing computers.

The commercial banks took a little time to sort themselves out and a little untidiness remains, but that does not detract from the impressive progress which has been made. Once again it was an empirical approach and it is doubtful whether anyone sat down with a blueprint or strategic design for the ultimate pattern of a clearing bank's involvement in leasing.

Successive credit squeezes had led the banks and finance houses to look for alternative means to finance their customers' requirements, but it was the publication of the Bank of England discussion paper, 'Competition and Credit Control' in 1971 which led to greater competition among the banks both in terms of their freedom to compete for deposits and the removal of the rigid structure of interest rates. New and profitable outlets for bank finance and banking skills were needed. If leasing had not existed, it would perhaps have had to be invented.

For the clearing banks the benefits of leasing are:

(a) the means of deploying funds on better terms from the banks' point of view than normal overdraft rates;

(b) the convenience and comparative safety of fixed contracts with built-in security and a regular rental cash flow;

(c) the opportunity for using funds which, for one reason or another, from time to time may not be applied through the more conventional banking channels;

(d) the facility for offering customers an attractive alternative source of finance;

(e) the fact that leasing can be done for non-customers of a bank – it does not depend on a continuing banking relationship and contracts may be won on a competitive basis regardless of existing connections.

From the lessee's point of view, we have already listed some of the main advantages of leasing. Some of those benefits do not apply, however, in relation to large companies with access to substantial financial resources and possibly a steady flow of taxable profits enabling them to secure for themselves the capital allowances. The decision whether to lease or buy is a matter of calculation. The finance department will have to take into account such factors as:

(a) the opportunity cost of capital, i.e. what the purchase price of the equipment would earn if used elsewhere in the company's business; or

(b) the current cost of borrowing elsewhere, discounted over the period in question; and

(c) the current (discounted) value of future tax allowances; and

(d) the discounted cost of meeting the annual or quarterly rental payments over the period of the lease.

In a situation where the capital allowances would be available equally to either the lessor or the company client and where there is equal access to finance at equivalent rates, leasing will be more costly than buying. The difference is the premium which one pays the lessor by way of his profit and administrative costs. Whether that premium is acceptable would be a matter of business judgment depending on the overall position of the company, other foreseeable calls on its resources, budgeting convenience, balance sheet considerations and even differing views of movements in interest and tax rates.

The growth in the use of leasing by British industry for financing purposes has been remarkable. It is understood that in 1967 new leasing contracts were being written at the rate of approximately £20 million per annum. In 1978, the corresponding figure was about £1,500 million and the Equipment Leasing Association (which accounts for about 90 per cent of all leasing business in the UK) has estimated in recent times that leasing contracts accounted for 7 per cent of all new investment in plant and equipment in the United Kingdom.

In fact, leasing now accounts for nearly twenty-five per cent of all external financing for new industrial plant and equipment in the UK. At the end of 1978, it was calculated that the total value of leased assets in the UK was as high as £3,000 million. The clearing banks have been very much associated with this growth situation. Approximately three-quarters of all new leasing business is undertaken by the English and Scottish clearing banks.

The statutory capital allowances are of course a particular feature of leasing in this country and have contributed to a marked degree to growth in this form of financing. For their part, the banks were well placed to enter the leasing business because, in the ordinary way, they would have very little benefit from capital allowances. Even if the taxation situation were to change materially, leasing would remain an important and developing feature of the financial scene because of the particular advantages outlined here. Competition for leasing business will increase, probably from overseas banks, and it remains to be seen whether the clearing banks will maintain their very substantial share of a form of financing which has much to commend it and which is here to stay.

## References and notes

1 'The Lease-Buy Decision'. British Institute of Management, 1976.
2 Refer to the Finance Acts 1971–1973.

'*. . . the trading . . . operations of the Pilgrim Fathers.*'

CHAPTER 15

# Factoring

Not for the first time in these pages we come to a subject which has no precise definition in this country. So far as the term is known to English law it means an agent who is employed to sell goods on behalf of his principal. The title is enshrined in the Factors Act 1889 although it is almost lost in the wider definition of 'mercantile agent', defined in the Act as 'having in the customary course of his business as such agent, authority to sell goods or to consign goods for the purpose of sale or to buy goods or to raise money on the security of goods'. In that sense the word has almost disappeared from our law and from our language except to the extent that it lives on in some parts of the country to indicate a specialist wholesaler, e.g. a cheese factor.

Factoring, as we know it today, is something quite different. It is the management and in some cases the purchase of business debts which, in the words of Mr Justice Mocatta, is 'the business nowadays somewhat confusingly called factoring'.[1] The word in its modern form came to us from the United States, but almost certainly had its origin in the older concept of a factor as an agent. The word may owe something to the agency contracts *facio ut facias* of the later Roman Empire. Certainly the Romans employed agents to manage businesses, including the recovery of debts due under contracts, and to take charge of trading ships for the purpose of managing contracts entered into on the voyage. In parts of Europe in the thirteenth and fourteenth centuries, agents were employed on a commission basis to sell goods and in some cases undertook responsibility for the credit-worthiness of the buyer. This became the origin of the 'del credere' agent who would receive an extra commission from his principal for guaranteeing the solvency of the customer to whom the goods were sold on credit.

Attempts have been made to show that modern factoring is related, perhaps a little tenuously, to the trading and financing operations of the Pilgrim Fathers on their arrival in America. What seems more certain is that with the upsurge of the textile industry in the United States at the turn of the century, the trading aspect of factoring diminished and the term was applied to the method of financing some of the newer industries, particularly that of textiles. Henceforth the factor would be more concerned with assessing the credit-worthiness of the buyer and in some cases would buy outright the debts receiable. In one of the few authoritative works on factoring in this country, Melvyn Westlake describes admirably the growth of factoring in America. He writes:

'Thus, the factor came into being with three distinctive functions: he assessed the credit-worthiness of the customers from whom orders had been received and in most cases he cashed the sales – that is bought these receivables outright without recourse: he made cash advances to textile mills, selling agents and converters against finished merchandise as security; in some cases he performed a group of special services such as providing space for display and storage of merchandise, handling insurance, billings, packaging, shipping and making city deliveries.'[2]

So it was that modern factoring was developed, but it remained a feature of the textile industry alone right through the years up to the Great Depression in the 1930s, and it was not until after the Second World War that factoring in America was extended to other industries.

Going back over 100 years or more, a number of American factoring companies provided factoring services for sales to the United States by a number of British companies in the Yorkshire woollen trade. This was, it seems, the first acquaintance with modern factoring in this country and it was not until 1960 that locally based factoring operations were set up here. In that year, Tozer Kemsley & Millbourn set up a factoring operation under the name of Towergate Securities, later to become International Factors (see p. 223). In the same year, Meinhard &

Co., one of the factoring houses in New York, commenced a factoring operation in the UK which, although not greatly successful in itself, sparked off considerable interest among other institutions. The National Provincial Bank, as it then was, became the first of the English clearing banks to enter the factoring field in 1968 and it was followed in turn by all the other major banks.

What then is factoring? There are three main aspects of the factoring function. They are:

1 An administrative service, under which the factor manages the trade debts of the client company. The factor will keep the sales ledger, issue the invoices, collect payment when due and generally relieve the client of the administrative burden of this side of his business.

2 A system of credit protection, by which the factor assumes responsibility for the trade debts due to the client company and thereby relieves the client of the risk of loss. This is the central, but not essential, aspect of factoring. In effect, the factor purchases the debts from the client company so that in the client's books one debt due from the factor takes the place of all the various trade debts due from the company's customers.

3 A method of financing in that the factor who takes over the client's trade debts will, in certain circumstances, advance a proportion of their value immediately and the balance on maturity of the debts. The client's liquidity is thus improved to the extent that a cash balance has been substituted for book debts.

There are other related aspects of factoring which are less important in the present context. They are:

(a) Invoice discounting: this is the purchase of a debt or a number of debts from a client, usually in order to improve the client's cash flow, and under the title of 'receivables financing' it is a service which has existed in the United States alongside factoring for a long time. Strictly speaking, it is not a factoring operation in the accepted sense because (i) the factor does not control the client company's sales ledger and (ii) invoice discounting is usually a 'one off' operation and does not involve the purchase by the factor of the entire sales turnover of the client. It has certain attributes of factoring in that the client is put in funds and there is a degree of credit insurance. (At least one major factoring company undertakes invoice discounting on a 'total turnover' basis on the assumption that this gives the factor a stronger legal position than with individual transactions.)

(b) 'With recourse' factoring: although a full factoring service will usually include the full underwriting of the client's trade debts, the factor may in exceptional circumstances wish to retain recourse against the client in the event of the failure of a debtor to meet his obligations. Such 'with recourse' arrangements may apply to particular transactions, e.g. above an agreed level, or to certain customers where the credit risk is not acceptable to the factor.

(c) 'Non-notification' factoring: it is doubtful whether this is strictly factoring at all because the client's debtors are not informed of the arrangement and the client continues to collect the debts himself, having sold them to the factor. It is similar to invoice discounting with the difference that it would normally apply to the entire sales turnover. Although it may have its usefulness in certain cases, it is not a form of factoring adopted by the clearing banks in this country. If a client company particularly wishes to conceal the factor's presence, an arrangement can be made for a company to be set up, owned by the factor, with a name similar to that of the client company. This is not 'non-notification' factoring, but a normal full factoring service with a company interposed for cosmetic reasons.

Let us return, therefore, to the three basic functions of factoring which for ease of reference we will call debt administration, credit insurance and factor financing.

## Debt administration

This is something more than the typical customer-billing service which a company might arrange through a computer bureau. Under a factoring contract the sales ledger of the client company will be managed by the factor. Thus the client will be saved the administrative costs of bookkeeping, invoicing, credit control and debt collection. The factoring company can usually handle these matters more economically because it will be organised on a large scale, it will be able to make more efficient use of computers, it will be trained in credit control and the size of the operation, the extent of the factor's risk and all other relevant aspects. A typical charge might be somewhere between ¾ per cent and 2 per cent of the annual turnover in the sales ledger. If the turnover is small, the charges may be disproportionately high, but, in general, factoring services are not suitable for companies with less than, say, £250,000 annual turnover although there would be exceptions below that figure. At that level of turnover, the client company might incur a fee of, say, £3,750 but would save the cost of the book-keeping clerk (including social security contributions and pension) and the not inconsiderable cost of stationery, postage and telephone charges. More particularly, management time would be saved, the company would be seen to have an efficient invoicing service and there could be substantial savings from the more speedy collection of debts. All in all, the small to medium sized company is able, at a very modest cost, to import a degree of professionalism in the management of its debts far beyond what it might otherwise achieve from its own resources.

## Credit protection

Just as the large factoring companies have the resources to manage sales ledgers in an efficient, large-scale operation, so they have the facilities for credit intelligence to enable them to assess credit risks and advise their clients accordingly. Indeed, debt protection is now an essential feature of factoring because, as we have said, it involves the purchase by the factor of the client's entire turnover of trade debts. In the comparatively rare instances of 'with recourse' factoring, the risk of bad debts remains with the client, but in a more typical 'without recourse' relationship the factor assumes the credit risk and therefore the entire responsibility for credit control. The extent of credit allowed by the client to individual customers will be approved by the factor and the monitoring of that customer's account will become part of the factor's day-to-day operations. The pursuit of outstanding debts may require careful handling, particularly if the customer is an important supplier of the factor's client. The factor is unlikely to take any precipitate action without consultation with the client and it may be in some cases that the client will assume the risk rather than see his customer sued. In the last resort, however, the decision to take legal action will be that of the factor to whom ownership of the debt has passed. The assessment of credit risk is something at which the factoring company will normally be much more expert than the client. The staff of the factoring house is trained in the assessment of credit-worthiness and will have access to very extensive information on the financial standing and credit rating of individual customers and corporations. The assumption of the credit risk is, of course, of considerable value to the client. No figures are available for the total bad debt experience for trading concerns in the United Kingdom, but the volume of trade debt is believed to be in excess of £20,000 million so that even a modest bad debt experience can amount to a very sustantial sum lost to British trading concerns in the course of a year. It would be wrong to think, however, that the factoring process merely transfers a bad debt experience from the client to the factor. When taking on a new client, the factor will examine the sales ledger closely and will not take on the responsibility for any debts which look 'doubtful'. A factoring house is not a debt collection agency and it cannot turn bad debts into good ones. What the factor does offer is credit control conducted in a very professional way from the outset of the client-factor relationship.

**Factor financing**

The third major aspect of the factoring role, although not an essential one, is the advancement of funds to the client against the debts which the factor has purchased. In this way the client turns a future debt into immediate cash. In earlier days the discounting of one's debts was looked upon as the last resort of a bankrupt trader – rather like taking one's watch to the pawnbroker. It was this attitude perhaps which gave a bad name to factoring, or more correctly invoice discounting, because in many instances it was not a factoring operation. However, in more enlightened times it is recognised that book debts are as important an asset as any other and in some instances, such as companies with a very large turnover but few tangible assets, the book debts will form the principal asset. We have said that the essence of factoring is the purchase by the factor of the entire turnover of the trading operation. If payment is made by the factor to the client as and when the debts mature, there is no element of financing. The factor is providing a sales accounting and credit insurance facility, as explained above. In most cases, however, the factor will be willing to advance a proportion, say 80 per cent, of the outstanding debts ahead of the maturity dates. In such instances, the factoring operation becomes an additional source of finance for the client. The factor will charge interest on the funds advanced, probably at a rate of between 2 per cent and 4 per cent over bank base rate. The suitability of this form of finance will depend, as with any financing operation, on the nature of the business and the purpose for which the money is used. For obvious reasons it would be quite unsuitable to finance long-term capital needs from the factoring of trade debts. On the other hand, if an advance from a factor will permit substantial discounts to be obtained from trade creditors, this could be a profitable operation. In other cases, factor finance (because it increases the availability of working capital) might enable a company to make use of spare capacity or otherwise expand turnover. The level of trade credit in the United Kingdom is considerably higher than the level of bank lending, but in recent years the gap has been considerably reduced. On average, trading companies in this country allow credit to their customers equivalent to approximately one-fifth of their annual turnover, or well over two months' credit. A survey conducted by the magazine *Business* a few years ago showed that although approximately three-quarters of all customers were asked to settle their debts within thirty days, less than 10 per cent actually did so and 25 per cent took two months or more. Rather as one would expect, the propensity to take extended credit increases in times of credit squeezes and other restrictions on bank lending. Certain industries traditionally allow, by force of circumstance, more trade credit than others. This is particularly true of the engineering industry, where in times of credit restriction, trade debts have been known to rise to levels of between 75 per cent and 100 per cent of the annual turnover. Three months' credit is not unusual among engineering concerns and it is not surprising therefore that such companies have turned increasingly to the factoring houses in recent years. It is obvious that a company which receives immediate payment (assuming for the moment 100 per cent finance) from a factor instead of waiting three months for customers to pay, is increasing its capital resources by a sum equal to 25 per cent of the annual turnover. Nor is this a once-for-all injection of capital because the product cycle is speeded up so long as the factoring operation continues. If in a typical case the cycle is six months from manufacture to date of payment, including three months' credit, the immediate factoring of the debt can reduce the product cycle by one-half or, in effect, double the circulation of capital in the business.

Not all companies are suitable candidates for factoring and, in general, the following would be excluded:

Small companies, e.g. those with an annual turnover of less than £250,000 and certainly those with less than £100,000 – in such cases the companies would normally find it more economical to run their own sales ledger.

Companies with large numbers of debtors for small amounts.

Companies with a speculative business.

Companies with unusual or highly specialist businesses where the factors would not have the experience to assess the credit risks.

Companies with an unusually high bad debt experience (although, if this arises from bad credit control, a factoring service may solve the problem).

Construction companies and others employing sub-contractors and requiring stage payments.

Companies selling a large range of small products to the general public.

Most factors would also exclude those companies where the management is patently inefficient and the supervision of the sales ledger could become a burden or even an embarrassment.

Some companies by nature lend themselves to the possibility of factoring. To quote one leading factor: 'Factoring is most suitable for goods which can be made, sold and forgotten.' In general terms, they are well-conducted, medium-sized companies selling not too diverse a range of products to a good spread of customers in a traditionally reliable sector. As we have seen, factoring began with the textile industry, but has long since been extended to a wide range of manufacturing and service operations. Although we have spoken here of client 'companies', a corporation as such is not a pre-requisite of factoring: some professional partnerships lend themselves to factoring, although such cases are more common on the continent of Europe than in this country.

As the business of factoring has grown in recent years, there has been a degree of specialisation among and within the factoring houses themselves. Factoring houses and officials within those houses continue to build up a wealth of experience of particular industries. They are also able to build up from their own experience a considerable fund of data which, in addition to the normal commercial sources of information, enables them to advise clients on specific credit risks.

## Some legal aspects

Just as our modern mercantile law has evolved from the Law Merchant, itself a reflection of the practice of merchants in the Middle Ages, so the business of factoring is a good example of a modern commercial practice which exists in advance of any legal framework. It is true of course that there is an established body of law on the subject of assignment of debt. A debt is, as the lawyers would say, a 'chose in action', that is to say an intangible asset the right to which may be enforced by means of action in the Courts. There are various classes of choses in action and a debt is among those which arise from a contractual relationship. Like other choses in action, contractual debt was not assignable historically in English law until the Judicature Act of 1873, the relevant part of which was re-enacted in Section 136 of the Law of Property Act 1925. Under the Act the assignment of a debt from one person to another will be effective provided that the assignment is in writing and that notice of the assignment has been given to the debtor. An assignment which thus satisfies the Law of Property Act would be a statutory assignment. Where, however, an assignment has been made in a form which does not satisfy the Act, it may still take effect 'in equity' as between the assignor and the assignee and would be classed as an equitable assignment. If, for example, the creditor fails to give notice to the debtor, the assignment cannot be a statutory one and the debtor would not be bound by the assignment. If, therefore, he subsequently paid the amount of the debt to the original creditor, he could not be required to pay it again. Whether an assignment is statutory or equitable, the assignor can only transfer rights that he possesses himself – *nemo dat quod non habet*. If, for example, the debt in question is subject to some counter-claim by the debtor, the creditor can transfer or assign the debt only subject to that claim.

Applying these rules to factoring, it would be simple enough in the ordinary way to ensure that the trade debts of a company are assigned in writing and that notice is given to the debtors concerned. However, under the Stamp Act of 1891, as amended by subsequent Finance Acts, such an assignment would require to be stamped at the current rate of stamp duty of up to 2 per cent on the value of the underlying debts. The cost of paying such a stamp duty would make factoring quite impossible in this country. In some cases the difficulty has been overcome by accepting an unstamped assignment (which would not be acceptable in evidence in civil proceedings), coupled with a power of attorney to the factor confirming the authority to execute a legal assignment in the factor's own favour (a document which would then be stamped if legal proceedings against the debtor became necessary). An alternative approach is that exemption from stamp duty may be claimed if the transaction is for a sum of money under £15,000 and does not form part of a series of transactions amounting in total to £15,000 or more. This exemption is secured by regarding each batch of invoices as a separate assignment.

In English law, factoring contracts and invoice discounting arrangements are essentially assignments of debt. The only other sphere of law – apart from bankruptcy and liquidation regulations – that relates to trade debts held for the benefit of a third party is a floating charge created under a debenture. Whereas a debenture is registrable, there is no provision in English law for the registration of debt assignments and it is, therefore, impossible to tell from any public source whether or not a company has entered into a factoring agreement. A factoring house which acquired the trade debts of a company after the company had given a duly registered debenture to its banker may be postponed to the bank in a receivership situation. The point is not entirely free from doubt because, in the ordinary way, a company which has given a floating charge may continue to dispose of its assets in the ordinary course of business and there is some legal authority for the view that the factoring of book debts is in the course of business. If, on the other hand, a floating charge (given, for example, in a debenture to a bank) prohibits the sale or factoring of debts subject to the charge, it is essential that the book debts be released from the floating charge by agreement with the debenture-holder if the factor is to have priority of title to the book debts. From the bank's point of view, the obligation of the factor to the client company under the factoring agreement will be caught under the debenture, representing a single and implicitly safer debt than would have been the case if the debts had not been factored.

In 1971, the Crowther Committee on Consumer Credit[3] recommended that all security interests should be the subject of public registration. This would enable the factoring houses to ascertain whether trade debts were in any way encumbered in priority to their own position as factors, and also to register their interest as assignees of the debts under the factoring agreement. However, the recommendation has not passed into law and in the meantime factors must continue to rely on their own investigations before entering into credit insurance arrangements.

## Involvement of the banks

In the United States, there had been a link between factoring and banking since the First World War, but there was some doubt about the legitimacy of this occupation for commercial banks in America until, in 1963, the US Comptroller of the Currency ruled that the national banks had authority to engage in factoring business.[4] There was also apparently some doubt as to whether there was a demand for factoring services to be provided by the banks. In his book, *Law and Practice of Credit Factoring*[5] (probably the most authoritative book on the technical aspects of factoring published in the UK), Peter Biscoe refers to the survey conducted by *Fortune Magazine* in 1965 on the question whether or not factoring, as a bank activity, was saleable. The result, in the terms of the four possible answers, was:

| **Answer** | **%** |
|---|---|
| Very saleable | 17·8 |
| Saleable | 62·8 |
| Not saleable | 10·4 |
| No answer | 9·0 |

Encouraged by this survey and the Comptroller of the Currency's ruling on the legal aspect, twelve American banks entered into factoring activities in the five years from 1965 to 1970. Since then many more banks have entered the field, to such an extent that most factors throughout America and Europe are now owned by or associated with banks.

Notwithstanding the developments in America, it came as something of a surprise to the financial world when, in 1968, the then National Provincial Bank acquired through its subsidiary, North Central Finance, 75 per cent of the capital of Portland Group Factors, a company which had been founded five years earlier and which had helped to pioneer factoring services in the United Kingdom. The venture was not entirely successful, partly because of the troubles afflicting a number of the earlier factoring operations in this country, and on the merger of National Provincial Bank with Westminster Bank there was a major reorganisation. In 1970, an entirely new company was formed, Credit Factoring, and by 1971 this was fully operational having taken over the residual business of Portland Group Factors. The new company concentrated on sales accounting and credit protection rather than the advancing of funds, and it was perhaps this aspect that enabled good progress to be made in attracting larger companies which were not particularly seeking additional sources of finance. Through an associated company, Credit Factoring International, the National Westminster Bank group was the first of the British banks to move into international factoring and at the end of 1974 the bank's chairman was able to report that Credit Factoring International 'has established itself as a leading company in its field'. Today it has factoring operations covering sixteen countries and services export sales on a worldwide basis. It is the largest factoring operation among the clearing banks and now has over 200 client companies.

The first step by National Provincial Bank was a momentous one. In many ways it was seen as a complete departure from traditional banking, but in other respects it displayed a rationale which has not always been apparent in relation to other services. Three essential aspects of factoring, viz. detailed administration on a large scale, credit assessment and provision of funds, were all familiar to traditional bankers, and in the event factoring has proved to be a natural and complementary development of the older services.

International Factors, originally Towergate Securities, is a factoring company formed in 1960 by Tozer Kemsley & Millbourn, M. Samuel & Co. (now part of Hill Samuel) and the First National Bank of Boston. It was to become the largest of the factoring operations before the clearing banks entered the scene, and in 1968 Lloyds Bank and the Royal Bank of Scotland (through their joint subsidiary, Lloyds and Scottish Finance) acquired a 70 per cent interest (later to become a 75 per cent interest) in International Factors. Of the original shareholders, only the First National Bank of Boston remains, with 25 per cent of the equity. By 1977, International Factors had 140 clients and an annual volume of approximately £125 million. As the name implies, the company has developed internationally and is now part of a worldwide network.

The Midland Bank group moved into factoring in 1970 jointly with the First National City Bank of New York, but the new offspring, Midland-Citibank Factors, grew but slowly and in 1973 Midland Bank bought out their American partners and transferred the factoring business to Shield Factors, in which Midland Bank acquired a 50 per cent interest jointly with one of the original shareholders of Shield, the Anglo-African Shipping Company. The following year, Midland Bank acquired the Anglo-African shareholding and thus Shield became 100 per cent owned by the Midland Bank, the name having been changed to Griffin Factors, and at the present day it is third in the field among the clearing bank factoring companies in terms of total annual volume.

Alone among the clearing banks, Barclays Bank chose to develop their factoring business from within their own organisation rather than by purchase of an existing operation or by way of a joint venture with a partner. A factoring division was set up in the bank's subsidiary company, Barclays Export & Finance Company, and it embarked on a steady programme of expansion under the trade name, Barclays Factoring. Barclays Bank already had an interest, however, in Mercantile Credit as a result of their acquisition of Martins Bank, and Mercantile Credit had been engaged in a factoring operation since the late 1960s. After the acquisition by Barclays Bank in 1976 of the balance of the equity of Mercantile Credit, it was appropriate to rationalise the factoring operations and they were brought together in a new subsidiary, Barclays Factoring, on 1 October 1978. At the time of writing, Barclays Factoring accounts for something in the region of 10 per cent of the total annual factoring volume in this country.

So each of the major English banks now has an interest, direct or indirect, in a substantial factoring activity. Of the eight major factoring companies in the United Kingdom, six are connected with a clearing bank, and it is estimated that these six subsidiaries account for approximately 80 per cent of the total factoring business, measured by turnover, in this country.

## The banker-factor relationship

In former days, a banker would not always view with equanimity the news that his customer was factoring his debts. There would be a vague assumption that the customer was *in extremis* and that in some undefined way the customer's last remaining assets were disappearing through the window. In fact, a customer in such dire circumstances would be extremely unlikely to find a factor to take him on. Factoring is not in any sense a rescue operation – it is not finance of last resort.

In similar vein, the banker of bygone years did not like to think that his customer was obtaining finance from any other source but himself. Here again, times have changed. Many well-run companies obtain finance for a variety of purposes from a variety of sources. The banker whose customer has negotiated a factoring contract will at least know that:

1 the factoring house has a good opinion of his customer – it used to be said that only one out of every thirty or so companies who applied to factors were accepted, but the proportion tends to be higher now that factoring is better understood;

2 his customer's sales ledger will be well managed and the customer will have the additional help of the factor in matters of credit information;

3 bad debts, if any, will be eliminated and debts paid on time;

4 the covenant of the factor is being substituted for the multiple covenants of the trade debtors;

5 if required, an extra source of finance is available to aid the growth of the business, to take advantage of discounts from

suppliers or, conceivably, to reduce the dependence on the bank.

The customer-banker relationship and the customer-factor relationship are not mutually exclusive – indeed they are complementary. This is particularly recognised now that the clearing banks are providing factoring services alongside their traditional banking function. From the standpoint of the banking group as a whole, the debt administration and credit control services are fee-earning operations which add strength to their customers' businesses and extend the influence of the bank. To the extent that finance is provided, the interest rate level is higher than that obtainable normally on bank overdrafts and the security is better than that which would otherwise be available to the bank on book debts.

If the roles of banker and factor are complementary, they are nevertheless different in concept. The banker lends money on the covenant and security of his customer. The factor, in so far as money may be advanced, is relying on the covenant and credit-worthiness of the client's debtors. Given that difference, the functions are compatible and the skills are similar. Factoring is a sensible and logical extension of the banker's role. It is here to stay and will no doubt be the subject of considerable growth in the coming years.

**The risks**

The early history of factoring in this country was a chequered one. Not only was the factoring of one's debts regarded, as we have said, as the last port of call before bankruptcy but the factoring companies themselves were not sufficiently selective. In some cases, the factored clients were quite unsuitable for a factoring service. On the clients' side there were instances of mismanagement or over-trading or failure to use the factor finance wisely or, in some cases, downright dishonesty. On the factors' side, there was a lack of experience of factoring in this country, inadequate administration on the sales ledger side, insufficient credit information and a general inexperience in matters of credit appraisal. In those early years, not all that long ago, considerable losses were written off by some of the factoring companies. In his book,[6] Melvyn Westlake has catalogued a number of case studies, not all failures by any means, which serve to illustrate some of the early mistakes.

Today the factoring houses, partly because of the influence of the banks, operate from better financial bases, have better back-up for their administrative services and have developed highly efficient systems of credit assessment and control. Nevertheless, factoring remains and always will be a risk business. Despite the systems of control, there is still the risk that through carelessness or fraud, invoices will be issued in respect of non-existent goods or to non-existent customers. Even the possibility of conspiracy to defraud on the part of the client company and the customer cannot be ruled out and has in fact been the cause of previous failures. However, the increased selectivity of the factoring houses has considerably reduced this area of risk. There remains the risk in 'with recourse' factoring of the failure of the client company or, in the more usual instances of 'without recourse' factoring, the failure of a major customer. As we have said, the factor is lending against the credit-worthiness of the customer, not of the client company (in a 'without recourse' situation) and even well-introduced, well-reported-on customers, have been known to fail. Here again, however, the processes of selectivity, aimed in part at seeking clients with a wide spread of customers, reduce the risk of an undue dependence on any one customer.

Lastly, there is the overall risk of business recession. The domino effect of business failures multiplies the factoring risk, particularly where (as was the case) factoring is concentrated on only a limited number of industries.

The risks are comparable to but no greater than those of traditional bank lending and the return in relation to resources employed can be as good or potentially better.

## Profitability

All the bank-owned factoring houses have shown sizeable profits in recent years, but the figures are of limited value unless related to the resources employed in this comparatively new line of business and unless one takes into account the opportunity costs of employing those same resources elsewhere in the banking group. Factoring's finance taken in isolation as a money-lending operation enjoys the benefit of marginally higher rates than traditional overdrafts and thus provides the banks with an opportunity of improving their margins. On the other hand, there can be no factoring without the sales accounting side and this is work with high routine content. It is labour-intensive or computer-intensive and in either case the costs are considerable. There is a similarity here to company registration work and pension fund administration, and indeed to the money transmission services of the banks. It is exceedingly difficult for banks to provide an adminstrative or routine service for customers on a profit-making basis. This is largely because of the high standard set by banks in the running of their operations, whether for themselves or for their customers, and this in turn means high costs in terms of salaries, pensions, premises, systems of control and high quality generally in all the accoutrements of business. Factoring, therefore, suffers to a degree from carrying the burden of a large routine operation. So it must be doubtful whether the sales administration side would stand as a profitable operation by itself despite the very real advantages to the client company. It depends very much on the level of turnover.

In all its aspects, factoring may, however, be viewed as a profitable enterprise and, so far as figures are available, it would seem that the return on resources employed is as satisfactory in this side of the business as in the more traditional forms of banking. In any case, factoring must be seen as part of the wider banking function – particularly, as we shall consider now, in relation to the factoring of overseas business.

## International factoring

'International factoring' is a loose expression denoting two or three developments of factoring business in overseas markets. It refers primarily to the factoring of exports from, say, the United Kingdom, the better term for which is probably 'export factoring'. It is also used to refer to the opening of offices or affiliates in other countries to undertake the factoring of both domestic and export business from those countries. Lastly, the term is used to describe the international groupings of the factors to undertake import-export factoring among trading nations generally, and this is more correctly referred to as 'multinational factoring'.

The factoring of export sales is fundamentally the same as for domestic business. The exporter may, however, have more need for factoring than in relation to his home trade. The problem is not necessarily one of finance, but rather of knowledge and expertise. The exporter may have no adequate means of assessing the credit-worthiness of his customer, and the language and documentation may be completely unfamiliar to him. There may be import duties and other local requirements, and the terms of trade may be much longer than those to which he is accustomed in this country. The factor who can take care of those problems as well as provide, as the larger houses do, information on local markets and introductions to agents and distributors, is giving the client a service which he would be hard put to match from his own resources. Thus it is that even the largest companies, who would not have recourse to factoring for their domestic business, have arranged to factor their exports.

For the factoring house, the work of export factoring opens up a whole new dimension, calling as it does for knowledge of overseas customs and the credit appraisal of the overseas buyers. The bank-controlled houses have perhaps a special advantage in this respect, drawing as they do on the international connections of the major banks. It was a natural extension of export factoring that the principal UK factors should set up offices in countries abroad.

Not surprisingly, the United States led the way in truly multi-national factoring. They were accustomed to the long distances and differing state laws of their own country and, in any case, were ahead of the rest of the world in having developed a modern factoring structure. Traditionally, the banks in the United States had not been involved in factoring apart from one or two minor instances before the Second World War. The First National Bank of Boston led the way in 1946, but it was not until the authorities finally approved factoring as a legitimate banking function in 1963 that the commercial banks in general moved into the field. Their involvement gave a great impetus to factoring in the United States in the following years, and at the present time over one-half of all factoring in the United States is undertaken by the bank-owned factoring houses.

The comparatively recent development of factoring in the United Kingdom was followed rapidly in most European countries, notably Sweden and West Germany. Factoring developed under the umbrella of existing financial institutions and was soon extended to a wide range of industries and professions.

International factoring has become centred on a handful of major groupings and it seems that this will continue to be the pattern. Three of the main groupings are the International Factors Group, dominated by the First National Bank of Boston but controlled as we have seen at the UK end by Lloyds Bank; the Walter E. Heller Overseas Corporation which is the largest factoring organisation in America; and Credit Factoring International, controlled by National Westminster group and having its world centre of operations in the United Kingdom. There is, additionally, a network of other leading factoring houses operating in association with each other under the title Factors Chain International. This 'association' of factors has approximately forty members throughout the world and has a permanent secretariat in Amsterdam. The aim is to achieve uniformity of standards and to assist members with legal and other technical information about the countries of operation. Factors Chain International enjoy a 'correspondent relationship' among their members, so that they are able to assist each other from their knowledge of the law, practice and language in each place, and the collection and guaranteeing of debts on behalf of members.

**The potential**

We have seen that not every company is suitable for factoring. Any sort of guess is probably meaningless, but it has been suggested that no more than 10 per cent of trading operations in this country would satisfy the stringent requirements of the factoring houses for the 'without recourse' factoring of their debts. Nevertheless, the market is very considerable and the arrival of the banks on the scene with their branch networks opened up possibilities that are reflected in the growth of factoring in this country in the last few years. (At the end of 1977, the total annual volume among factoring houses in the UK was nearly £800 million excluding invoice discounting; the clearing bank groups accounting for approximately 90 per cent of the market.)

If the potential for domestic factoring is considerable, that for multi-national factoring is absolutely vast. Only a small proportion of the total of world trade is so far factored. The large British and American banks with their worldwide networks have immense opportunities for facilitating world trade through their factoring operations. The biggest deterrents to world trade are ignorance of the markets, unfamiliarity with the procedures and the financial risk. The international factor can probably do more than anyone else to remove those impediments and oil the wheels for increased trade.

## References

1 Hamilton Finance Co. Ltd v Coverley, Westray, Walbaum & Tosetti Ltd, and Portland Finance Co. Ltd (1969) 1 Lloyds Rep. 53, at p. 58.
2 M. Westlake: *Factoring*. Pitman, 1975.
3 Report of the Committee on Consumer Credit [Chairman: Lord Crowther], Cmnd. 4596. HMSO, 1971.
4 US Comptrollers' Manual for National Banks, 1 June 1963. para. 1105.
5 P. M. Biscoe: *Law and Practice of Credit Factoring*. Butterworths, 1975.
6 M. Westlake: op. cit.

CHAPTER 16

# Hire Purchase

The system of hire purchase, according to the Report of the Crowther Committee on Consumer Credit, 'has been one of the chief contributory causes of the great rise in the material standard of living of the British people in the last generation'.[1] The same Report expressed the belief that 'the first principle of social policy should be to treat the users of consumer credit as adults who are fully capable of managing their own financial affairs and not to restrict their freedom of access to it in order to protect the relatively small minority who get into difficulties'.[2] Thus hire purchase, which had been viewed with mistrust and suspicion for over 100 years in this country, received the accolade of an official Committee of Inquiry and the majority of those who might default in their hire purchase commitments were categorised as 'inadequate people who never quite face up to reality, are incapable of managing their own affairs and never seem to be able to predict the consequences of what they are doing' whilst others 'have become overwhelmed by a burden of debt through illness, unemployment or other misfortune and some over-commit themselves through not budgeting'.[3]

Hire purchase is a particular aspect of instalment credit. This is the provision of finance to be repaid by instalments over a period in accordance with a contractual arrangement. Thus occasional credit granted by a local shopkeeper is not instalment credit as such, nor is the allowing of 'time to pay' in the case of a debt which is overdue. Using the language of the same Crowther Report, consumer credit like all credit may be classified as 'lender' or 'vendor' credit. The former is the lending of money, usually for a particular purpose, such as a bank overdraft or personal loan. The latter is an arrangement made with the vendor of goods or property whereby the purchase price is to remain outstanding over a period and repaid on an agreed basis. Hire purchase is the largest single category of instalment credit in this country and is a perfect example of vendor credit, although the distinction has become blurred in modern times when the finance for a hire purchase sale has in fact come from an outside source. (In fact, the distinction introduced in the Consumer Credit Act 1974 is between 'debtor-creditor' agreements and 'debtor-creditor-supplier' agreements.)

Whilst the lending of money or chattels goes back to the beginning of mankind and has never been the subject of any great moral strictures, the charging of interest, i.e. usury, finds a degree of condemnation in the codes of Judaism, early Christianity and Islam. Down the ages, however, various devices and fictions were adopted to avoid the usury laws and throughout Europe over the years various statutory constraints were imposed on the rate of interest which might be charged. Interest could not legally be charged in England until it was permitted by an Act of 1545, and then could not exceed 10 per cent. There were many variations over the next 400 years or so, culminating in the comparatively permissive Moneylenders Act 1927, by which a transaction was presumed to be 'harsh and unconscionable', if the interest rate exceeded 48 per cent per annum.

Primitive communities are preoccupied with the production rather than the purchase of goods and it is only in the more developed communities that consumer credit as such has any meaning. In the UK it appears to have been in the sixteenth century that the lending of money, and indeed the lending of goods, became common, usually on a personal basis, between the more well-to-do members of society, such as farmers, tailors, grocers, mercers and parsons, for the benefit of the less well-to-do. What we do not often appreciate nowadays is that during the seventeenth and eighteenth centuries goods were almost invariably sold on credit, a practice which led to endless entanglements and an ascendancy of trader over customer often manifested in short weight, excessive charging, the ultimate impoverishment of the consumer and his imprisonment for debt. We are told that:

*'A transaction was deemed to be harsh and unconscionable.'*

'It was no uncommon thing for a family to be in debt to an unscrupulous chandler who allowed increasingly short weight at increasingly extortionate prices, so that while they dare not desert his shop, they worked only to enrich him and drive themselves even more hopelessly into his power.'[4]

Indeed, in 1780, a London bookseller, James Lackington, was ridiculed for attempting to run his business on a cash sale basis.

The term hire purchase has its origin in the 'hire and purchase' of goods and it was introduced into England in the 1840s, principally for the sale of pianos and subsequently of sewing machines. It appears that the practice had its origin in the hiring of furniture in France and the United States on a temporary basis – perhaps to equip a town house during the 'season' – a practice which is more akin to our modern leasing contracts than hire purchase as such. The essence of 'hire and purchase' was that the hirer had the option to purchase the goods at the end of the hiring period. Because the hirer did not have title to the goods, he could not pass a good title even to a purchaser in good faith – a principle established in the leading case of Helby v Matthews,[5] which virtually set the pattern for hire purchase contracts right down to the present day.

In the early days of hire purchase, each transaction was financed by the supplier or manufacturer of the goods in question. If that had remained the situation there could never have been the tremendous growth in hire purchase to the level which exists today, because makers and suppliers of goods would not have had the resources to finance consumer demand on such a scale. It was the arrival on the scene of the third party financier which set the pattern for future hire purchase development in Britain, and the massive finance house industry of the present day has its origins in the entrepreneurial instincts of a small group of Victorian businessmen in the North of England. It was in 1861 that the North Central Wagon Company was formed in Rotherham. The objects of the company were 'the purchasing, hiring and manufacturing of railway wagons (sic) Railway Companies, Coal Proprietors and other persons'. Such was the insatiable demand for coal, both for domestic and industrial purposes, in the late nineteenth century that neither the railway companies nor the colliery companies could afford to provide the necessary wagons and a number of wagon companies were formed to manufacture or purchase wagons and hire them to the railway companies and collieries. In its concept, this arrangement was similar to our modern leasing contracts. The wagons bore the name of the wagon company and remained in their ownership, but this soon developed into a 'hire and purchase' arrangement and thus was the beginning of our modern industrial hire purchase business.

By 1900, North Central Wagon Company had 25,000 railway wagons on hire to its customers. Not surprisingly, it took its house symbol from coal, the 'black diamond'. As we have seen (see p. 206) the company was acquired in 1958 by National Provincial Bank and in 1971 merged with Lombard Banking as part of the National Westminster Bank group under the name Lombard North Central. It is believed to be the oldest hire purchase company in the world and in its crest under the L (or £ sign) for Lombard, still retains the black diamond of the past. With the nationalisation of the railways in 1948 all rolling stock on the railways became vested in the Transport Commission and thus ended a highly successful, and indeed romantic, chapter in British financial history.

It was in 1934 that the Southern Counties Finance Corporation (following its acquisition by North Central Wagon and Finance Company) 'noted with concern' a proposal to undertake the hire purchase of motor cars. It suggested that any such transactions should be limited to business cars. The comment was perhaps prophetic in relation to the vast business of financing the purchase of car fleets for business purposes in more recent years, but more particularly it was symbolic of the transfer of interest from the railway wagons to the motor car. It is believed that the first instance of a motor car being bought on hire purchase was in 1912, but it was not until the 1930s that car hire purchase developed rapidly.

There were two other factors contributing to the growth of finance house business in this country. The one was the arrival of American companies for the purpose of financing consumer credit and the other, the setting up by the larger manufacturing companies of their own finance companies. The Finance Houses Association was formed in 1945 and now consists of thirty-nine members who together account for 90 per cent of the hire purchase business undertaken by finance houses in the United Kingdom. The aims of the Association are to promote the interests of the members; to act as a channel of communication between members and government departments, local and other public authorities, trade associations and the press; to establish and maintain good relations with the public; and to promote good business practice among members of the Association and disseminate information of interest to the credit industry.

There is no legal definition of a finance house. Historically they have been associated with hire purchase, but nowadays the larger finance houses not only conduct hire purchase business in all its forms, but a wide range of other credit operations including, as we have seen, leasing and factoring. Some of the larger ones are statutory banks and most of them engage in deposit-taking activities to finance their lending business. A number of them grant personal loans as part of their consumer credit operations, even though this may be seen by some as being in competition with a parent bank.

It was estimated by the Crowther Committee that there were as many as 1,900 finance houses in the United Kingdom, but of these only 1,000 or so were thought to be in active operation. Apart from those finance houses which grew up independently as financial institutions, there are those which were established as subsidiaries of manufacturing companies and retail stores. At the end of 1977, the total hire purchase and instalment credit liability in Great Britain was approximately £3,054 million, of which approximately £2,026 million had been advanced by the finance houses direct, the remaining £1,000 million or so being outstanding to retail stores, mail order companies and co-operative societies. During the summer months of 1978, the level of hire purchase debt increased considerably to approximately £3,900 million by the end of August and, at the time of writing, is probably well in excess of £4,000 million.[6]

Hire purchase in the broad sense of the term covers a number of different instalment credit arrangements, of which there are three in common use:

1. Hire purchase in the strict sense of the term where goods are hired to the customer over a period and, as we have seen, no title passes until he is deemed to purchase the goods at the end of the hire period.

2 Credit sale agreements, which are strictly an arrangement by which the purchase price of goods is paid by instalments. It is 'vendor' credit rather than 'lender' credit in that there is not a loan as such, but an agreement for deferred payment over a period.

3 Conditional sale, which is an arrangement by which the vendor agrees to sell goods to the customer, the title to the goods to pass on payment of the last instalment of the price. Under this arrangement the finance house lends the price of the goods and the credit charge is interest on the loan. Until the change in the taxation laws introduced by the Finance Act 1969, the interest thus paid by the consumer was allowed for tax purposes. Although this relief was withdrawn, a large part of instalment credit business is still conducted in this way.

For most practical and legal purposes, these differences in consumer credit arrangements are no longer significant. Both credit sale agreements and conditional sale agreements are brought within the scope of the Hire Purchase Act 1965 where the purchase price does not exceed £5,000. Similarly, the distinction is no longer material for the purpose of the Consumer Credit Act 1974. A more important distinction to be drawn in hire purchase business is that between consumer hire purchase and what is usually called industrial hire purchase. In broad terms, the first is instalment credit for the private individual: the latter is instalment credit for businesses. In 1969, for example, some 65 per cent of all instalment credit provided by finance houses was for private consumers but nowadays, as we shall see, the comparative figures have been more or less reversed.

## Consumer hire purchase

When a finance house provides the finance for consumer business, it often does so through an umbrella agreement with the manufacturer or supplier of the goods. The purchaser acquiring goods on hire purchase may be under the impression at the outset that the agreement is with the supplier, but this is rarely so: normally it will be a triangular arrangement bringing in a finance house – which will be either a captive finance house set up by the manufacturer or supplier of the goods or an independent financial institution. The hire purchase agreement will be between the finance house and the purchaser. In some cases a supplier will deal with two or more finance companies, but this is an inconvenience to the supplier because it means that he must be familiar with two or more sets of forms and with the varying special requirements of different houses.

Although the hire purchase contract is between the finance house and the purchaser, great reliance must be placed by the finance house on the good sense and experience of the supplier and the quality of his business generally. Although the normal enquiries will be made by the finance house on the creditworthiness of the purchaser and the finance house will have the security of the goods, the strength of the finance house's loan portfolio will depend very much on the standing and integrity of the suppliers with whom they deal.

It is a feature of consumer hire purchase that the finance houses hardly, if ever, meet the consumers with whom they do business. It is not the personal, subjective lending of a clearing bank, but a detached, clinical and even mathematical assessment of facts and figures set out on a piece of paper. Because of this, the security aspect is important and the interest costs can be relatively high. Although the legal relationship with the customer continues during the currency of the hire purchase agreement, there is not usually a continuing customer relationship as such, nor would this always be possible. In practice, the finance house 'customer' is often the dealer.

Consumer hire purchase, beginning with pianos and sewing machines over a century ago, now extends to virtually all forms of consumer durable goods. The following table shows the breakdown of *new* hire purchase credit, by category of purchase, among the finance houses in 1977.[7]

| | **£m** |
|---|---|
| Private cars | 1,029 |
| Motor cycles | 71 |
| Caravans | 55 |
| Household goods | 116 |
| Other goods | 315 |
| | £1,586 |

To this figure we can add the total new credit extended by retailers (as distinct from the finance houses) of approximately £3,000 million, resulting in total new consumer credit during 1977 of nearly £4,600 million. It must be borne in mind, however, that a very high proportion of private cars, approximately 60 per cent, are purchased for business use and, to that extent, these 'consumer' figures include instalment credit which properly belongs to the industrial and commercial section.

**Industrial hire purchase**

Turning to industrial hire purchase, we have already noted the growth in this side of the business as a component of the finance houses instalment credit activity. It has outstripped the growth of consumer hire purchase to a point where the industrial or business side now accounts for approximately 56 per cent of all finance house business and in one or two of the larger institutions the proportion is very much greater.

To an industrial or commercial concern hire purchase is another source of possible finance. It is in many ways akin to leasing, with the important difference that under a hire purchase contract the customer company becomes in due time the owner of the goods and thus is able to claim the capital allowances for corporation tax purposes. For a company with sufficient taxable profits a hire purchase transaction may therefore be more attractive than a leasing one.

A company seeking to renew its car fleet or instal or replace any equipment of a reasonably movable nature might well find it an advantage to do so by hire purchase. The particular benefits may be summarised briefly as follow:

1 Capital allowances may be obtainable, as mentioned above.

2 The company's working capital will not be strained, nor its existing overdraft arrangements disturbed.

3 Budgeting will be facilitated by the fixed and regular nature of the instalments and, if desired, by a fixed rate of interest.

4 Individual assets can be seen to earn their keep.

5 Hire purchase contracts have the advantage of simplicity.

Industrial hire purchase is now commonly available for the purchase of industrial and agricultural equipment, plant and machinery, and business assets generally. As with consumer finance, the equipment in question is purchased by the finance house and hired to the customer to whom ownership of the equipment passes on payment of the last instalment.

Although it has been a feature of hire purchase finance that the rate of interest is fixed at the date of the contract and remains constant throughout its term, it has been the custom in the case of some of the larger industrial contracts to quote a variable rate of interest. Some company customers have shown a preference for this arrangement, particularly if they were entering into a hire purchase commitment at a time of comparatively high interest rates.

From the standpoint of the finance houses both consumer and industrial finance have been areas of considerable growth, but this has not been achieved without some problems. During the secondary bank crises of the early 1970s some of the finance companies went through a difficult time and in some cases recovery was a long, slow process. The changed climate of today brings its own difficulties, not least the difficulty of funding a major hire purchase operation in the face of intense competition for medium-term finance. Among the finance houses themselves competition for consumer and industrial business is keen and, on the whole, there is no particular loyalty among suppliers to one or other finance house. At first sight the rates earned by finance houses seem generous in relation to traditional rates for, say, bank credit. At the present time, a hire purchase contract might yield 18 to 20 per cent on a day-to-day basis (and correspondingly higher in times of high interest rates), but against this one must take into account (a) the comparatively high present-day costs of a labour-intensive business; (b) the commissions paid to dealers which amount on average to approximately 15 per cent of the finance houses charges and may on occasions be as high as 25 per cent; (c) the comparatively high costs of maintaining a marketing-orientated business; and (d) the bad debts experience which, although not high, is above the level for bank finance.

With improved conditions and the steady growth in business, the profits of the finance houses have increased considerably and, although individual figures are not always available, it would seem that profits overall show a very satisfactory return on resources employed. Those houses which are subsidiaries of the major banks claim to show a better return per unit of staff employed than their parent companies.

The major finance houses are outward-looking organisations which know that they must work hard to maintain their share of the market. The branches throughout the country are primarily marketing outlets, and in its branches or regional control office a large finance house may have 500 or more sales people. They are pensionable staff paid on a salary basis, and are separately recruited and highly trained for their work. As one senior official remarked: 'Our people are selling and it's hard work.'

## The market for hire purchase business

Let us turn now to the market for hire purchase business in the United Kingdom. Here we must differentiate again between personal consumer credit and industrial hire purchase, meaning in the latter case hire purchase lending for industrial and commercial purposes to companies or private firms.

The motives which prompt an individual to resort to consumer credit were categorised in the Crowther Report:

'First, it enables him to achieve great practical convenience in paying for the purchase of goods and services. Secondly, it enables him to bridge the gap between income and spending in the intervals between the receipt of income, be it a week, a month or longer. Thirdly, it enables him to purchase goods and services for current consumption over a period longer than the normal interval between income receipts. Fourthly, it enables him to purchase real and financial assets in excess of the amount permitted by his own savings.'

The first three of these needs are met by *account* credit in its various forms, e.g. bank overdrafts, personal loans, budget accounts and credit cards. The fourth need or motive – the acquisition of assets in excess of current savings (or because of a desire not to disturb current savings) – constitutes the main *raison d'être* of the consumer credit movement.

Any understanding of the consumer credit market involves a consideration of some deeply entrenched social attitudes. It is, for example, widely accepted that a householder will buy his home on mortgage (usually justified on the grounds that this is an appreciating asset, although it was not always so), but conventionally it would not be so widely accepted that he should furnish his home with capital assets also acquired on credit. The NOP Market Research survey, commissioned by the Crowther Committee, showed that up to 1969 only 49 per cent of the population had ever used hire purchase. The profile of the typical hire purchase customer was not very precisely defined. Not surprisingly, the twenty-five to forty-four age group had the highest proportion of credit, and among the various income groups the highest percentage of borrowers was among those who were above the subsistence level but whose incomes did not exceed £1,500. In fact, however, the percentage of credit customers above that level was not significantly lower. Only half of those making use of hire purchase had banking accounts.

After hire purchase (used by 49 per cent of the population, as mentioned above) there was a sharp drop in the proportion which had ever used other forms of consumer credit. About 37 per cent had, at some time, rented their television sets; 28 per cent had made use of mail order on credit; and 12 per cent had bought goods by means of check trading, mostly in the North of England. It is interesting that the same survey revealed bank borrowing as high on the list (second only to borrowing from a moneylender) of sources of credit thought to be undesirable by the public. It was regarded as socially embarrassing for it to be known that one had a bank overdraft, compared with, say, hire purchase credit.

Apart from such social attitudes, the survey showed a remarkable degree of ignorance on the subject of consumer finance generally. Although all the people interviewed had heard of hire purchase, television rental and house mortgages, about half of the sample had little or no knowledge on the subject of second mortgages, approximately a third had not heard of credit sales and a tenth did not know of the existence of bank overdrafts. It is perhaps not surprising that about 20 per cent of those questioned had little or no knowledge of the basic nature of the various credit contracts, and it is well known, of course, that a considerable number of credit customers are unaware of the true rate of interest being paid.

It was another conclusion of the Crowther Report that 'consumers display a considerable amount of inertia in their buying habits and, even if they are aware of differences in the cost of credit, prefer the convenience of dealing with familiar suppliers'. The Report goes on to say that 'many consumers, through a failure to shop around, are simply unaware of existing variations in the cost and availability of various forms of credit'.

The result of such attitudes, whether due to social inhibitions, ignorance or an unwillingness to 'shop around', is a very imperfect market. There was, and to a degree still is, a wide disparity in interest rates quoted for comparable forms of credit. For example, the Crowther Report, quoting the Consumers' Association, showed that in a specimen year, 1969, interest rates at electrical showrooms varied from 6·3 per cent to 17 per cent and in furniture shops from 3·3 per cent to 110·9 per cent! It is not surprising that the Committee concluded that 'competitive forces are weak'. The Finance Houses Association has done much to improve consumer education in matters of instalment credit and the Consumer Credit Act 1974, itself a result of the Crowther Report, now requires the licensing of credit brokers, i.e. those engaged at any time in advising members of the public on credit facilities. (In other words, all dealers who offer finance house facilities have to be licensed as credit brokers.)

We have said that the total hire purchase and instalment credit debt outstanding at the end of 1978 was probably in the region of £4,000 million, approximately two-thirds of which has been advanced by the finance houses.

In fact, however, the level of personal consumer credit has probably no more than kept up with inflation in recent years, notwithstanding the increased strength of the finance houses following the alignment of some of the larger ones with the major banks. Successive government controls and, more particularly, the years of pay restraint and general recession have kept in check what would otherwise almost certainly have been a period of boom in consumer credit.

In September 1968, approximately 23 per cent of the total instalment debt in Great Britain was attributable to business assets.[8] By the end of 1977, approximately 51 per cent of instalment credit extended by finance houses was for business purposes. In recent years, the larger finance houses have seen a considerable increase in their industrial hire purchase business, principally as a result of their deliberate cultivation of this field. Although it is a competitive market, the amounts involved are much greater than in the field of personal consumer credit and the rewards can be appreciably higher. Among the larger finance houses, figures in the region of 75 per cent of total business have been suggested as representing the industrial proportion of their business.

It remains only to summarise the involvement of the British clearing banks in the hire purchase field. Differing reasons have been advanced for the banks' entry into hire purchase and it is probably fair to say that at the outset it was not so much a desire to engage in hire purchase business as such, but rather to broaden the lending base during periods of credit control and, more particularly, to be able to lend through subsidiary or associated companies at rates of interest outside the clearing bank cartel. Reference has already been made to the initial investment by the major banks in hire purchase companies by way of minority shareholdings and it was very largely the subsequent mergers and the desire to tidy up some anomalous situations that led to the present-day position. Today, Barclays Bank own Mercantile Credit Company; Midland Bank own Forward Trust; National Westminster Bank own Lombard North Central; Lloyds Bank and the Royal Bank of Scotland are the principal shareholders in Lloyds and Scottish; and the Bank of Scotland owns North West Securities.

Thus, by varying routes the banks have augmented their traditional skills to include a new competence in the field of instalment credit. Whilst to many it must seem a natural extension of the clearing banks' role, it is nevertheless an area with which the banks have had little acquaintance until recent years. The market, the marketing approach, the lending skills and even the accounting systems differ from those of the traditional banks, but by their acquisition of finance houses the banks have been able to move into this new dimension in an effective and profitable way. Through their associated finance companies, the banks now reach out to a market which they might not otherwise have entered and are able, at one remove, to lend considerable sums of money, fully secured, at higher rates of interest than might have been possible through the traditional banking outlets. Indeed, as much as 60 per cent of the total business of the Finance Houses Association is accounted for by those members which are owned by banks.

As for the finance companies which are now part of the banking groups, they are rightly proud of their history and they have retained a considerable degree of autonomy and perhaps, more than any other single enterprise, have brought a whole new dimension of activity to the clearing banks in Great Britain.

## References

1 Report of the Committee on Consumer Credit [Chairman: Lord Crowther], Cmnd. 4596. HMSO, 1971. p. 69.
2 Ibid, p. 153.
3 Ibid, p. 145.
4 Dorothy Davis: *A History of Shopping*. Routledge, 1966.
5 Helby v Matthews (1895) A.C. 471; (1895–1899) All E. Rep. 821.
6 Source: Department of Industry.
7 R. J. Barnes: 'Instalment Credit Business of Finance Houses'. *Credit Quarterly Review*, December 1977.
8 Research Report No. 4 of the (Bolton) Committee of Inquiry on Small Firms. HMSO, 1971.

'. . . *an American shopping in Harrods.*'

CHAPTER 17

# Credit Cards

If an American shopping in Harrods presents a Visa credit card, perhaps for a substantial purchase, the store will telephone Barclaycard at Northampton who will in turn contact the Visa Centre in California by means of a permanent transatlantic link. A computer in San Mateo will, if necessary, check the customer's credit rating with the bank that issued the card, which could for example be in Chicago. It is the proud claim of the Visa Group that the entire process, whilst Harrods wait on the line for an answer, takes but seven seconds. It is a telling commentary, not only on the universality of the modern credit card system but on the advanced electronic network which supports it.

The development of the credit card is probably the most significant phenomenon of the modern banking scene. It embodies two essential aspects of a basic banking function – the transmission of payments and the granting of credit. It is such a departure, however, from traditional banking that it merits a place in any survey of the newer banking services.

Mr Frank Snushall, the present Head of Barclaycard, has pointed out that the first credit card of a kind was introduced by the Provident Clothing Group in this country in the 1880s.[1] It was the earliest 'check trading' scheme – customers were issued with vouchers which they could use at shops on the approved list and payment for the vouchers was made on a weekly instalment basis to the Provident Clothing representative who called at the customer's home. It was the forerunner of credit cards in two respects, in that payment was made by a voucher and the customer enjoyed the benefit of revolving credit.

It was in the United States, however, that the credit card as we know it today was developed. In the early days of the century some of the American department stores issued credit coins or tokens which enabled customers to pay for goods, and the oil companies introduced 'courtesy cards' to be honoured at their gasoline stations. To this day, the largest issuers of credit cards* are the retail stores in North America, but their cards differ from the bank cards in that their use is limited to purchases from the store issuing the card and associated stores. Mr John Biggins of the Flatbush National Bank, New York, is credited with introducing the bank credit card. Under his 'Charge-It' plan, the credit for retail purchases was provided by the bank. That was in 1946 and in the next few years cards were introduced by The Diner's Club, American Express and Carte Blanche. These were primarily for travel and entertainment purposes and became known as 'T and E' cards. They were a method of payment rather than a source of credit and did not provide a credit limit as such.

The first bank credit card as we know it today was issued by Franklin National Bank in 1952 and numerous bank cards were issued in the following years. The Bank of America issued Bank Americard in 1958 and eight years later, in 1966, the banks comprising the Western States Bankcard Association issued the Mastercharge Card. Bank Americard and Mastercharge became the focal points for the eventual groupings of all bank cards throughout the world, with the exception of Bankcard set up by the Australian banks which has remained independent but may well become associated with the major groups in time. Today, the Visa card is issued by approximately 9,000 banks throughout the world and a slightly larger number of banks issue the Interbank card. There are now about 115 million cardholders from these two groups.

In the United Kingdom, there are three categories of cards associated with the clearing banks. These are (a) travel and entertainment cards, (b) cheque cards and (c) credit cards. (Cash dispenser cards are in a different category, being no

---

* It has recently been estimated that out of 600 million credit cards in use in the United States, 85 per cent are issued by non-banking groups.

more than an extension of the traditional counter service.)

In the first category, as already mentioned, The Diner's Club card was the first to appear in America and was introduced to Great Britain in 1951, a year after its launch in America. In 1965, the then Westminster Bank took a minority shareholding in The Diner's Club in the UK, increasing this holding to 47·8 per cent of the equity in the following year. Thus, Westminster Bank, now National Westminster Bank, became the only British bank with a significant interest in a travel and entertainment card as such. It now has 49·7 per cent of the UK based operations of The Diner's Club.

American Express opened offices in England in 1963 and a few years later entered into an arrangement for the promotion of its cards through Lloyds Bank and Martins Bank, but this move was overtaken by and overshadowed by the subsequent development of card business among the clearing banks. It is interesting that ten years later American Express had 4·8 million cardholders around the world generating over $4,000 million of business per annum. The number of cardholders was doubling every two years or so, but nevertheless the 'T and E' cards were not destined to grow at the rate of bank credit cards as such in this country, and at the time of writing The Diner's Club has approximately 200,000 UK cardholders and American Express has approximately 350,000. A charge is normally made for travel and entertainment cards.

The second category of card is the cheque card. The purpose of a bank cheque card is, in effect, to guarantee payment of a cheque within prescribed limits, whether presented for cash at a branch of the paying bank or to a trader for goods or services. The first cheque card was introduced by National Provincial Bank in October 1965, guaranteeing payment of cheques up to £30. In March the following year Midland Bank introduced their cheque card, and in the following month Lloyds Bank, Martins Bank, Williams Deacon's Bank, National Bank, Yorkshire Bank, Glyn Mills & Co., Lewis's Bank, Bank of Scotland, Royal Bank of Scotland, National Commercial Bank of Scotland, Bank of Ireland and Hibernian Bank, representing in all 4,600 branches, issued their joint 'Bankers' Card', similarly guaranteeing payment of cheques up to £30. In 1969, it was estimated that 1 million cheque cards were in use in Great Britain. With the merger of Barclays Bank and Martins Bank that year, the Bankers' Card was withdrawn from the former Martins Bank customers (Barclays Bank having already issued their Barclaycard, although at that stage this was not a cheque card).

An inevitable corollary of the cheque card's arrival was the reluctance of traders to accept cheques without a supporting card. To many this seemed a backward step, particularly as in pre-merger days there had been only eleven clearing banks whose cheques were familiar pieces of paper in the UK, and whose 10 million or so customers operated their accounts very satisfactorily. It was suggested in *The Banker* that:

'The decline in the cheque's acceptability is in part connected with the growing number of people with bank accounts. Until fairly recently, banks served a rather privileged section of the community – the same section as, rightly or wrongly, shopkeepers deferentially expected to be honest. The extension of the market has been accompanied by an increase of dud cheques and a greater degree of suspicion on the part of shopkeepers.'[2]

For a few years after the re-alignment of the banks in the post-merger period, only Barclays Bank operated without a cheque card as such. This led to the strange but perhaps predictable result that some traders refused to accept Barclays Bank cheques. As a result, Barclays Bank arranged for Barclaycards to serve the dual role of credit card and cheque card, and thus nowadays cheque cards are available in support of cheques issued by all the British clearing banks. The limit of the 'guarantee' is £50, whether for cash withdrawals over a bank counter or for the purchase of goods and services. By the end of 1976, there were nearly 9,500,000 cheque cards in issue in the United Kingdom, including Barclaycards. Recently, Barclaycard have announced the intention to introduce a new cash advance service, which will enable cardholders to draw cash up to £100 a day at any one of the 61,500 branches of banks belonging to the Visa International scheme.

The third category of card, and our main subject of discussion in this chapter, is the credit card. The first bank credit card issued in Great Britain was Barclaycard, launched in 1966 in co-operation with Bank Americard. Commenting on the development, as Chairman of Barclays Bank that year, Sir John Thomson said of Barclaycard:

'We look upon this as a natural extension of ordinary banking facilities. For a long time we have had the cheque; more recently the credit transfer; and now we have the Barclaycard as a convenient and easy way for the everyday shopper to make his payments for all kinds of goods and services without the use of cash. We particularly want the use of the Card to be widespread throughout all sections of the community.'

By 1972, six years later, Barclaycard had over 1·7 million cardholders and 52,000 merchant outlets. That same year the other leading banks announced the introduction of the Access Card. The original sponsors were National Westminster Bank, Midland Bank and Lloyds Bank. Together the three banks promoted the Joint Credit Card Company, in which they share the equity. Before the launch, Williams and Glyn's Bank, Clydesdale Bank, Northern Bank, Ulster Bank and Royal Bank of Scotland joined in the scheme. Within the first year, Access had 3·3 million cardholders and 65,000 merchant outlets. The following year, 1973, the group negotiated an agreement with Eurocard which gave a link with a further 60,000 shops, hotels and restaurants throughout Europe. The truly international nature of the card was established with effect from March 1975 when Access became a member of the Interbank Card Association with, then, 32 million cardholders around the world.

At the present time, there are approximately 4 million Barclaycard holders (including those who use Barclaycard as a cheque card only) and approximately 3·6 million Access cardholders.

There are three quite distinct parties to a credit card operation and it may help if we consider these in turn. They are the cardholder, the merchant and the bank or other card-issuing organisation.

Any credit-worthy adult may be a credit cardholder. In Britain, he or she will tend to be a middle class person who probably, but not necessarily, has a banking account already. In fact, between 70 per cent and 80 per cent of Access and Barclaycard holders are believed to be in the A B and C1 socio-economic groups.[3] Over 80 per cent of the adult population do not possess a credit card and among people with incomes of £5,000 or over, approximately half of them possess a credit card. Approximately 70 per cent of all Access and Barclaycard holders are between twenty-five and fifty-five years of age and in each case, over half of the cardholders live in London or the south-east of England.[4]

When a person applies for a credit card, he will be asked to supply details of his financial circumstances and, subject to satisfactory references, he will be given a card with an appropriate credit limit. Some limits, for example in the case of student cardholders, are very small, but very substantial limits may be allowed for cardholders of considerable personal means. Many cardholders will have applied for a card not in order to obtain credit as such, as a means of postponing payment for goods, but in order to have the convenience of a card as a method of payment as an alternative to cash or cheques. In the early days of credit cards in this country one of the major banks reported that the majority of cardholders 'continue to settle their accounts monthly' and were not availing themselves of continuing credit. In more recent times, however, another major group has estimated that about 70 per cent of its cardholders use their cards as a means of obtaining instalment credit.

There is in any case an element of free credit granted to cardholders because (a) accounts are sent out monthly covering purchases of goods or services since the last monthly statement and (b) the cardholder is allowed twenty-five days from the date of his monthly statement in which to settle the outstanding amount. It follows that if a cardholder's statement is normally sent out on, say, the 15th of the month, any purchases he makes on the 16th of the month could carry the benefit of fifty-five days' free credit.

The advantages to a cardholder under the credit card system may be summarised thus:

1 A card is a convenient method of payment as an alternative to cash or cheques. It is simple to operate, convenient to carry and reasonably immune to financial loss compared with losing cash or a cheque book.

2 It is a convenient source of credit if desired, involving no formalities and no 'headmaster' type meeting with the bank manager. Owing to the revolving nature of the credit, the

customer can take advantage of it as and when he pleases within, of course, the overall limit.

3 Because all monthly purchases are covered by one payment, the activity on the customer's banking account is considerably reduced with possible savings in commission charges.

4 It is an aid to budgeting because the cardholder can pay a fixed amount each month according to his circumstances, and plan accordingly.

5 The monthly statements in narrative form are a great help to domestic and even business bookkeeping.

6 The acceptability of the leading cards in so many countries of the world is an aid to business and holiday travel.

7 Under the Consumer Credit Act 1974 (s. 75) the credit card companies may be held jointly and severally liable with the supplier in respect of defects in goods purchased on credit cards where the purchase price exceeds £30 and is not more than £10,000. This added protection is at least available to those who became cardholders after the relevant section of the Act came into force on 1 July 1977.

Notwithstanding these very real advantages of the credit card system and the fact that cards are widely held, it has been estimated that less than 2 per cent of retail sales in this country are financed by the use of credit cards. The typical credit cardholder uses his card on average about fourteen times a year and according to some calculations by the *Daily Telegraph* (14 November 1977), the average purchase is between £11 and £14. There is certainly great scope here for the credit card issuing houses to encourage the greater use of the cards already in issue.

It is no doubt inevitable that a large number of cards get lost and some get stolen. If the finder or thief uses the card fraudulently, the cardholder may be held responsible for the first £25 of loss up to the time that he reports the circumstances to the card company. The machinery within the card companies for dealing with the fraudulent use of cards is very impressive and the financial loss from this source is kept to very modest proportions.

The second 'party' to the credit card transaction is the merchant. There are more than 100,000 merchant outlets in the United Kingdom who accept credit cards in payment for their goods or services. From the merchants' point of view, there are a number of advantages in operating a credit card system:

1 By accepting a credit card, the merchant has a guarantee of payment and his account is immediately credited with the cleared funds on payment of the vouchers into his bank.

2 He can use the card system as an alternative to other means of allowing credit and thus avoid bad debts.

3 The acceptance of a card in lieu of cash reduces the security risk.

4 A merchant who accepts credit cards may expect to increase his turnover, as more and more people accept the practical advantages of credit cards and turn to those traders who will accept cards in settlement.

5 A credit card system permits the merchant to offer his customers the facility of taking credit without involving himself in the expense , administration or risk of setting up his own credit arrangements.

6 The merchant is able to expand his business to include overseas visitors.

7 He will also have the support of the credit card company in advertising campaigns and other promotional activities.

8 The credit card record of purchases is a convenience for bookkeeping.

Each retailer will be given by the card company an agreed 'floor limit' up to which he may accept customers' cards at his own discretion. Beyond that, he must telephone one of the principal card centres where a twenty-four-hour service is operated, to confirm whether or not a card may be accepted for a particular purchase.

The cardholder does not pay a fee for his card, but the merchant will pay a service charge of up to 5 per cent on his credit card turnover.

The level of charge will vary according to the nature of the business. In general, goods sold on a small margin but with a rapid turnover will suffer a lower service charge than, say, luxury items with a wider margin of profit. So far, credit cards are not normally acceptable in food supermarkets because the profit margins on many items are too low to bear a service charge in favour of the card company, and partly because of a lingering view that people should not be encouraged to buy food by means of a credit card.

Finally, let us return to the third party in the triangle, the card companies themselves. In recent times, the two principal card schemes in the United Kingdom have been able to report a trading profit on their operations. This was not always the case, however, and in the early years the administrative developments, and to a considerable extent the credit regulations imposed by the Government, caused substantial losses in the card companies.

The service charge paid by merchants provides some income towards meeting the costs of running a credit card scheme, but the real source of profit to a card company lies in the interest charge made to customers who use their cards to take extended credit. If all cardholders paid their monthly accounts within the stipulated period, there would be little profit to the companies and indeed they would probably operate at a loss. It is estimated that the average period of credit taken by cardholders is between four and six months, and it is certainly in the interests of the card companies to encourage cardholders not only to make more use of their cards but to avail themselves of the revolving credit facility.

The introduction of credit cards into Britain was a major marketing operation and despite the enormous initial costs it may be rated as a highly successful exercise in terms of the market penetration which was achieved and the ultimate profitability. In broad terms, the marketing effort of the credit card industry is pointed in three directions. There is the market among merchants, there is the market among potential cardholders and there is the marketing drive to encourage existing cardholders to make greater use of their cards.

Taking first the market among merchants, the view has been advanced that this market is approaching saturation point. With a few notable exceptions, virtually all the major retail trading groups in the United Kingdom accept payment by credit card. In most cases, these retailers will accept the cards of either of the two main card-issuing groups in the UK. There may still be scope for expansion of the market into, for example, the food trade and certain non-trading areas such as local authorities for the payment of rates; and there are also a large number of small shops and other retail houses which do not accept credit cards, but for the most part their turnover is so small or their margins so narrow that they are outside the credit card market. Thus the main marketing thrust so far as the merchants are concerned lies in servicing and developing the existing merchanting outlets. Each of the major card groups has one hundred or so salesmen who pay regular visits to the merchants in order to assist with administrative problems and the training of staff. The card companies also take a close interest in the marketing of the trader's merchandise and will assist with advertising campaigns or displays in order to improve the merchant's turnover and thus enhance the return to the card company.

As for the market among cardholders, there is no question of having reached saturation point, but the number of cardholders may well have reached a plateau for the time being. Six or seven million cardholders is not a very high proportion of the total adult population of the UK, but it amounts to about one-third of the population who have developed a banking habit. Whilst it is not necessary to have a banking account before possessing a credit card, the main market for cardholders so far as the banking groups are concerned is among their own customers. Although the card groups will no doubt continue to encourage as many people as possible to carry credit cards, there could well be a diminishing return in relation to the marketing costs involved. There is still a fair amount of misunderstanding and indeed prejudice in relation to credit cards. Even some well-informed people fail to recognise that a credit card is a convenient, safe and efficient method of payment as an alternative to a cheque. Instead it is too often regarded as merely a means of consumer credit and shunned by those who regard a credit facility as an undesirable temptation, whether to themselves or their fellow men.

The potential number of cardholders in the United Kingdom was given a significant boost by the trustee savings banks coming into the Visa family. The new 'Trustcard' in the blue, white and gold of the Visa Group was introduced in November 1978, bringing to the UK credit card scene an ultimate potential of more than 10 million additional cardholders.

Probably the main growth area for the card companies, however, lies in the increased use of cards by the existing cardholders, which in turn would lead to an increase in the amount of credit taken. Even if the average use of credit cards merely doubled from, say, one purchase per person per month to an average of two purchases per month, with a doubling in the value of the credit taken, the effect on the profits of the credit card companies would be dramatic. Administrative costs would not increase proportionately and even if the average credit period did not increase beyond the present figure of four to six months, the increase in interest earnings would double. It is very much in the interests of the card companies, therefore, to encourage greater activity among their 5 million or so active cardholders.

There is yet another main growth area which, at this point in time, is only just beginning. It is the development of credit card schemes among retailers, i.e. the introduction of the in-house card. We have already said that the largest issuers of cards in America are the department stores, whereas in the UK it has been a predominantly bank-dominated industry. We are now seeing the introduction of a number of in-house schemes in this country, but with the difference that they are administered and financed by the banks and the major card groups. In August 1978 Marks & Spencer announced their own credit card scheme in co-operation with Citibank. More recently, Barclays launched a special service under the name Barclaycare for the purpose of running in-house schemes for companies who wish to have their own card. Access have also announced their intention of supplying a similar service. That forerunner of the credit card industry in this country, the Provident Financial Group also provides, under the name Unicredit, a number of tailor-made schemes for companies operating in the retail sector, including in particular the recently announced scheme for Woolworths. Considerable activity in the in-house card front is expected in the next year or so.

The credit card business is not without its risks. The original risk was that the conservative British public might not respond to the vastly expensive campaigns launched to introduce credit cards into this country. In the event, the confidence of the pioneer promoters in the United Kingdom, notably Barclays Bank, was well repaid. It was a major business decision and the risks were considerable, but the operation was well timed and well executed. The hazards which remain are those which are inherent in this type of business, viz. legislative controls, fraud and bad debts.

To the extent that the card companies are in the credit business, they are inevitably exposed to the varying monetary controls introduced from time to time by successive Chancellors of the Exchequer. Any major restraints on credit or on credit repayment terms (such as have been a recurring feature of the UK economy) can be a burden to the credit card business, both in terms of administrative costs and the impact on interest earnings. It is a hazard which must be accepted as part of the environment in which the companies operate. Other legislative hurdles are the Consumer Credit Act 1974, with the already mentioned attendant liability on credit card companies for defects in goods purchased by cardholders and the provisions of the Fair Trading Act 1973 under which the major card companies are currently the subject of a reference to the Monopolies Commission. It is noteworthy that under the United States anti-trust laws, the member banks of the two major card groups in the US may now issue each other's cards if they so wish, thus introducing a degree of 'duality' in the card business in America. The major credit card groupings are now multi-national businesses (although dedicated only to serving the interests of their member banks) and as they develop they may well be faced increasingly with local hazards in one country or another, whether it be in terms of credit control, consumerism, anti-monopoly rules, exchange control or a variety of other local requirements and attitudes.

A more truly operational risk is that of fraud. In this we can include theft, forgery and general misuse of credit cards or of the credit card system. The risks are considerable and must inevitably become greater with the international growth of credit card business. Readers of Arthur Hailey's *The Moneychangers*[5] will recall the bank losses occasioned by mammoth-sized credit card forgeries, but such risks are not confined to the pages of novels. The scope for the fraudulent use of cards is considerable, but the anti-fraud organisations of the major British card companies are very impressive and have been highly successful in keeping losses of this nature to a very low level.

The last risk area is fundamental to the business – the risk of bad debts. Here again, the experience of the major card companies in the United Kingdom is very encouraging. The two large groups lend on credit card transactions in the course of a year sums well in excess of £1,000 million. That money is lent to complete strangers who are unknown in any personal sense to the credit card companies and with whom, unlike traditional banking, no continuing business relationship will necessarily have been established. The money is lent without security and without guarantees, and it says much for the integrity of the great majority of cardholders on the one hand and the efficiency of the card companies' debt-collecting procedures on the other that the bad debt experience is so modest and is, in fact, significantly below that sometimes encountered in other forms of consumer credit. It has been said that losses occasioned by fraud in the case of American card companies can be as high as 4 per cent of the sums outstanding at any one time. In the United Kingdom, the combined losses from both fraud and bad debts is significantly below that percentage.

What of the future? Here we may pose a number of questions, but the card industry is a fast-moving business and the questions we ask today will be replaced by a variety of others next year or the year after. Some have called in question, for example, the practice by which credit cards (as distinct from the travel and entertainment cards) are issued free, with free credit being allowed to cardholders, as we have seen, for up to nearly two months. This is only possible, so the argument goes, if those who take extended credit are charged a high rate of interest. In other words, the borrowers subsidise the remainder of the cardholders. An opposing argument is that by issuing cards free and not charging for short-term credit, the card companies are able to operate on a larger scale with lower administrative costs and therefore greater efficiency in everyone's interests. Nevertheless, it is a matter which may well remain the subject of debate, and it could be that cardholders will at least be required to pay for the privilege of holding a card and thus contribute to the cost of the otherwise free credit. Indeed, cardholders may be encouraged to make greater use of their cards if they were required to pay for them in the first instance.

One may also question whether the development of the credit card is consistent with the introduction of cheque cards. There are those who regret the introduction of cheque cards because in the United Kingdom cheques on the clearing banks used to be widely accepted in payment for goods and services, whereas today a cheque is seldom accepted without a supporting cheque card. Is there in fact any good reason why a bank should guarantee payment of its cheques by means of a cheque card? Why should the bank accept the risk of loss on the transaction between customer and merchant when there is no other direct benefit to the bank itself? Admittedly, the wider use of cheques encourages current account banking with valuable free balances, but it must be doubtful whether the introduction of cheque cards as such encourages the banking habit. The need for cheque cards is perhaps even more questionable in an age when the major banks issue credit cards to creditworthy customers. Is it not possible that without the introduction of cheque cards, the two leading credit cards – Access and Barclaycard – would have come even more into their own as acceptable methods of payment for goods, quite regardless of the credit aspect? Might this not have been desirable? It would presumably have diminished the volume of cheques in circulation and helped to pave the way for the next stage in payment transmission, the linking of credit cards to electronic data systems.

This last subject must in itself be one of the major issues for the bank credit card industry. Already the combined use of credit card and telephone (e.g. the ordering of theatre seats) has become an acceptable feature of our society. Much more exciting is the possibility of using the plastic credit cards as a means of instruction to computer terminals in shops, airports, hotels, travel agencies and the like, virtually dispensing with all paperwork. All this has been perfectly possible for some years and will no doubt come about in whatever way may be deemed to be commercially suitable. In some respects, the linking-up of credit card companies internationally has resulted in electronic equipment of a sophistication which exceeds that in normal banking. The international settlement of card liabilities is already achieved to a large extent by electronic means. In the case of Barclaycard, for instance, transactions generated by overseas cards in this country or by domestic Barclaycards used overseas are settled not by the despatch of paper around the world, but by electronic data transmission. The San Mateo computer provides the

Barclaycard organisation with daily settlement in dollars, notwithstanding that the original transactions may be made in any of fifty or more currencies.

Whether by accident or design the credit card business has usurped some of the older and more routine functions of traditional banking. As Mr D. V. Weyer has written:

'Customers, helped by external cash dispensers and by credit cards can get along surprisingly well without often visiting their bank.'[6]

This was not entirely unforeseen and, in particular, the architects of Barclaycard emphasised its merits as a convenient method of payment and foresaw its contribution to the 'cashless society' (although a 'chequeless society' is the more likely).

Some readers and students might care to debate the hypothesis that plastic cards which can be used (a) for transmitting payments, (b) for withdrawing cash, (c) for borrowing money (whether in cash or as credit for goods), (d) for depositing cash and (e) for issuing instructions or requests to one's banker – all by means of a computer terminal in some central place – might well replace quite a number of High Street branches, at least in their more traditional roles. Indeed, at the time of writing, the Clydesdale Bank in Scotland has successfully concluded a pilot scheme entailing the use of a plastic card, the Autobank card, for over-the-counter transactions, thereby dispensing with cheques and paying-in-slips in due time at the 370 or so branches of the bank, all of which will be on-line to the Autobank Centre. It is not of course a credit card operation as such, but the implications are exciting in terms of money transmission.

Nor will such changes apply only to banking. Retail purchases and the processes of settling domestic bills may well be effected from the comfort of the home by means of a keyboard terminal within reach of the armchair. Already the world of science fiction has been brought nearer by the Post Office announcement of the Viewdata scheme, by which the linking of a telephone line to a home television set will permit a vast array of goods and services to be offered on the screen. By means of a keyboard no larger than a pocket calculator, the consumer will be able to make his purchases without stirring from his chair, payment being made instantly if desired by debiting a credit card account. One will have to be careful, of course, when buying a second-hand car from a robot!

No doubt in the United Kingdom both the credit card groups and the domestic banks will each continue to develop along their established lines, finding here and there some particular point of contact, some mutual development of their systems and integration of ideas. On the international front, however, the credit card groups have become much more a business unto themselves and, largely treading new ground, they have achieved a degree of co-operation and harmonisation which is exciting to observe. At the time of writing, the two worldwide groupings – Interbank and Visa – have over 100 million cards in issue and these are acceptable to something like 2½ million merchants around the world. It is indeed the phenomenon of our time.

## References

1 F. Snushall: Credit Cards *in* Credit Management Handbook, 1975.
2 The Decline of the Cheque. *The Banker*, November 1973, p. 1411.
3 Target Group Index, 1976.
4 Ibid.
5 A. Hailey: *The Moneychangers*. Michael Joseph, 1975.
6 D. Vander Weyer: 'Clearing Bank Marketing: the Practical Issues Today'. *The Banker*, October 1970.

CHAPTER 18

# Off-shore Services

At a stroke of the legislature's pen, any person who left the United Kingdom and became domiciled in the Channel Islands or the Isle of Man after 10 December 1974 is deemed, subject to certain exceptions, still to be domiciled in the United Kingdom. In a brief and slightly desperate clause of the Finance Act 1975 (section 45), the Government of the day sought to stop what it regarded as a drain of personal wealth to the off-shore islands, to the detriment of the Exchequer. Thus, overnight, a new dimension to the meaning of the word *domicile* was introduced, in relation to what the Act refers to as 'the Islands'. Although the concept of domicile has given rise to a great variety of interesting law cases over the years, the basic meaning is clear enough. In simple terms, it is the fact of residence in a particular country with the intention of remaining there. In relation to 'the Islands', however, Parliament has decreed, like Humpty-Dumpty, that the word means what they choose it to mean. Some would say that this modest little section is bad law because (a) it is selective (it applies only to those persons seeking to take up domicile in the Islands), and (b) it is largely ineffective (provided that such persons take all their taxable resources with them).

Good or bad, the section typifies a popular view that the offshore islands of the British Isles are populated by wealthy Britons who, having made their fortunes in this country, put themselves beyond the tax-collecting arm of successive governments. This popular image is not wholly without justification. But there are of course far more people who have left the United Kingdom to live in other tax-favourable countries around the world than have moved to the Channel Islands and the Isle of Man. The point is, however, that a large number of people have for tax reasons chosen to leave the United Kingdom and taken up residence and domicile in the off-shore islands, thus enjoying the freedom of exchange within the sterling area, the continuation of a predominantly British way of life, the convenience of frequent visits to the home country and, in some cases, the facility for running their UK businesses from a safe distance. Partly because of section 45, but perhaps more particularly because of the internal rules of the off-shore islands as regards new residents, the flow of those who come, as they say in the Isle of Man, from 'across' had dwindled to a trickle. Whether or not the tax loss to the Inland Revenue is of significant proportions will no doubt continue to be a matter of debate. Such is the constitutional independence of the Islands, however, that the introduction of any system by which they could become tax-gatherers for the UK Inland Revenue is extremely unlikely.

To the extent that the Islands are seen as sanctuaries for fugitives from the British tax system, it must seem strange that the English and Scottish banks have established off-shore bases in the Channel Islands, as indeed they have in other so-called tax havens around the world. The truth is, however, that the British banks have refused to allow their off-shore services to be used for tax-avoidance purposes for persons of continuing UK residence and have certainly not taken a positive role in encouraging people to forsake the UK and remove to the off-shore islands. Intending residents of the Islands will be given every assistance by the local subsidiaries of the UK banks in matters of local information and, as in this country, will be helped in arranging their affairs to the best advantage. There has been for many years, however, a 'gentleman's agreement' between the English clearing banks and the States of Jersey that the off-shore subsidiaries would not be used to assist UK residents in the avoidance of taxation. Additionally, there was a firm understanding between the Channel Island States and the UK Inland Revenue that companies would not be registered in the Channel Islands for the purpose of avoiding UK tax liabilities.

Any contemplation of these matters requires some definition of the terms used. In everyday parlance, the Channel Islands

*'. . . prefer to be called Financial Centres.'*

and the Isle of Man and other similar locations around the world are referred to as 'tax havens'. This is a slightly emotive term suggesting an element of escape, or at least refuge, and understandably enough the Islands prefer to be called financial centres. This latter description is no doubt reasonable in relation to the principal off-shore centres around the world, but is a little euphemistic when referring to some of the wind-swept isles which claim to be 'low tax areas'.

The expression 'off-shore' has also acquired its own special meaning in the financial world. Naturally enough it was of geographical origin. People who moved their residence or their business affairs from some political land mass to a nearby tax-efficient base were usually moving to the nearest convenient haven within reach. It was literally off-shore – the British to the Channel Islands, the Americans to the Bahamas, the Chinese to Hong Kong and the Australians to the New Hebrides. In time, however, the term acquired a wider significance and was used to apply to any centre where international business may be done in a favourable tax climate. This may be an on-shore independent state, e.g. Panama, Liberia, Liechtenstein, but it may also be a state within a state – usually a situation where a country allows international business to be conducted free from the burden of its own tax laws. For example, non-resident companies may operate in Jersey free from Jersey's own income tax (modest though it is) and in a number of countries it is possible for overseas nationals, whether personal or corporate, to conduct business in a way which is reasonably free from the local fiscal legislation. Indeed, it is argued by some that the United Kingdom is one of the best 'off-shore' centres in the world because there is more international business conducted there, untrammelled by British taxation or other restrictions, than in any other place.

In general terms, we may say that there are three categories of business in which British banks and other international financial institutions engage in the various financial off-shore centres of the world. They are:

1 Personal financial services, whether for the local residents of the off-shore centre or, more likely, for the residents of other countries around the world.

2 Corporate financial services for those institutions in various parts of the world who can with advantage conduct some part of their business from an off-shore centre.

3 Those activities which, for the convenience of banks or other financial institutions themselves, may better be conducted off-shore.

Taking first the broad area of personal financial business, we should note the particular requirements of the typical international customer. They are:

(a) He wishes his affairs to be managed in a low tax area in order to minimise the effect of income taxes, inheritance taxes and capital gains tax.

(b) He expects a standard of expertise which may only be available in the more sophisticated off-shore centres.

(c) The local currency should be reasonably stable, or it should be possible to conduct transactions in the currency of the customer's choice.

(d) There must be politically stable conditions.

(e) The off-shore centre should be sufficiently agreeable scenically and climatically, and enjoy sufficiently good communications to encourage the customer either to live where his money is, or at least to make occasional visits.

(f) Complete confidentiality is essential.

Some typical examples of personal off-shore business are:

1 The management of personal trusts set up by the customer for the benefit of himself, his family or other persons. It may be to the advantage of the settlor not only that the settled funds enjoy a favourable tax climate, but also that the trust funds may be beyond the reach of the political system of his own country. To some extent, a trust may do the work of a will in so far as it facilitates the transfer of assets on death without incurring the time and expense of proving title and changing the title to assets in a number of different countries.

2 The management of investment companies. In those centres where there is a degree of personal taxation, but little or no tax on companies, it may be an advantage to the customer concerned to have his or her investments or other assets held in a company in the off-shore centre.

3 The management of investments. Most of the off-shore centres conduct portfolio management for private clients on an international basis, offering secrecy, international expertise, freedom from local taxation and to varying degrees, freedom from exchange control restrictions.

4 The management of mutual funds and unit trusts. These have been set up in most of the principal off-shore centres, partly because of the freedom from local taxation and partly, in the case of UK promoters, to facilitate transactions in non-sterling securities without the need for payment of the dollar premium. This is only possible of course for bona fide, non-UK investors and such funds cannot be used by British investors for the purpose of avoiding the investment currency premium.

These various activities are very much the same as each other in substance. They provide a worldwide service to enable customers of means to locate some part of their personal resources in a politically stable environment with a favourable taxation system.

The second category of activity, corporate services, or perhaps more correctly called business services, is more sophisticated and in some cases more tortuous. An increasing number of business houses are finding it an advantage to centre some part of their activities in off-shore locations, perhaps to avoid recording taxable profits in the parent company or perhaps to circumvent some other legal requirement of the company's country of origin. The following are examples of services offered by the off-shore centres to international or multinational businesses:

1 Company registration services

These include the setting up of subsidiary companies for international companies and the provision of secretarial arrangements and sometimes the provision of local directors, to enable companies to establish some part of their business in a tax-favourable area. Although it may not always be possible to transfer a manufacturing process to a tax haven, there are instances where consultancy services and intellectual property such as copyrights and patents, have been transferred off-shore in order to allow royalties to build up in a tax-free situation.

In the Channel Islands and the Isle of Man, companies set up in this way (or investment companies, as described on page

267) are referred to as 'corporation tax companies'. This is because they are not subject to income tax on profits, except locally earned profits, but pay a flat rate of corporation tax, currently £300 per annum in the Channel Islands and £200 per annum in the Isle of Man. At the time of writing, there are well over 11,000 companies registered in Jersey and new registrations are running at a level of approximately 1,500 a year.

2 Invoicing
In its simplest form this involves the routing of invoices through an off-shore centre where a further margin is added to the price in order to accumulate profits in the neutral tax area. In other instances, the invoicing or re-invoicing procedure is used to circumvent exchange control regulations in the principal country of operation. The banks will not of course lend their name or assistance to any scheme which transgresses the local laws of any of the countries concerned.

3 Captive insurance companies
This type of company has been known in the United States of America for fifty years or more, and in more recent times has been introduced to other parts of the world. A so-called 'captive' insurance company is usually a subsidiary company set up by a large corporation to handle the group's insurance risks. In other words, the group undertakes its own insurance, thereby retaining for itself the profit element of the insurance contracts, although larger risks would be laid off in the reinsurance market. It has become the fashion to establish a captive company in such places as Bermuda, Guernsey or the Bahamas in order that the company may operate in a tax-free environment and build up untaxed reserves for the benefit of the group generally. There are many advantages of setting up captive insurance companies, although this is not perhaps the place to pursue the subject in detail. It is noteworthy, however, that there has been a considerable growth in this type of business in recent years with consequent benefit to the off-shore centres.

4 Cash management
One of the problems of multinational companies is the management of cash flow in the various countries of operation and the 'netting' of cash balances in order to achieve maximum benefit from the group's liquid resources.

At least one international bank operates a worldwide clearing system to enable inter-company payments to be made in local currencies on a settlement day each month (or more frequently, if desired). The inter-company and group liquidity position is available at a glance from a computer print-out and so maximum use can be made of cash resources. Similarly, it is possible to operate a collection system for trade debts by the use of a single account in each customer country, the worldwide balances being netted by the bank operating the service. Thus it is possible to obtain a daily cash position for the group as a whole, notwithstanding the variety of currencies in which transactions have been conducted. If services of this kind are operated through a company set up for the purpose in one of the off-shore centres, it is possible for net balances to be built up for investment purposes in a neutral tax situation.

These are but examples of services which are being developed on an increasing scale for international companies. As world trade develops, more and more companies are attracted to the possibilities of channelling some part of their business through those centres which have a favourable tax climate. In some cases, this merely postpones the payment of tax until such time as the profits are remitted to the home country, but in other instances it permits the accumulation of tax-free reserves for the further development of a group's international business without any occasion to repatriate funds to a high-tax country.

What then is the role of the British banks in all this? Most of the UK banks have subsidiary companies operating in the principal off-shore centres throughout the world, partly as a service to local residents but more particularly, in modern times, for the development of such international services as we have described. It must be emphasised again that the banks will not lend their name or support to any transactions which are illegal in any of the countries involved. More than that, however, the banks will not participate in any activities which, although strictly legal, are contrary to the known views of the governments or central banks of the countries involved. The British banks are themselves concerned, to varying degrees, in international banking activities and thus will not prejudice their own presence or potential presence in particular countries by operating nefarious schemes to the detriment of those countries. For example, an international bank represented in, say, Italy will not do its image any good by encouraging Italian companies to operate elaborate re-invoicing schemes off-shore in order to defeat the Italian taxation laws or exchange control regulations. Similarly, in the area of personal wealth the banks will not facilitate the flight of capital across national boundaries in contravention of local regulations.

Nevertheless, as the world contracts, more and more people will seek to develop their personal fortunes in the most favourable fiscal climates; and corporations, in the pursuit of international business, will seek to administer it from, or channel it through, those parts of the world which offer the most attractive return. One may indeed argue that world trade is encouraged by the particular facilities which the off-shore centres offer.

So it is that the British banks have sought to provide a complete range of legitimate services, not only in the immediate off-shore bases of the Channel Islands and the Isle of Man, but in the Bahamas, Bermuda, the New Hebrides, Hong Kong, the Cayman Islands and even the small island and former German colony of Nauru in the Central Pacific.

The third aspect of off-shore business is that which relates to the business of the banks themselves as distinct from services to customers. One of the earliest examples of this was the setting up by the British banks of finance companies in the Channel Islands at the time of the interest rate cartel on the mainland. The finance companies were not governed by the agreement on interest rates, nor indeed were they subject to the liquidity ratios then applying to the clearing banks. It was possible for these finance company subsidiaries to offer a service not only to the local population and other overseas depositors, but also to residents of the United Kingdom who were thus able to obtain a higher rate of interest than was available in this country. That was a minor example of a use which the banks made of the off-shore centres for their own bookkeeping purposes.

Of far greater importance at the present time is the practice of international banks of 'booking' substantial loans in the off-shore centres, whether for reasons of tax efficiency or in order to take advantage of the freedom from regulatory provisions in a bank's home country. The result has been a considerable upsurge of business on the books of the principal off-shore centres, notwithstanding that the effective control of the lending has remained with New York or London or elsewhere. A particular example of this occurred in the Bahamas in 1976 following an increase in New York State bank taxes in the previous year. It was reported that in the first half of 1976 more loans by American banks were 'booked' in the Bahamas than in London. In the same year, UK bank loans 'booked' in the Bahamas increased by over 28 per cent and deposits taken through the Bahamas increased by 77 per cent. At the end of 1976, the deposits taken by UK banks from the off-shore centres (outside the sterling area) amounted to over £12,000 million compared with only £1,300 million five years previously. Loans recorded by the UK banks in the non-sterling off-shore centres during 1976 totalled £17,000 million – over eight times the corresponding figure five years earlier.

From the standpoint of international banking, the choice of an off-shore centre will depend on such factors as (a) local exchange control regulations, (b) the freedom of foreign banks to operate, (c) the freedom to operate in non-local currencies, (d) the freedom from onerous local taxes, whether direct taxes or withholding taxes, and (e) the freedom from reserve ratios or other regulatory provisions in relation to international business.

There will always be off-shore financial centres. Like water finding its own level, entrepreneurial business, when constrained in one place, will emerge in another. When the restrictions in one place become too burdensome, too discouraging and perhaps too punitive, the businessman will look elsewhere. Ship owners soon appreciated the taxation advantages of registering their vessels in Liberia or Panama. Mutual fund operators found they could set up their funds in centres where there was no capital gains tax and no withholding tax. The equalisation tax and domestic interest rate regulations in New York led to the development of London as the centre for the Eurodollar and Eurobond markets. If bearer securities cannot be issued in one place, they will be issued in another. And so on. As one door closes, another is opened. Even within the off-shore centres themselves the rules change from time to time. What is possible today in the Bahamas, Bermuda, Jersey or Grand

Cayman, may not be possible tomorrow. The term 'off-shore' shorn of its original meaning will no doubt continue until someone finds a better one. As with flags of convenience, perhaps we ought to call them countries of convenience – countries where we can run businesses or manage our private finances in a way which seems advantageous to us at the moment and which is denied to us somewhere else. One thing is certain, that the banks will wish to be where the action is. They will seek to meet a demand and cultivate a demand wherever there is the opportunity of doing legitimate business for themselves and their customers – whether it be in Bermuda or Bootle.

*'Money and travel go nicely hand in hand.'*

CHAPTER 19

# Money and Travel

'Much have I travel'd', wrote the poet Keats, 'in the realms of gold'. Certainly nowadays he would not have travelled very far without gold or its modern equivalent. Travel and money are like intersecting circles which overlap very considerably, for it is almost impossible to contemplate modern travel without both the provision of money and the problems of money. The traveller abroad must pay for his tickets, he requires currency for the journey, he needs the wherewithal to pay hotels and restaurants and personal shopping bills, perhaps in a succession of countries, he needs (or should have) baggage and health insurance, he must know the rules of the game and he should have a lifeline in case of need.

The banks respond to these needs of the traveller by issuing him with currency and travellers' cheques at his local branch, advising on exchange control regulations and marking his passport appropriately, opening credits with foreign banks, supplying credit cards with almost worldwide acceptance, opening airport branches and *bureaux de change* en route and generally instructing, counselling and sometimes rescuing the traveller in all the financial aspects of his visit. For the business traveller, one may add the supply of economic data, advice on local markets and in all probability some worthwhile local introductions. Thus, money and travel go nicely hand-in-hand.

It was no doubt the awareness of this relationship which prompted the debate over many years as to whether or not the British banks should engage directly in travel business. For long enough the Australian banks had conducted their own travel departments; in some respects they were among the first to appreciate the needs of the traveller and to provide lounges for the comfort of foreign visitors in some of the principal cities around the world. A number of American banks have travel departments or travel agencies and perhaps one need look no further than Wells Fargo for an historic link between travel and money. Some of the German banks have direct interests in travel agencies and in Scandinavia, the Netherlands and France the banks allow facilities in their branches for tour operators and travel agents.

Although no one doubts the financial needs of the traveller, one must question the philosophy of banks in the travel business. To provide travellers' cheques, currency, credit cards and to advise generally on the financial arrangements may be seen as part of the total financial service of the commercial bank. To book rail tickets, air tickets, hotel rooms and the like is essentially a different business. It is not of course banking and it is not strictly a financial service at all. It stands alone in the gallery of services described in this book as a non-financial operation. Perhaps such a nice distinction is unfair and even irrelevant. After all, two of the principal operators in the travel business, Thomas Cook and Son and American Express, have for long been bankers in their own right. Nevertheless, as a matter of pedantry if nothing more, perhaps we may be allowed the proposition that travel business is not service banking.

Whatever the philosophy may be, the fact remains that many banks around the world have found it convenient and profitable to engage directly or indirectly in the provision of travel facilities. It was not surprising, therefore, that the clearing banks in this country showed interest when, in 1972, the government announced its proposals for selling off Thomas Cook and Son from the government-owned transport holding company. At the conclusion of the tendering process, the company was acquired by a consortium of Midland Bank, Trust Houses Forte and the Automobile Association. Thus the Midland Bank acquired a direct interest in one of the best known and oldest established travel businesses in the world. In 1977, Midland Bank bought out the minority shareholdings of the other members of the consortium and now own the entire share capital. The attractions of Thomas Cook to a bank buyer were no doubt its name, its worldwide outlets, its banking and travellers' cheque business and the expertise of its staff.

Of the other clearing banks, Barclays Bank also has a direct interest in the travel business through its wholly-owned subsidiary, Travel Enterprises. Originally developed as a captive travel agency to deal with the very considerable travel requirements of the Barclays group, its services are nevertheless available to business customers through the bank's branches. It is of course a modest sized operation in relation to the giant Thomas Cook.

From a bank's point of view there are a number of advantages to be gained from involvement in the travel business. The first and principal benefit must be that of profits and it is generally accepted that there are good profits to be made among travel operators, although in the past there have been some very lean years and some failures. The combination of a well-established travel group with an international bank must, it is thought, have a very worthwhile profit potential. Secondly, a bank like any business house must be on the lookout for valid opportunities of extending its influence and the travel business offers a very real way of doing this. The tourist industry is very big business indeed and now constitutes the largest single item in the analysis of world trade. In 1977, international tourist receipts in the twelve leading industrialised countries reached \$40½ billion, i.e. 20 per cent higher than in the previous year. Thirdly, the close contact between a travel agency and its travelling customers provides considerable opportunity for gaining new accounts for the associated bank; and fourthly, the same extensive connections present cross-selling opportunities for a wide range of the bank's other services.

On the other side of the coin, there are of course some possible disadvantages. We have already said that the travel business has had its troubles and can, at times, be particularly exposed to extraneous factors, such as bad weather, strikes, unemployment, credit and exchange control restrictions and to some extent also to changes in fashion. In addition, there is the danger of some unfortunate travel experience 'rubbing off' on the operator or agent who made the arrangements and if this happened to be a bank, some unfavourable publicity could result. From a bank's point of view, there is also the disadvantage that the travel business tends to be labour-intensive with the administrative organisation which that entails and the consequential high costs. Lastly, it could perhaps be said that for a bank to obtain the full benefit from an affiliated travel business, the services of the latter should be available in the bank's branches – something which is difficult, but not impossible to organise, within the framework of banking hours in the United Kingdom.

In a speech in 1973 to the Financial Times Conference on World Tourism and Travel,[1] Mr Malcolm Wilcox, then Assistant Chief General Manager of Midland Bank and Deputy Chairman of Thomas Cook, outlined with great lucidity the three fundamental aspects of travel business, viz. the 'originating sector' (the travel agents and tour operators who book the trains, flights and hotels, put together the packages and sell the tickets); the transportation sector (the air and shipping lines and railways); and the accommodation sector (the hotels, holiday villages, etc.). At the front end of the total operation, i.e. the travel agency section, it is not difficult to see the affinity between banks and the travel people. They have reciprocal, or at least complementary, marketing strengths, and as we have already mentioned there is much common ground between them. In the middle section, that of transportation, the banks are already involved, as Mr Wilcox points out, in the leasing of ships and aircraft (although it must be acknowledged that this is a far cry from being involved in the transportation business at first hand). In the final category, at the accommodation end, the banks are already accustomed to financing hotels and similar leisure complexes.

It must remain very doubtful, however, whether the banks would ever wish to become involved at first hand in either the transportation or accommodation business. They are both highly specialised activities and both areas have suffered serious setbacks over the years. It may be that the banks will participate to a degree in the provision of hotels and aircraft, but this must surely, at its most, be no more than a trade investment and one would expect any significant involvement by the banks to be at the originating end of the operation, as agents for the operators, if there is going to be any direct involvement in travel business.

One particular aspect of travel business has undergone a

boom in this country in recent years, that is the provision of *bureau de change* facilities. The growth of tourism in London during the past few years (and no doubt the closing of the banks on Saturday mornings) has led to the development of independent *bureaux de change* in London and, to a lesser degree, in the provinces. According to one recent estimate, there were approximately 170 shops, stores and hotels offering *bureau de change* facilities in London and other centres in the UK. Naturally enough, the banks have not stood aside from this development. Barclays Bank opened its first bureau in Oxford Street in September 1977 to provide a six-day service from 8 o'clock in the morning until 10 o'clock in the evening. Lloyds Bank, through their subsidiary Lewis's Bank, offer *bureau de change* facilities at fourteen of the Lewis's Group stores and Midland Bank, of course, offer exchange facilities through Thomas Cook. Apart from these 'separate' *bureaux de change*, the banks have made a move to extend banking branch opening hours to provide exchange facilities. In March 1978, National Westminster Bank extended the opening hours of its Shaftesbury Avenue Branch and later in the year, Barclays Bank reached agreement with the staff side for the opening of four branches on Saturday mornings to provide bureau services with the intention, subject to demand, of developing a small network of exchange bureaux operating from bank branches on Saturday mornings. Midland Bank too, augmented its existing Thomas Cook outlets by opening a Thomas Cook bureau in the bank's Leicester Square Branch. It is a self-contained unit within the branch and is open six days a week until 10.00 p.m. and also open for most of Sunday.

The provision of travel services through the banks is a subject of continuing interest and one in which some major developments might well be seen in the coming years. It must be said, however, that the banks have not yet solved the problem of being financial supermarkets in those areas of activity which are second nature to them. It may be some little time, therefore, before they are all open for business over the travel counter.

## Reference

1 M. G. Wilcox: Banks and the Travel Business, *Journal of The Institute of Bankers*, October 1973.

CHAPTER 20

# Selling the Services

This final chapter is in the nature of a tailpiece to what has gone before, for it seems appropriate that some reference should be made to the methods of selling bank services and to some of the problems involved. The point must, however, be made that we are concerned here only with selling, not with the total marketing concept. Selling is merely part of marketing. Marketing, as the distinguished business philosopher, Peter Drucker, has said: 'encompasses the entire business. It is the whole business seen from the point of view of its final result, that is, from the customer's point of view.'[1] It is too vast a subject to deal with here and in any case would be outside the scope and purpose of this book.

It is, indeed, a pity that so far no major work on the subject of bank marketing in the United Kingdom has been published, although such a book has now been commissioned by The Institute of Bankers.[2] Even in the United States, there was such a comparative shortage of literature on the subject that in 1974 Professor Leonard Berry and Mr L. A. Capaldini recognised the need for a marketing book which 'puts it all together' for the bank executive.[3]

As we have already said, the term 'marketing' was unknown in British banking until the late 1960s. In fact it was not in much earlier use in North America. It was only in the early 1960s that marketing attitudes and the language of marketing were introduced into American banks. The so-called marketing mix (not to be confused with the product mix) refers to the major ingredients of the marketing concept. They have been defined for bankers in the same phraseology now used in the marketing world in general: they are the four Ps of marketing – product, place, promotion and price.[4]

Marketing as applied to banking has been defined by Lord Seebohm[5] as:

(i) identifying present and future markets for services;

(ii) selecting which markets to serve and identifying customer needs within them;

(iii) setting long- and short-term goals for the progress of existing and new services;

(iv) managing the services so as to persuade customers to use them at a profit, and controlling of success in so doing.

These matters and indeed the whole approach to marketing in the clearing banks will repay detailed study. What would no doubt emerge is the extent of the pragmatism (and also conservatism) and the sensitivity (and also inconsistency) which has characterised the rapid development of bank services. Here, however, we are concerned only with the P of promotion – the selling of the products.

Just as this book is concerned only with the non-traditional banking services, so these comments on selling must logically be confined to those services and not to banking as a whole. Such a distinction is not easy to preserve because, to use the National Westminster Bank's terminology, these 'related' bank services are very much related to the traditional banking function when it comes to the processes of selling.

Some bankers are good salesmen by nature, others would never be good salesmen in a thousand years. Some regard selling as fun, some regard it as vaguely unclean. There are those who, long before 'marketing' was introduced to banking, regarded themselves as salesmen – and some were better salesmen than bankers. There are others who to this day, with Ralph Emerson, believe that if a man offers a better service than his neighbour 'though he build his house in the woods, the world will make a beaten path to his door'.

The traditional view was summed up long ago by George Rae:[6]

'. . . it is for its customers to come to a bank, and not for the bank to go to them . . . the Manager has to be as much a fixture in the office, during the business hours of every business day, as the office desks or the bank counter.'

And again:
'You ask, if you are thus to pass the remainder of your days inside your office, how are you to push the business? But banking is a business to which the business of pushing must be applied, if at all, with the utmost circumspection.'

Bank officials on both sides of the Atlantic were not on the whole regarded as salesmen. The typical view was given light-hearted expression in an article published in 1965 by the Financial Public Relations Association from which the following is a short extract:

'Our bank offices are nice and my chair is soft. I like my chair and its softness. People come to my desk to see me and I make lots of loans and open their accounts – all in my chair. I don't like to leave my chair.

'We have lots of customers all over town. I know they like my bank as much as I do because we are so nice. Almost everyone likes us. Some customers send people to the bank for them and have no more contact with us than their monthly statement. Some nervy people from those other banks go to call on *our* customers and ask for their business. But they won't get it because we are such nice folks. I understand some of those other banks even go out to see prospective customers instead of letting them come in themselves. We have branches all over town. It is convenient for them so they will come to see us at our nice offices.

'Some of those other banks even have *officers* who go out to "sell" bank services. Anyone knows a BANK OFFICER IS NOT A SALESMAN. Salesmen are pests. We're executives. I've even heard that some banks have special meetings to promote selling of bank services. They show films and talk about "prospects". None of those gimmicks for me. I'm a bank officer and people come to me and my bank because we're nice.

'But, where have they been lately?'

There were good reasons why bank managers should not be seen in the role of salesmen. We shall consider in a moment the ways in which their role has changed, but it must be recognised that historically the bank manager saw himself as a professional man offering a professional service. He was similar to the solicitor or accountant or doctor or surveyor. He was not running a shop and he did not see himself in charge of an emporium with row upon row of shelves full of various products.

Perhaps understandably something of the traditional attitude still lingers. We have referred earlier (see p. 189) to a recent survey of twenty-three bank branches in London whose customers included over 8,000 small firms. The survey tells us that 'one subject on which there was almost unanimous agreement was their (the bank managers') dislike of the marketing approach that they consider was being forced on them'.

Amongst banks in the United Kingdom, the need for aggressive selling may be attributed to three main causes:

1 The historical inability to compete on interest rates, coupled with long periods of credit restriction in the 1950s and 1960s when it was equally impossible to compete as lenders. It seemed, without justification in the event, that traditional banking was to be proscribed for ever.

2 The disclosure of bank profits which brought a sharper edge to competitiveness with an increased profit awareness on all sides.

3 The changes brought about in 1971 under the heading of 'competition and credit control', which as we have already mentioned brought about freedom from the interest rate cartel, uniformity of liquidity ratios among banking houses generally and a greater encouragement to compete for business.

It was the first of these factors which gave rise to the proliferation of banking services, but the two subsequent developments gave new emphasis to the need for developing those services in an energetic and profitable way.

The markets for these services are considerable and in some cases almost infinite. The first and obvious point is that there is not one market but many. The market for personal taxation advice is not the market for leasing or factoring. The market for world travel may overlap only slightly with the market for executorship work. The market for linked life assurance has no relevance to the market for large funded pension schemes. And so on. In short, the size and location of each market will vary from service to service and readers may wish to make their own calculations and draw their own conclusions on the size and nature of the different markets.

It would be tedious to recite here the extent of the market for each of the services listed and perhaps a few examples will suffice. By way of illustration, let us examine the market for the administration of estates. At first sight, the market consists of everyone who makes a will as well as everyone who dies without doing so. If one assumes that, as part of the marketing plan, every adult is encouraged to make a will, the market first consists of every person of full age and sound mind who can be persuaded to make a will appointing the X Bank as executor. The rest of the market are those who have died, having failed to make such a will, but whose beneficiaries (in loose terms) authorise the X Bank to act as administrator. Approximately 600,000 adults die every year and in marketing terms the sale is not 'clinched' until the death or, more correctly, until a short time afterwards, because (a) the testator might change his mind at any time before death and (b) even after death the family may prevail upon the executor bank to renounce the appointment. Thus, it would be nice and easy to say that the market for executorship services among the banks is approximately 40 million adult persons (ignoring the insane ones), trusting that when they have all appointed the banks, they, or ultimately their families for them, do not change their minds. Such a situation would give a steady flow of approximately 600,000 new cases per annum. But of course all this is nonsense. First, with few exceptions, the banks can look only to their own customers for executorship business. Thus if the market comprises some 15 million customers and if X Bank has approximately one-third of the banking market, the figure is reduced to 5 million. Secondly, not everyone has resources of sufficient dimensions to justify the appointment of a bank as executor; and, thirdly, even with the benefit of minimum fees the banks do not wish to attract business below a certain level because to do so would be unprofitable. There is probably no great point in anyone with less than, say, £20,000 worth of assets at death appointing a bank as executor because the fees would bear unduly on an estate of this amount and, from the bank's point of view, an undue proportion of such estates would be unprofitable to administer. The total number of people in the United Kingdom with personal wealth in excess of £20,000 has been estimated at 1·4 million,[7] and the figure for England and Wales is approximately 1·2 million.[8] We can assume for all practical purposes that most people with personal wealth of that order will have an account with one of the clearing banks. Thus a clearing bank, with one-third of the banking business in England and Wales, seeking to develop its executorship business among customers worth £20,000 or more, would effectively have a market of only, say, 400,000 (i.e. one-third of 1·2 million). In practical terms, the target will be much smaller still, if one allows for those customers who have made wills appointing someone other than their bank as executor and have no occasion to change their wills, and those people who, regardless of the banks' efforts, will die intestate.

In terms of a marketing plan, it becomes apparent that the size of the market does not justify large-scale advertising, and that in terms of the branch network the great majority of the customers at each branch will have insufficient personal wealth to be within the target group. There are, in fact, quite a number of bank branches in the United Kingdom that have comparatively few customers with personal wealth of more than £20,000.

The profit from the administration of estates is only modest and in some cases non-existent. Fees are not taken until an estate is in course of administration, although the marketing effort to secure the appointment of a bank will have taken place some years before. It has also been estimated that on average a period of twelve years elapses between making one's last will and the date of death. Whatever the period, today's marketing costs for executorship business must be set against the discounted value of future earnings, and in many cases that discounted value will be negligible. The scope for worthwhile promotional activity is therefore extremely limited.

If we consider another service, the market for instalment finance is very considerable indeed. The total hire purchase debt outstanding in the United Kingdom in 1977 was of the order of £3,000 million. If we assume that approximately 30 per cent of this is related to business assets, the level of personal hire purchase is about £2,000 million. This is less than $2\frac{1}{2}$ per cent of personal disposable income in the UK.[9] The Crowther Report showed that consumer hire purchase in this country had never exceeded 5 per cent of personal disposable income and had reached that figure only during a period of freedom from credit control. The typical figure for the post-war years was of the order of 4 per cent. In the United States, however, outstanding debt on consumer goods, including motor cars, is typically around 9 per cent or 10 per cent, in Australia a little lower and in Canada up to 12 per cent.

It seems reasonable to suggest that the total market for consumer hire purchase is that proportion of the adult population who wish to purchase capital assets in excess of the amount permitted by their savings (or in order not to disturb their savings) and it has been suggested that this tends to be at least once in a consumer's life cycle, usually at the time of marriage.[10] Given the facts that only 49 per cent of the British people have ever used hire purchase – that those who do, suffer from ignorance and inertia (see p. 242) – that as a country we incur less than half the proportion of disposable income which other comparable countries incur in consumer debt – and that the need to borrow for capital assets arises at least once in a typical life cycle, we can perhaps deduce that the banks have a vast market to go at and a market in which, to quote Crowther, 'competitive forces are weak'.

Turning to factoring, the domestic market consists of every trading company and partnership in the United Kingdom consisting, as we have seen, of over 2 million enterprises – or at least as many of them as are well-managed and who have a well-ordered and widely based pattern of trade debts. Of course, only a small proportion of the whole will ever factor their debts, but the home market is considerable and the international market offers even wider opportunities.

Similarly with leasing, the extent of the market at home and abroad is so considerable that the statistics cease to have any meaning. The limiting factors on the growth of the business are the availability of finance and of taxable capacity on the part of potential lessors, and also the supply of specialist staff to service the operation.

Some services – for example, trusts and estates, taxation advice, company registrarships and insurance broking – tend to follow the existing banker-customer relationship. They are services designed primarily but not exclusively for existing customers. Many other services however – for example, instalment credit, factoring, leasing, travel services and life assurance – cut across the banker-customer relationship in that they are offered equally to customers of other banks and are available to the world at large. Thus, a city corporation may bank with A but lease equipment through Bank B; a private customer of Bank C may buy his car through the hire purchase company of Bank D; the traveller may carry the travellers cheques of Bank E; but book his holiday through the travel agency associated with banking group F.

Defining the individual markets is one thing: identifying the market responses and attitudes is something different. Quite a lot of market research has been done in the field of traditional banking and other organisations have financed a considerable amount of research into savings habits generally. Only a modest amount of research has been undertaken so far in relation to the newer banking services. Some of the banks have undertaken 'in depth' surveys with random groups in order to define consumer attitudes to banks and banking. Transcripts of the tapes make remarkable reading, but the samples are inevitably small and are of limited value. It is comparatively easy to find out why Smith banks with a clearing bank: it is difficult to establish accurately why Jones does not.

If it is difficult to establish consumer attitudes to traditional bank services, it is seemingly impossible at the present time to establish a meaningful cross-section of responses to all the other services. The potential consumers for the majority of bank services are so unaware of the nature and scope of those services that the problem is primarily one of education. In many instances, the need has not yet become a demand.

'Salesmanship,' says Dr Paul Nystrom in his *Handbook on Marketing*, 'is the skill or art of presentation of goods so as to convert neutral or even negative attitudes into positive wants or demands.' The salesmanship of the clearing banks is conducted through four main channels and these we will consider in turn. They are (a) the branch network, (b) advertising, (c) direct mail and (d) extra-branch salesmen.

The network of 12,000 or so branches operated by the English clearing banks is, or ought to be, the envy of every retail business. They are in prime locations in virtually every town and a good many villages. The systems of regional or district control are highly developed and the staff are of a high standard of intellect and integrity, but the style of the premises and the hours of business are not necessarily conducive to the development of the business and, as we have questioned elsewhere, 'is there any other trading organisation which would retain 11,000 or 12,000 properties in town centres all over the country and open the doors for a mere thirty hours a week?'[11]

Mr D. V. Weyer, now Vice-Chairman of Barclays Bank, summed the matter up when he said:

'If 20 years ago the industry had thought of itself as running a huge network of retail outlets, it might have developed on a shop hours basis.'[12]

More recently, the Price Commission in a report on bank charges suggested that 'there should be greater flexibility with regard to opening hours so that retail bank services can be available to the public whenever there is a commercially justifiable demand'.[13] Since the publication of the report, one or two banks have experimented with extended opening hours on weekdays and limited opening on Saturdays. At the time of writing, Lloyds Bank has perhaps gone further than other banks in announcing its plans to open between fifty and sixty branches on Saturday mornings for personal banking business in high demand areas. Both Barclays Bank and Midland Bank have also announced limited experiments in extended hours in various parts of the country and it will be interesting to observe the outcome in due time.

The banks are of course well aware of the problem and recognise that the branch network, as constituted, is not necessarily the right one for modern retail banking. A few years ago, *The Economist* magazine estimated that 'about 40 per cent of those branches, on expensive sites in so many High Streets, are already losing money'.[14] The estimate may not have been accurate, but the underlying point was valid. Nevertheless, the physical presence in so many towns is and must remain a vital feature of the banks' marketing strategy.

The location of a branch may be important in developing the

basic banking business in the town, but it is the customer list which is important when it comes to developing the related services. The bank branches around the country have a captive market of approximately 15 million customers. For the most part those customers, a little anachronistically perhaps, consider that they bank personally with their branch in the High Street and not with Barclays Bank or Midland Bank or whatever bank. They think, however absurdly, that their money is deposited in that place and that their overdraft (if they have one) was granted, out of the local kitty. Thus, there is a local banker-customer relationship, on which the banks would have been foolish not to build as they developed their new services.

The key figure is essentially the manager and his role is so important that we shall look at it separately in a moment. As Mr L. C. Mather has said:

'More than ever before, the bank manager, supported by his branch team, will have to be the marketeer ever on his toes to produce new business for the entire family group.'[15]

It is part of his everyday task to offer to his captive market the ever-growing services of his bank. He will do this in conversation and in correspondence. He will take opportunities and he will make opportunities. He will seek tirelessly to recognise his customers' needs and to match them with the services on his shelf. When reviewing an overdraft, he may mention opportunities for insurance, savings plans or taxation advice; when talking about holidays, he will mention the related travel agency and the need for insurance; when talking about the burden of taxation, he will mention Capital Transfer Tax and the need to make a will; when talking about future retirement, he will suggest a pension plan. And because the manager, even in the best ordered branch cannot hope to meet all his customers, he will teach his staff to take or make the same opportunities over the counter.

In very recent times, Barclays Bank has introduced a new 'Personal Banker' service in selected branches. These will be the large, predominantly urban branches where it is difficult for the manager to maintain personal contact with his customers. Under the Personal Banker scheme, customers will receive a plastic card bearing the name of the member of the banking branch staff who will look after that particular customer's requirements. These 'personal bankers' will normally be seated at desks in the banking hall and not behind the counter, and will assist customers with all their banking enquiries.

In all banks there are those customers, an increasing number, who do not visit their branches, but receive the occasional leaflet – irreverently known as 'a stuffer' – with their bank statement. It will pinpoint some appropriate service, and invite further enquiry and discussion. Those customers who do visit their branches will see from time to time the visual displays mounted nowadays by the banks in relation to their varied services. On other occasions, a little more formally, they will be invited to receptions or 'bank-in's' either in the bank's premises or at a local hotel, where they can partake of a sherry and chat or be chatted to about unit trusts, life assurance, financial planning, household insurance, investment management and everything else that the bank has to offer.

All in all, it amounts to a careful cultivating of the existing connections, to the advantage of bank and customers alike, seeking to make the best use of the bank's presence in that place.

Like Goldsmith's village schoolmaster ('And still they gaz'd and still the wonder grew, that one small head could carry all he knew'), the bank manager has the impossible task of seeking to be up-to-date and well-informed on all his bank's services. In this he is aided not only by a steady flow of circulars and handbooks, but by the specialist help of others in the group. In Barclays Bank, for example, the local manager may call on the help of the local consultant representing the bank's insurance broking subsidiary, the area manager of the unit trust company, the representative of the in-house life office, the local manager of the business advisory service, the local representative of Mercantile Credit Company, a regional director of Barclays Merchant Bank and the local Trust Company manager (for matters of investment, taxation, testamentary arrangements and pensions).

Obviously, the manager must have sufficient 'product knowledge' to recognise the customer's need before he can call in the specialist. He has a daunting task.

If the spearhead of the marketing attack is the branch network, it is advertising which provides the main support role. In advertising everyone is his own expert. There are few subjects on which there are so many diverse opinions and so many inconclusive answers. Despite the use of modern scientific aids, advertising remains very unscientific. The results of advertising are unpredictable and often unquantifiable. The combined advertising budgets of the clearing banks in a typical year might these days amount to some £7 million. The view is sometimes advanced that if the banks agreed among themselves to cease advertising, only the agencies and the media would lose. There may have been an element of truth in this at one time, but less so nowadays. The banks are in competition, not only among themselves and not only collectively for the business of non-banked customers; they are also in competition with a considerable number of institutions, including foreign banks, for a wide range of services.

Bank advertising falls into a number of different categories. In the first place, considerable expenditure is incurred merely to keep the name before the public. This is sometimes known as prestige advertising and, in other spheres of activity, is usually undertaken to establish a brand name or maintain a brand image. It is difficult to see that this is so necessary among the handful of well-established clearing banks in the United Kingdom. It is unlikely that anyone will ever say: 'Whatever happened to the Natwest Bank?' Nevertheless, the experts can show that when a name disappears from the advertisement pages, there is sooner or later a falling off in business. Secondly, there is the advertising of specific products, usually to establish a new service in the market, but thereafter to maintain and improve its competitive position. Thus the banks advertise their various advisory services, their credit cards, their instalment credit facilities and so on. Thirdly, there is an element of 'instant response' advertising, although financial services in general are not the subject of impulse buying and an advertisement on television is unlikely to produce a queue at the High Street branch to open new accounts the following morning. Some services lend themselves, however, to coupon advertising, i.e. advertisements requesting the completion of a coupon asking for further information, and in some cases it is possible to include an application form inviting an immediate response. The latter would apply particularly in advertisements for unit trusts and single premium life policies. Fourthly, a considerable amount of bank advertising in recent years has been aimed at 'product awareness'. One of the biggest obstacles to the development of bank services is the lack of market awareness of the products being offered. Many companies do not appreciate that banks can help them with their pensions problems, or the issuing of capital, or the provision of alternative forms of finance such as leasing or factoring. Many private customers have but a hazy knowledge of the investment services or the insurance broking facilities offered by their banks. In many cases, they are not aware of a basic need such as the importance of making a will. In other cases, they are aware of a problem but are confused by the number of products on the market.

The fifth and last area of bank advertising is that undertaken from time to time by the banks collectively such as the 'bank manager in the cupboard' advertising undertaken as a counter to the possible threat from the National Giro, and (in more recent times) the advertising campaign against bank nationalisation. Using the established methods for measuring consumer response, the 'feedback' on such advertising has been good but it is of course outside the field of advertising of bank services as such. This category of advertising is more in the area of public relations and has been used, for example, by the insurance industry in an effective way to show the socially desirable ways in which insurance company funds are invested.

One American critic of bank advertising, Mr N. W. Pope, has written:[16]

'Bank advertising has been traditionally noted for its obvious, almost intentional lack of creativity. Most bankers felt, perhaps wisely and perhaps not, that a bank's image through its advertising must be conservative, straight-arrow, soft-sell or no real sell at all. Any so-called "off-beat", creative approach would degrade the bank, its offices, personnel and maybe even its customers.'

And more stringently:

'Too few bankers who spend money to advertise genuinely understand advertising's purposes. Too often, the bank's money goes towards advertising creation and placement as a reaction to the competition, or in panic. Many banks advertise to advertise. It is accepted as the thing to do. It is expected.

Therefore we run ads. And in so doing we often waste a good deal more than we produce. Then the obvious occurs. Someone in authority becomes upset and arbitrarily blames advertising per se for the failure.'

This last, aimed at American banks a few years ago, would certainly not be true of UK banks today. They are very much aware of what advertising is all about and employ some highly skilled people in their advertising and marketing departments. At the same time, because many of the services we are concerned with are new, the advertising of those services is new. It is in a formative period and to some extent its success or otherwise cannot yet be judged.

In some areas, as we have said, the response can be measured. If, for example, a unit trust advertisement contains an application form, the response can be measured in terms of the number of applications returned. Better still, the profitability of the advertisement can immediately be gauged. During the comparatively euphoric unit trust period of the late 1960s and early 1970s, it would be rare for a unit trust advertisement not to produce sufficient applications and sufficient immediate income to show a profit even after allowing for an elementary costing of unallocated overheads. On the other hand, television advertising for linked life assurance has been known on occasions to produce no identifiable response. The cost may have been justified in terms of building up a brand image, but that kind of advertising requires some very shrewd and carefully controlled budgeting.

Many of the services dealt with in this book show such a narrow profit potential that extensive advertising would be prohibitive. We have already seen that the main selling thrust is in any case through the branch network, and a lot of bank advertising is in support of the selling effort put in by the bank branches. If a full allocation of branch costs were taken into account in the marketing of the individual services, there would certainly be little to spare for advertising, particularly with the increase of advertising costs in recent years.

The purpose of advertising is to inform. The aim is to tell the potential consumer about the product in such a way that he becomes aware of his own need and of the suitability of the product to meet that need. That process must go on and to some extent it has hardly begun. Relatively few people are aware of the range and variety of modern bank services and their suitability to meet the varying needs of individuals and corporations alike. Even the bank staffs up to quite senior levels are comparatively uninformed in terms of product knowledge.

Many of the markets for the individual services are hardly tapped and none is near saturation. With many of the services, to borrow a phrase from an old advertisement, the world is indeed 'our market'. If advertising is too expensive for some individual products, they may have to be included in packages and advertised, as it were, in bulk. Some traditional forms of advertisement may have to be discarded and new ones adopted. Research will continue on consumer attitudes and consumer responses in order to find out which advertisements 'get through' to the market. But the need for advertising will continue as part of the total marketing process. The basic need will remain – to inform, inform, inform.

After the two main selling weapons – the branch network and advertising – we come to two methods of direct selling which are comparatively new in the banking world: they are direct mail and the employment of sales representatives. Some form of advertising is of course direct selling, but generally advertising is mass communication through the mass media: it is not selective except in a broad sense. A so-called 'mail shot' is much more selective. It is aimed at individuals because of certain known facts about them. A section of the market will be isolated because it displays certain common characteristics. It may be merely that they are all customers of a particular bank or of a particular branch, and they may perhaps receive what we have already referred to as 'stuffers' with their bank statements. On the other hand, the target group may be existing shareholders of a bank unit trust, in which case they may receive a communication inviting them to buy more shares or units. Yet another example would be a 'mail shot' to the bank's credit card holders with information about some new insurance package put together by the bank's broking subsidiary.

The particular advantage of direct mail is that it is comparatively selective. It is good marketing in that the opportunity is taken of building on an existing relationship. Although postage and printing costs are high, direct mail is proving itself to be much more cost effective than many other forms of selling. It does not depend on expensive branch outlets and it is not so wasteful as blanket advertising through the mass media.

Mr David Ogilvy, of Ogilvy & Mather International, speaking at a London conference of the British Direct Mail Marketing Association, was critical of missed opportunities in the field of direct response advertising. He said:

'I have three life insurance policies. Do my insurance companies ever write to me and sell me more insurance? Never. All they send me are notices that my premiums are overdue.'

And again:

'I own two cars. Do the manufacturers of these cars ever use the mail to sell me a new model? Never.'

On the other hand, unsolicited mail can cause offence and damage existing connections, and also there are occasions when customers become caught in the cross-fire of a number of bank departments or subsidiaries seeking to sell their own wares. These are perhaps no more than the normal hazards of zealous salesmanship.

An extension of the 'mail shot' is the circulation of newsletters or magazines designed to promote the bank's business. There have been a number of these promoted by the clearing banks and on the whole they have not been a great success. This may be no more than a failure to strike the right note. Other organisations have successfully developed the concept of a regular magazine as a means of promoting their goods or services. The contents should be down-to-earth and appropriate to the needs of the consumer. Esoteric articles on the state of distant economies are too remote for the High Street customer and 'fluffy' articles written by humorous celebrities probably do little to convince the customer of the seriousness of the bank's products. The television studios teach one not to smile when expounding on the subjects of religion, death or money – particularly money, which for most people is a serious matter.

Lastly, we come to direct selling by representatives. We have discussed this at some length in connection with life assurance, but the banks also employ salesmen in the development of their credit card and hire purchase activities. Similarly, the insurance broking consultants or representatives are also engaged in direct selling, but in their case it is to a professional sector of the market rather than to the general public. A highly trained and well-controlled sales force can be very effective; a good salesman will often achieve better results than, say, a bank manager who may not have the right temperament, probably has not had the right training and in any case has other things to think about. The professional salesman does not enjoy the respect in our society which he deserves. According to a survey among 3,000 college students in America, the words which most came to mind in connection with the word 'salesman' were 'travel', 'money', 'personality', 'sales', 'fast talker', 'commission'.[17] The public concept of direct selling is very often that of persuading people to buy something they do not want. To quote, however, from the July 1976 issue of the Royal Bank of Canada monthly letter:

'The top-ranking salesman is a gold-mine of information and help. He has studied the merchandise he sells until he is an expert judge of quality, fit, good taste and appropriateness. He has absorbed ideas from the experience of customers. His function, as he sees it, is to help the buyer get the best for his money. He has respect for what he is selling and that respect is contagious.'

The presence of a professional sales force lies a little uncomfortably among professional bankers. Furthermore, direct sales organisations have become rather expensive. By their nature they are labour-intensive and the costs of salaries and commissions, social security and pensions, training and supervision have escalated in recent years. There is a tendency among insurance companies to move away from this method of selling, but it may well become more common in one or two particular areas of bank services. Whilst a sales force is cheaper to maintain than a branch network, the banks are not faced with that choice. The branch network already exists and an independent sales force is not only an extra expense but it does not fit easily into the established structure of banking in this country.

This is perhaps a good point to turn from the professional salesman to the role of the bank manager in promoting the proliferation of bank services.

The traditional role of the bank manager is that of lending

banker. He has of course to manage the bank branch as such, but his technical training over the years has been in the lending of money. It would no doubt be generally agreed that he now has to have a wider knowledge of financial matters. This is partly because the financial scene has become more diverse and partly because the manager has more services to offer. As we have seen, he has always acted in an advisory way to his customers and now when a customer has a financial problem, a manager is very often offering a solution from his own stock-in-trade. As a result, there are those who say that the manager of a bank branch should be primarily a salesman. We would respectfully disagree with this view, although it is of course a matter for the individual banks to determine the function of their managers. We prefer the view that the bank manager is running a business – a business which consists of matching a wide range of financial products to the needs of a variety of customers.

We have said that the bank manager's place in the local town has been that of a professional man, not unlike that of the solicitor, doctor and accountant. His professional skill has been, in a broad sense, the care of his depositors' money, the conduct of their banking arrangements and, more specifically, the lending of money. In a comparatively short space of time, he has been required to be much more than that. Whilst discarding none of his traditional skills, he now has to run a shop: he has to mix the professional skills of lending money and giving advice with the trade of selling products from his shelf. He need not of course do all this himself. His task as the manager of the business in that place is to see that it is done, and to organise his staff and other resources to that end.

It is not an easy task and there are those who would regard it as near-impossible. The running of a branch usually involves the strictest attention to internal disciplines and compliance with a massive book of instructions, and one may add to this the responsibility for lending money in a variety of situations in varying economic climates and the need to assist customers generally with their everyday financial affairs. That is the established picture of the bank manager. One must now add to it the need for him to have an up-to-date knowledge of almost every aspect of personal and corporate finance; the facility for recognising the need for such services, whether it be the leasing of an executive aircraft or the comparatively simple matter of holiday insurance; and on top of this there is now the overall need to develop all those services in an energetic way in his immediate area. The surprising thing is that all this is done so well, and it says much for the capacity of the British bank manager.

Recognising the difficulty of the manager's task and the costliness of the existing branch system, the banks have experimented in varying degrees with plans for concentrating certain services in particular branches. If there be a natural division among the multiplicity of modern bank services, it must lie between those which are of a corporate nature and those which are designed for the individual. To some extent, that pattern has been followed throughout these pages. It can never, however, be a clear-cut distinction. For example, in considering the affairs of a director of a private company, it is impossible to divorce his own personal situation from the fortunes of the company as such. Nevertheless, one can draw a line between business needs and for personal financial needs. Midland Bank, in particular, conducted an experiment in Newcastle, Sunderland and Southampton, and subsequently extended this to other areas of the country. This involved setting up centralised Area Offices to deal with the more specialised needs of business customers, leaving the other branches to operate as so-called 'service branches'. Somewhat similar schemes are being tried in other banks. The concept is not by any means new, having been introduced in some North American banks many years ago. The concentration of particular services in one office must lead to an accumulation of the relevant skills in that place. The knowledge and experience of the bank staff is not spread so thinly and, therefore, there will be a better use of resources. In time, such schemes will no doubt lead to some 'streaming' or categorising of bank officials according to whether they are equipped to manage 'business' or 'service' branches. It remains to be seen whether this is practicable and, in the meantime, no doubt all career staff will be required, as hitherto, to acquaint themselves, through professional education and internal training, with the total banking scene.

Although the bank manager remains the focal point, he is in some cases no more than a source of introduction to certain of

*'It says much for the capacity of the British bank manager . . .'*

his group's services. A continuing problem of bank marketing is the offering of the relevant services at the right level to the right customer in the right area. This also has led to the division of the market into the two main areas for personal and corporate services. A private customer may well look to his local bank manager for a variety of personal financial services, but the large corporate body will probably deal with the bank at a higher level and it is at that level that the channel must be found for the cross-selling of corporate services. So it is that some of the banks have created a number of 'account executives' – senior officials with the responsibility for the financial needs of a number of companies and institutions. In the ordinary way, the official would expect to be kept informed of the various contacts throughout the group with the customers on his list and he, rather than the local bank manager, will become the focal point for co-ordinating the various services as between the bank and those particular customers.

In similar vein and for similar reasons the banks have moved increasingly towards the packaging of customer services. Private customers will be offered for example, insurance packages to cover a variety of their insurance needs. One bank offers a combination of investment advice and financial planning. Another bank has offered a package of investment management and taxation advice. On the corporate side, attempts have been made to win accounts or to cultivate existing connections by offering all-in packages embracing such services as corporate advice, company registrarship and pension fund management. However, many of the services do not lend themselves to packaging. In each bank there are many different profit centres and cost centres, and it becomes a mammoth task of so-called transfer pricing to mix a number of services at an all-in rate. Furthermore, many customers resist packages. They sometimes feel that they are being offered, and therefore would have to pay for, more services than they require, and in any case most people and institutions prefer to look at each item in isolation, and in some cases to 'shop around' for particular services.

Whether or not packaging is the answer, the banking groups all have a similar aim – to be the all-purpose bank for their private and corporate customers. Ideally, for the private customer, the bank would be the modern counterpart of the

Victorian 'man of affairs' – the bank would be on hand to help the customer with every imaginable financial problem. Much modern advertising is directed in this way. Similarly, with corporate customers, the aim is that the all-purpose bank will look after the institution's every need, drawing as necessary on the considerable resources of the banking group at home and abroad. It may be in that situation that the provision of traditional facilities will have a less than paramount place. We said at the beginning that many of the services described in these pages were often termed 'ancillary'. But in fact, in the total concept of bank services, the basic banker-customer relationship may become subsidiary. There are two aspects of modern banking which the student or observer of these matters may wish to consider.

The first is that a new relationship has been created quite outside the legal relationship of banker and customer. The bank manager looks upon each customer as 'his' customer and quite reasonably has tended to consider all other banking services as subsidiary to that basic relationship. He feels aggrieved if his customer is sold a life policy or is offered computer services or receives financial planning advice from elsewhere in the group without his knowledge. This may be a commendable possessiveness on the manager's part, but it must be realised that many of the new relationships cannot be appended to the traditional one of banker and customer. In the new order of things, the banks enter into a great variety of relationships, including the following:

Lessor and lessee
Trustee and beneficiary
Factor and client
Credit card promoter and merchant
Investment manager and client
Insurer and insured
Broker and client
Travel agent and client
Computer bureau and client
Pension fund manager and client
Registrar and company
Unit trust manager and unitholder.

None of these necessarily depends on an underlying

banker-customer relationship. Many such services are offered by institutions who are not in any sense bankers. In the case of credit card holders, the relationship may still be that of banker and customer but it is *sui generis* – it is not dependent on any other underlying relationship. A large number of the 7 million or so card holders in the United Kingdom will not necessarily have a banking account with the group whose card they carry. A very large number of them will never have been seen face to face by anyone from that group.

In other words, the banks are all the time entering into a number of diverse relationships with people and institutions and, in some instances, those relationships will be very long term. For example, a life policy may be for twenty-five or thirty years. In many cases, the local bank manager will have no particular part to play in that continuing relationship, although he may at the outset have been responsible for the introduction of the business to the group. In many cases, the particular service in question may be taken up by someone who is not a customer of the banking group. This will apply frequently, for example, in the case of unit trusts, insurance policies, hire purchase finance, credit cards and leasing contracts. This may apply even more so in the case of international services where, for example, factoring contracts, the sale of off-shore funds and credit card operations may be entered into where the banking group has no retail outlet and there is no question of an existing banker-customer relationship. Thus, we may note one of the major changes in modern banking – that many of the newer services have no particular relevance to and certainly are not dependent on the traditional banker – customer connection.

The second point for consideration is that in the total concept of financial management, the operation of a banking account is no longer the most important item in the eyes of the customer, whether the customer is a private person or institution. Taking the case of a private individual who has all his financial needs provided by his clearing bank – including such matters as life assurance, car and household insurance, investment and taxation advice, pensions advice and executorship arrangements, overseas travel and, if desired, advice on his business – the day-to-day operation of his banking account becomes of comparatively minor importance. This is particularly so if he makes frequent use of credit cards. Even in the case of an institution, although the operation of a current account and the provision of overdraft facilities will always be important, they will not necessarily have any special priority in the mind of the company customer which may also be receiving from its bank certain computer services, company registration services, and pensions services, and may well have entered into major leasing contracts and factored its debts (which reduces the activity on the current banking account), and may even be engaged on a major capital issue or merger situation with the assistance of the merchant banking arm of the group.

If that be so, what does it matter? There is no reason why it should matter: indeed, in these various ways the UK banks have extended their business influence. It does mean, however, that some major re-thinking may be necessary in relation to bank marketing in general. At present, people go into the High Street branches of the clearing banks only if they are customers. It may become important that banks should open their doors in a more welcoming way to allcomers – to anyone who may have occasion to use the services we have sought to describe, regardless of whether or not they have a banking account. Bank branches are designed primarily for the pupose of receiving and paying out cash and it could be that the counter may have to be pushed to one side. Perhaps a time will come when the public will 'drop in' on the banks in the High Street as they might visit the supermarket, not necessarily because they are already a 'customer' there but because they have a financial problem and from somewhere on their shelves the bank can provide the answer. That will indeed be service banking.

## References

1 P. F. Drucker: *The Practice of Management*. Pan, 1968.
2 C. McIver and G. Naylor: *The Marketing of Financial Services* – to be published by The Institute of Bankers in Autumn 1979.
3 L. L. Berry and L. A. Capaldini: *Marketing for the Bank Executive*. Leviathan House, 1974.
4 J. S. Hensel: The Essential Nature of the Marketing Management Process: An Overview *in* L. L. Berry.

5 Sir Frederick Seebohm (now Lord Seebohm): The Marketing Programme *in* 'The Marketing of Bank Services', Cambridge Seminar 1971, The Institute of Bankers.
6 G. Rae: *The Country Banker*. Murray, 1885.
7 Royal Commission on the Distribution of Income and Wealth. [Chairman: Lord Diamond] Report No. 1: Initial report on the standing reference cmnd. 6171. HMSO, 1975.
8 Board of Inland Revenue: Inland Revenue Statistics. HMSO, 1977.
9 *Financial Statistics*, September 1977.
10 A. Enthoven: 'The growth of instalment credit and the future of prosperity'. *American Economic Review* 47, 1857, p. 913.
11 D. G. Hanson: Money Shops – or Not? *Journal of the Institute of Bankers,* April 1973.
12 D. Vander Weyer: Clearing Bank Marketing: 'The Practical Issues Today'. *The Banker*, October 1970.
13 Price Commission: 'Banks; charges for money transmission services'. HMSO, 1978.
14 'The Banking Revolution'. *The Economist*, 18 September 1971.
15 L. C. Mather: Commercial Banks: Evolution of Services *in* International Banking Summer School, *Banking in the 1970's*. The Institute of Bankers, 1970.
16 N. W. Pope: A Philosophy of Bank Advertising *in* L. L. Berry and L. A. Capaldini, *Marketing for the Bank Executive*. Leviathan House, 1974.
17 *Harvard Business Review*, January 1972.

## Comparative Growth of Deposit Holdings

Sterling deposits of UK residents

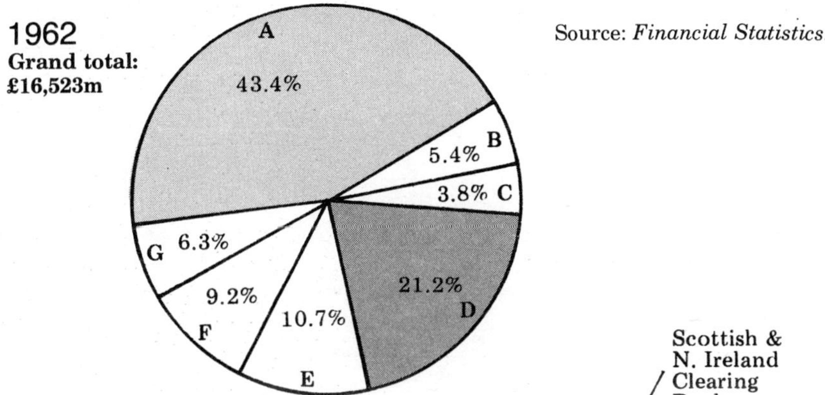


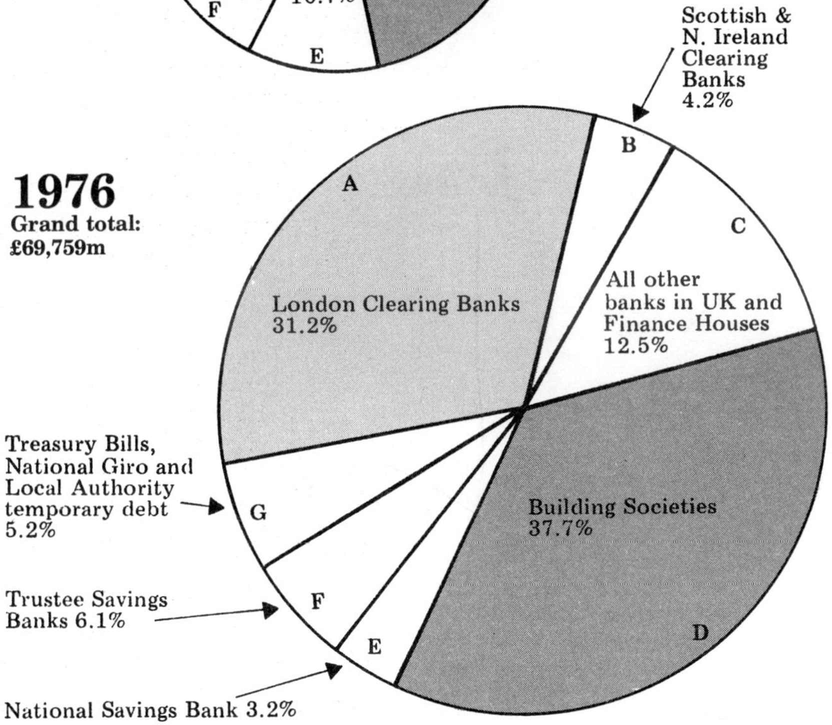

# Appendix B

## Personal Holdings of Financial Assets

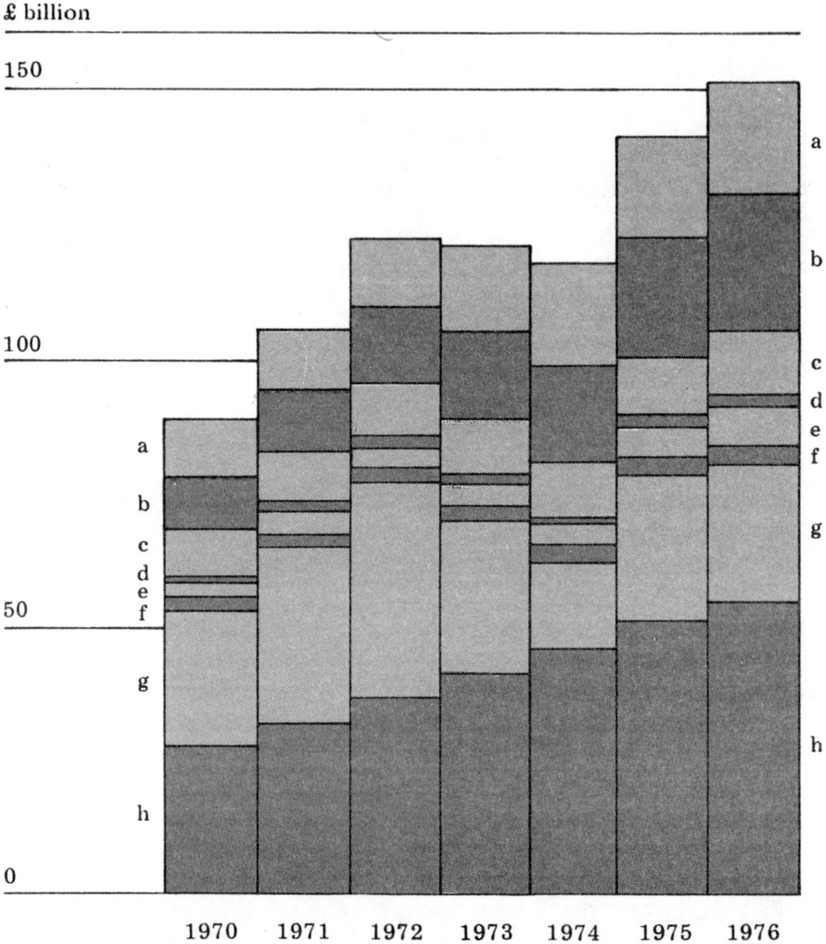


| | | | | | | | |
|---|---|---|---|---|---|---|---|
| a. Bank deposits[1] | 10·1 | 11·0 | 12·9 | 16·3 | 19·3 | 19·4 | 20·6 |
| | 11·4 | 10·4 | 10·5 | 13·4 | 16·3 | 13·6 | 13·5 |
| b. Building societies | 10·1 | 12·0 | 14·2 | 16·3 | 18·3 | 22·5 | 26·1 |
| | 11·4 | 11·4 | 11·6 | 13·4 | 15·5 | 15·8 | 17·2 |

| | | | | | | | |
|---|---|---|---|---|---|---|---|
| c. National savings[2] | 8·4 | 9·0 | 9·8 | 10·1 | 10·1 | 10·7 | 11·5 |
| | 9·5 | 8·5 | 8·0 | 8·3 | 8·5 | 7·5 | 7·6 |
| d. Unit trusts | 1·4 | 2·0 | 2·6 | 2·1 | 1·4 | 2·5 | 2·7 |
| | 1·6 | 1·9 | 2·1 | 1·7 | 1·2 | 1·8 | 1·8 |
| e. UK government stocks[3] | 2·6 | 3·4 | 3·1 | 3·5 | 3·4 | 5·0 | 6·7 |
| | 2·9 | 3·2 | 2·5 | 2·9 | 2·9 | 3·5 | 4·4 |
| f. Local authority debt[3] | 3·1 | 3·0 | 2·9 | 3·1 | 3·9 | 3·7 | 4·0 |
| | 3·5 | 2·9 | 2·4 | 2·6 | 3·3 | 2·6 | 2·6 |
| g. Company and overseas securities[3] | 24·7 | 32·8 | 39·4 | 28·4 | 15·9 | 27·0 | 25·4 |
| | 27·8 | 31·1 | 32·2 | 23·4 | 13·5 | 19·0 | 16·7 |
| h. Life policy and pension rights[4] | 28·3 | 32·2 | 37·5 | 41·6 | 45·9 | 51·5 | 55·0 |
| | 31·9 | 30·6 | 30·7 | 34·3 | 38·8 | 36·2 | 36·2 |
| **Total financial assets** | **88·7** | **105·4** | **122·4** | **121·4** | **118·2** | **142·3** | **152·0** |
| | 100·0 | 100·0 | 100·0 | 100·0 | 100·0 | 100·0 | 100·0 |

[1]Includes deposit banks, National Giro,accepting houses, overseas and other banks and discount market, less 2½ per cent to allow for non-profit-making institutions.

[2]Includes National Savings Bank, Trustee Savings Banks, National Savings Certificates, Save-as-you-Earn, Premium Savings Bonds, etc.

[3]Estimated market values.

[4]Includes Government Actuary Department's estimates of occupational pension rights.

*Source: Appendices B and C* The London Clearing Banks: Evidence by the Committee of London Clearing Bankers to the (Wilson) Committee to Review the Functioning of Financial Institutions. November 1977.

# Appendix C

## Composition of UK Clearing Bank Groups

## Balance sheet totals at latest accounting date

| **main activity**<br>£m | **Barclays**<br>19,320 | **Lloyds**<br>11,788 | **Midland**<br>11,843 | **National Westminster**<br>17,070 | **Williams & Glyn's**<br>1,721 |
|---|---|---|---|---|---|
| Domestic banking | Barclays Bank<br>8,547 | Lloyds Bank<br>5,410<br>Lewis's Bank<br>21 | Midland Bank<br>9,068<br>Clydesdale Bank<br>899<br>Northern Bank<br>722 | National Westminster Bank<br>9,886<br>Coutts & Co<br>365<br>Ulster Bank<br>614<br>Isle of Man Bank<br>79 | Williams & Glyn's Bank<br>1,584 |
| International banking† | Barclays Bank International<br>10,129 | Lloyds Bank International<br>4,329<br>Lloyds Bank California<br>863<br>National Bank of New Zealand<br>497 | †See note below | International Westminster Bank<br>4,652<br>Handelsbank NW<br>261<br>Global Bank<br>146 | †See note below |
| Merchant and 'wholesale' banking | Barclays Merchant Bank<br>813 | Lloyds Associated Banking Company<br>1,507 | Samuel Montagu<br>980 | County Bank<br>495<br>Coutts Finance<br>387 | Williams, Glyn & Co<br>22 |
| Instalment credit, etc. | Mercantile Credit<br>371<br>Barclays Mercantile Industrial Finance<br>Barclays Export & Finance Company<br>144<br>Barclays Factoring | Lloyds Leasing<br>122<br>Lloyds Associated Air Leasing<br>11 | Forward Trust<br>250<br>Midland Montagu Leasing<br>84<br>Griffin Factors | Lombard North Central<br>1,080<br>Credit Factoring International | St Margaret's Trust<br>24<br>William's & Glyn's Leasing<br>18 |
| Other | Barclays Bank Trust Company<br>Barclays Insurance Services<br>Barclays Insurance Brokers International | Lloyds Bank Unit Trust Managers<br>Exporters Refinance Corporation<br>Beehive Life Assurance Company | Midland Bank Trust Company<br>Midland Bank Insurance Services<br>Bland Payne<br>Thomas Cook Group<br>London American Finance Corporation | National Westminster Unit Trust Managers<br>National Westminster Insurance Services<br>Centre-File | Williams & Glyn's Trust Company<br>Williams & Glyn's Insurance Consultants |

# Further Reading

A list of books and articles that readers of this book may find helpful and interesting.


### 1 Trustee Work

**Books**

D. R. Marsh: *Corporate Trustees*. Europa, 1952.
M. Sladen: *Practical Trust Administration*. Europa, 1977.

### 2 Investment (Services) Including Share Registration

**Books**

R. J. Briston: *The Stock Exchange*. Allen and Unwin, 1975.
M. J. Day and P. I. Harris: *Unit Trusts*. Oyez, 1974.
T. G. Goff: *Theory and Practice of Investment*. Heinemann, 1978.
R. R. Pennington: *Investor and the Law*. MacGibbon and Kee, 1968.
*Unit Trust Year Book*.
Committee to Review the Functioning of Financial Institutions (Chairman: Sir Harold Wilson). *Evidence on the Financing of Industry and Trade*. Vol. 3: Stock Exchange Evidence. HMSO, 1978.

### 3 Insurance (Services)

**Books**

G. Clayton: *British Insurance*. Elek, 1971.
W. A. Dinsdale and O. C. McMurdie: *Elements of Insurance*. Pitman, 1971.
Committee to Review the Functioning of Financial Institutions (Chairman: Sir Harold Wilson). *Evidence on the Financing of Industry and Trade*. Vol. 3: Insurance Company Associations Evidence. HMSO, 1978.
Government Actuary's Reports.
*Report of the Committee on Property Bonds and Equity-Linked Life Assurance*. (Chairman: Sir Hilary Scott). Cmnd. 5281. HMSO, 1973.

**Article**

D. G. Hanson: 'Banks in the Insurance Field – How far should they go?' *Journal of The Institute of Bankers*, December 1974.

### 4 Pension

**Books**

G. A. Hosking: *Pension Schemes and Retirement Benefits*. Sweet and Maxwell, 1977.
M. Pilch and V. Wood: *Managing Pension Schemes*. Gower, 1974.
M. Pilch and V. Wood: *Company Pensions and the new Act*. Gower, 1975.
Committee to Review the Functioning of Financial Institutions (Chairman: Sir Harold Wilson). *Evidence on the Financing of Industry and Trade*. Vol. 3: National Association of Pension Funds Evidence. HMSO, 1978.

## 5 Personal Advisory Services/Taxation

### Books

M. Allen: *The Money Book: Your Money And Your Life*. Sidgwick and Jackson, 1977.
R. Glynne-Williams: *Elements of Taxation*. Cassell and Collier, 1973.

### Articles

*Money Which?* Published quarterly by the Consumers Association.

## 6 Merchant Banking

### Books

C. J. J. Clay and B. S. Wheble: *Modern Merchant Banking*. Woodhead-Faulkner, 1977.
R. Kellett: *Merchant Banking Arena*. Macmillan, 1967.

### Articles

J. Padovan: 'New Influences in Merchant Banking.' *Journal of The Institute of Bankers*, August 1977.
J. Padovan: 'Raising Finance: the Merchant Banks' Changing Role.' *Journal of The Institute of Bankers*, October 1977.

## 7 Business Advisory Services

### Books

*Sources of Finance for the Small Company*. Institute of Directors, 1978.
*Report of the Committee of Inquiry on Small Firms* (Chairman: J. E. Bolton). HMSO, 1971.

### Article

E. Parry-Williams: 'Bank Services, multinational needs.' *Bankers' Magazine*, April 1976.

## 8 Leasing

### Books

T. M. Clark: *Leasing*. McGraw-Hill, 1978.
A. Sykes: *The Lease-buy Decision. A survey of current practice in 202 companies*. British Institute of Management, 1975.
R. F. Vancil: *Leasing of Industrial Equipment*. McGraw-Hill, 1963.

### Articles

M. Craig: 'Lending? – Why not lease?' *The Bankers' Magazine*, July 1977.
S. Maran: 'Equipment Leading in the UK.' *The Accountant's Magazine*, April 1978.

## 9 Factoring

### Books

P. M. Biscoe: *Law and Practice of Credit Factoring*. Butterworths, 1975.
M. Forman and J. Gilbert: *Factoring and Finance*. Heinemann, 1976.
M. Westlake: *Factoring*. Pitman, 1975.

### Article

M. Craig: 'Factoring . . . Respectable.' *The Bankers' Magazine*, August 1977.

## 10 Hire Purchase

**Books**

F. R. Ryder: *Consumer Credit Act: The present stage with special reference to banking*. Kings College, 1978.
*Report of the Committee on Consumer Credit* (Chairman: Lord Crowther). HMSO, 1971.

## 11 Credit Cards

**Books**

L. Mandell and N. B. Murphy: *Bank Cards*. American Institute of Banking, 1976.
D. W. Richardson: *Electric Money: evolutions of an electronic funds transfer system*. Cambridge (Mass.) and London MIT, 1970.

**Article**

H. Morris: 'A Billion Credit Cards by 1985?' *Burroughs Clearing House*, June 1978.

## 12 Off-shore Services

**Books**

E. Chambost: *Using Tax Havens Successfully*. Institute for International Research, 1978.
J. F. Chown and T. F. Kelen: *Offshore Investment Centre*. Barker Research Unit, 1977.
C. Doggart: *Tax Havens and their uses*. Economist Intelligence Unit, 1975.

## 13 Money and Travel

**Books**

G. M. Macleod and J. E. McGookey: *Travel — a logical banking service*. Financial Publishing Co., 1972.

**Article**

M. G. Wilcox: 'Banks and the Travel Business.' *Journal of The Institute of Bankers*, October 1973.

## 14 Marketing

**Books**

L. L. Berry and L. A. Capaldini: *Marketing for the Bank Executive*. Mason and Lipscombe, 1974.
L. L. Berry and J. H. Donnelly: *Marketing for Bankers*. Institute of Banking/American Bankers Association, 1975; *Marketing of Bank Services*. The Institute of Bankers, 1971.
C. McIver and G. Naylor: *The Marketing of Financial Services*. To be published by The Institute of Bankers, Autumn 1979.

**Article**

D. G. Hanson: 'Money Shops – Or Not?' *Journal of The Institute of Bankers*, April 1973.

# Index

# Notes